Abductive Reasoning

Abductive Reasoning

Douglas Walton

THE UNIVERSITY OF ALABAMA PRESS
Tuscaloosa

Typeface is Bembo

∞

The paper on which this book is printed meets the minimum requirements of American National Standard for Information Science—Permanence of Paper for Printed Library Materials, ANSI Z39.48-1984.

Library of Congress Cataloging-in-Publication Data

Walton, Douglas N.
    Abductive reasoning / Douglas Walton.
        p. cm.
    Includes bibliographical references and index.
    ISBN 0-8173-1441-5 (cloth : alk. paper) 1. Abduction (Logic) 2. Reasoning. I. Title.
    BC199.A26W35 2004
    160—dc22

                                                                2004008797

For Karen, with Love

Contents

Acknowledgments

I would like to thank the Social Sciences and Humanities Research Council of Canada for a research grant that made writing this book possible. The motivation to tackle abduction as an important research topic for both argumentation and computing was stimulated by participation in the Symposium on Argument and Computation at Bonskeid House in Perthshire, Scotland, in June and July of 2000. I would especially like to thank Tim Norman and Chris Reed for organizing the conference and for what they taught me during the tutorials and discussions, both formal and informal, at the conference. The following conference participants also deserve thanks for informing me about the state of the art of artificial intelligence and clarifying many questions related to abduction: Trevor Bench-Capon, Daniela Carbogim, Jim Crosswhite, Aspassia Daskalopulu, John Fox, Jim Freeman, Janne Maaike Gerlofs, Michael Gilbert, Rod Girle, Floriana Grasso, Leo Groarke, Corin Gurr, David Hitchcock, Hanns Hohmann, Erik Krabbe, Peter McBurney, Henry Prakken, Theodore Scaltsas, Simone Stumpf, and Bart Verheij. Recent collaborative research work with Chris Reed and Henry Prakken has proved to be very influential in shaping my current views in the area of argumentation, law, and computing and has helped to refine my approach to abductive reasoning in too many ways to acknowledge specifically. I would also like to thank Erik Krabbe, Frank Veltman, Frans van Eemeren, Eveline Feteris, Taeda Jovicic, and Jan Albert van Laar for comments and discussions during an invited talk given at the University of Groningen in June 2003.

Some parts of chapter 1 have been reprinted (in revised form) from my article titled "Abductive, Presumptive and Plausible Arguments," *Informal Logic* 21 (2001): 141–69. Some parts of chapter 5 have been reprinted (in revised form) from my article titled "Are Some *Modus*

Ponens Arguments Deductively Invalid?" *Informal Logic* 22 (2002): 19–46. Thanks to the editors for their permission to reprint these sections.

I would like to thank Chris Reed and Floriana Grasso for organizing the workshop "Computational Models of Rational Argument" at the European Conference on Artificial Intelligence held on July 22, 2002, in Lyon, France. Discussions during the workshop were valuable in helping me to learn about the latest developments in artificial intelligence concerning connections of multiagent computing with argumentation. In addition to Chris and Floriana, I would like to thank Subrata Das, Tangming Yuan, David Moore, Alec Grierson, Henry Prakken, Francisca Snoek Henkemans, John Fox, Helmut Horacek, Antonis Kakas, Pavlos Moraitis, Fiorella de Rosis, and Giuseppe Carenini.

Input from colleagues who are specialists in law and computing has been extremely helpful during all phases of the book, and indeed the book would not have been possible without it. At various times, discussions with Tom Gordon, Bart Verheij, and Arno Lodder have proved to be valuable. For discussions at the Second Joseph Bell Center Workshop on the Evaluation of Evidence held at the University of Edinburgh from June 30 to July 2, 2003, I would like to thank John Zeleznikow, Jeroen Keppens, Moshe Koppel, Uri Schild, Sacha Iskovic, Andrew Aberdein, and Gary Davis. For some useful input through conversations at the University of Dundee in the summer of 2003, I would like to thank Chris Reed, Simon Wells, Glenn Rowe, and Joel Katzav. I would like to thank Craig Callen for organizing and chairing the conference "Visions of Rationality in Evidence Law," held at the DCL College of Law, Michigan State University, April 3–6, 2003. My work on abductive reasoning in evidence law benefited from discussions with participants in the conference, and I would especially like to thank Richard Friedman, Erica Beecher-Monas, Mike Redmayne, Greg Mitchell, Michael Risinger, Michael Saks, Roger Park, Ron Allen, Myrna Raeder, Eleanor Swift, and Bruce Burns. Comments from the two anonymous referees of The University of Alabama Press enabled me to improve a number of my arguments and prevented me from making some serious mistakes.

My thanks to The University of Alabama Press for editorial advice that proved helpful to the project, to Bill Dray and David Godden for help with proofreading and editing at various stages of the manuscript preparation, and to Rita Campbell for composing the index. Finally, I would like to thank my wife, Karen, for her tolerant attitude toward my work.

Introduction

Abductive inference, commonly called inference to the best explanation, is reasoning from given data to a hypothesis that explains the data. Abductive inference is very common in forensic evidence. For example, if pieces of a knife blade are found in the window frame of a house where a burglary occurred, the best explanation may be that entry took place by someone's prying open the window with a knife. Abductive inference has been recognized as centrally important in artificial intelligence (AI), but many in the social sciences and argumentation are not familiar with abduction or have only an unclear or uncertain idea of it. This book presents a clear account of abduction accessible to non-specialists in the philosophy of science or computing.

Abductive inference has most often been seen as an important kind of reasoning used at the discovery stage of scientific hypothesis formation and testing. Charles S. Peirce, the American pragmatic philosopher and scientist who coined the term "abduction," emphasized its scientific importance. The recent book on abduction by Magnani (2001) has concentrated on abductive reasoning in scientific discovery. An earlier book on inference to the best explanation (Lipton, 1991) also, understandably, stressed the scientific uses of abductive inference. Lipton admitted (p. 4) that he left a gap when he "neglected the various approaches that workers in Artificial Intelligence have taken to describing inference." Two technical books have been written on abductive inference from a point of view of AI: Peng and Reggia (1990) and Josephson and Josephson (1994). The present book fills a gap not only by giving a clear explanation of the approaches taken in recent work in AI but also by considering the role of abductive inference in everyday argumentation. In contrast to the belief-revision approach taken by Magnani, this book takes a commitment-based approach of a kind that has been developed in recent work in argumentation theory and computing. Although the new theory is applied to cases of scientific and medical reasoning, it takes more of its data from examples of abductive reasoning from Anglo-American evidence law.

Chapter 1 introduces the reader to abduction by showing not only how the idea was presented by Charles S. Peirce but also how the notion evolved historically. Chapter 1 surveys the literature on scientific discovery and introduces the reader to some of the tools of argumentation analysis needed to understand abductive reasoning. Abduction is analyzed as inference to the best explanation of a given set of facts, and thus the notion of explanation is central to it. But previous attempts to give any analysis of abduction have been obstructed by the very large problem of how to explain explanation. Chapter 2 draws on recent techniques used in AI, especially in the areas of expert systems, multiagent systems, and plan recognition technologies, to develop a new dialogue model of explanation. For example, it has been found in the development of expert systems that the user must sometimes be able to ask the system for an explanation, and, to provide it, the system must offer a reply to the user's question that the user understands. In this model an explanation is defined as a process in which a respondent gives understanding to a dialogue partner who has sought it by asking a question. This new and powerful dialogue model of explanation yields a much deeper analysis of abductive reasoning than was heretofore possible. This model of explanation is central to a new field called computational dialectics, which provides formal models of types of dialogue in which rational agents communicate with each other. Computational dialectics provides the framework for the new theory of procedural rationality presented in chapter 3.

The analysis uses a new software system of argument diagramming called Araucaria to analyze defeasible (nonmonotonic) arguments of a kind familiar in AI. A common sort of example from medical diagnostics is the following argument: "If Bob has red spots, Bob has the measles; Bob has red spots; therefore Bob has the measles." The structure of this common form of argumentation is analyzed in chapter 4. Such arguments are closely tied to causal explanations in many instances. The problem is that no theory of causality is widely accepted in science or philosophy, and previous attempts to define causality have proved to have insuperable difficulties. Chapter 5 shows how viewing causal reasoning as a form of abductive inference provides an approach that removes many of these difficulties. The new approach is illustrated by legal examples of trace evidence and disputes about causation in torts. This chapter shows how the abductive model throws new light on such causal fallacies as the *post hoc* fallacy, the error of leaping too quickly from an observed correlation between two events to the conclusion that one caused the other.

The method for evaluating abductive arguments set out in chapter 6 is built around two argumentation schemes applied to forward and backward reasoning in a dialogue process. The model portrays query-driven abduction as a dialogue process of discovery in which a question is asked by the forming of a hypothesis, and answers are given in the form of explanations. Explanations are elicited from facts as these facts are pieced together and marshaled in sets of statements called accounts, filled out by inserting implicit assumptions as new data are collected in an investigation. The best explanation is selected out of this process. Chapter 7 presents several unsolved problems that can be better formulated in light of the new theory of abduction set out in the previous chapters. Chapters 6 and 7 open new avenues to solving these problems by revealing how abductive reasoning provides evidence to support a hypothesis through a discovery process of questioning and answering in which competing accounts are examined by probing into the weaknesses in them.

Abductive, Presumptive, and Plausible Arguments

Three kinds of inference—abductive argument, presumptive argument, and plausible argument—are often confused. And it is not too surprising that they are confused. They seem to be quite similar in representing a kind of uncertain and tentative reasoning that is very common in everyday thinking, as well as in special contexts such as legal argumentation and scientific hypothesis construction. And although there is quite a bit of writing on all three types of argument in logic, artificial intelligence (AI), philosophy of science, and cognitive science, there seems at this point to be no widely agreed upon systematic theory that clearly distinguishes between (or among) the three in any precise way. A related notion in the same category is inference to the best explanation, now widely taken (see below) to be the same as abductive argument. The purpose of chapter 1 is to survey how these related terms are used in the literature and to determine what the main differences are between (or among) them. The aim is thereby to elicit a basis for making a clear distinction between (or among) them that should help to explain and clarify these differences. On the basis of this survey and analysis, tentative definitions of all these related concepts will be proposed. The definitions are not meant to be the final word that closes off all discussion of the matter. They are put forward as tentative hypotheses meant to clarify the discussion and move it forward constructively.

   The current convention is typically to postulate three kinds of argument—deductive, inductive, and the variously named third category: abductive, presumptive, defeasible, or plausibilistic.[1] This convention poses an important question. Should one of these variously named types fit in as the third kind of inference contrasting with the other two? Or should all of them fit into that category? Or should some subset of them fit? Or should some of them be nested under others as subcategories? The situation is complicated, and the terminology is unsettled. Many logic textbooks either do not recognize the third category at all or show uncertainty about what to call it. Recent work in argumentation theory has studied forms of argument fitting into the third category. These forms are called argumentation schemes. The arguments fitting the schemes appear to be neither deductive nor inductive. Could they be classified as abductive, or is that the wrong word? These questions are perplexing, but seem to be very important not only for logic and computer science but also for many other fields, such as law, where such arguments are so commonly used as evidence. Another question is how abduction is related to argumentation schemes. These stereotypical forms of argument, such as argument from witness testimony and argument from expert opinion, have traditionally been classified as fallacies but can often be reasonable forms of argument used as legal evidence. Some examples of schemes are introduced in this chapter, and it is shown how they can be used in a new automated method of argument diagramming.

ABDUCTIVE INFERENCE

To begin, it is useful to review the definitions of "deductive argument" and "inductive argument" offered in the most widely used logic textbook. According to Hurley (2000, p. 33), a deductive argument is "an argument in which the premises are claimed to support the conclusion in such a way that it is *impossible* for the premises to be true and the conclusion false." Or to put it another way, if the premises are true, then necessarily the conclusion is true, where the adverb "necessarily" applies to the inferential link between the premises and the conclusion. An inductive argument (Hurley, 2000, p. 33) is "an argument in which the premises are claimed to support the conclusion in such a way that it is improbable that the premises be true and the conclusion false." The inferential link between the premises and the conclusion here is not one of necessity but of probability. But what is probability? Although logic textbooks generally agree on how they define a deductively valid argument, there are many differences on how they define probability. The most popular approach is called the Bayesian interpretation, which defines probability in terms of degrees of belief about events. In the Bayesian formalism, measures of belief follow the basic axioms of the probability calculus (Pearl, 2000, p. 3). One is that probability is measured as a fraction between zero and one. Another is that the probability of an event not occurring is defined as one minus the probability that the event does occur. Conditional probability, the probability of one event given the probability of another, is a very important defining characteristic of the Bayesian approach.[2] Independence of events is assumed as a requirement of applying the Bayesian formalism to them. When it is said that event A is independent of event B, it means that our belief in A remains unchanged on learning the truth of B (Pearl, 2000, p. 3). To apply Bayesian probability to a set of data to infer a conclusion, one has to assume that each event in the data set is independent of the other events. At any rate, this rough account gives the beginner a basis to contrast the abductive type of inference to what can be taken, on commonly held criteria, to be deductive and inductive inference.

Abductive inference is a notion that has become familiar to some of us, but the idea is a relative newcomer as something that is widely known or accepted in logic. There seems to be quite a bit of uncertainty about exactly how the notion should be defined. It is thought that the American philosopher Charles Saunders Peirce was the originator of the notion of abduction. But that, too, is somewhat uncertain, in my opinion, even though Peirce's work on abduction is strikingly original and deep.[3] An article by Harman (1965) is also often assumed to introduce the notion of abduction to philosophy. Harman's article makes no specific mention of Peirce's work on abduction. Perhaps Peirce's work had not been "rediscovered" in 1965. Many readers of this book may have only a fuzzy notion about what abduction is, or is taken to be, although they can be expected to have firm opinions on how to define deductive and inductive inference.[4] Hence the best way of introducing the notion is to begin by describing some examples used by Peirce to contrast abductive inference with deductive and inductive inference.

The definitions from Hurley above are about premises "claimed" to support a conclusion. But such claims contain success conditions. A good point at which to begin is to describe what are usually taken to be the success criteria for all three types of inference.[5] In a deductively valid inference, it is impossible for the premises to be true and the conclusion false. In an inductively strong inference, it is improbable (to some degree) that the conclusion is false given that the premises are true. In an abductively weighty inference, it is implausible that the premises are true and the conclusion is false.[6] The abductive type of inference tends to be the weakest of the three kinds. A conclusion drawn by abductive inference is an intelligent guess. But it is still a guess, because it is tied to an incomplete body of evidence. As new evidence comes in, the guess could be shown to be wrong. Logicians have tended to be not very welcoming to the idea of allowing abductive inference as part of logic, because logic is supposed to be an exact science, and abductive inference appears to be inexact. Certainly it is not final. It would seem to be more fallible and conjectural than the other two types of inference.

Abductive inference has often been equated with inference to the best explanation. Harman (1965, pp. 88–89) wrote that "inference to the best explanation corresponds approximately to what others have called abduction." According to Harman, various kinds of reasoning can be shown to be instances of inference to the best explanation. One kind he cited is that of a detective who puts the evidence together to arrive at the conclusion that in a murder case the butler did it (p.89). Another kind of case is that of a scientist inferring the existence of atoms and other subatomic particles (p. 89). Another is the use of witness testimony in which we infer that the witness is telling the truth (p. 89). Harman explicated the latter case of inference to the best explanation as follows (p. 89). Our confidence in the testimony is supported by there being no other plausible explanation than that the person actually did witness the situation described. Hence we draw the conclusion, by inference, that the witness is telling the truth of the matter. It is interesting to note that two of the three kinds of cases cited by Harman show the fundamental importance of abductive inference in legal argumentation.

Abduction is often associated with the kind of reasoning used in the construction of hypotheses in the discovery stage of scientific evidence. A good idea of how abductive inference works in scientific reasoning can be gotten by examining Peirce's remarks on the subject. Peirce (1965II, p. 375) described abduction as a process "where we find some very curious circumstance, which would be explained by the supposition that it was a case of a certain general rule, and thereupon adopt that supposition." The description given by Peirce suggests that abduction is based on explanation of a given fact or finding, a "curious circumstance." The words "supposition" and "adopt" suggest the tentative nature of abduction. As noted above, you can accept an abductively derived conclusion as a provisional commitment even if it is subject to retraction in the future. The expression "general rule" is significant. Abductive inferences are derived from the way things can normally be expected to go in a familiar kind of situation, or as a "general rule." A general rule may not hold in all cases of a certain kind. It is not based on a warrant of "for all x," as deductive inferences so often are. It is not even based on a finding of most or countably many cases, as inductive inferences so often are. It holds only for normal or familiar cases and may fall outside this range of "general rule" cases.

Archeology provides many excellent examples of abductive reasoning. Leakey and Lewin (1992, pp. 28–29) described how a fossil hunter recognized a partially exposed bone fragment as part of a *hominid* skull. It was flattish, the slight curvature indicating it was part of a skull of a large-brained animal. The other observation pointing to the conclusion that the skull was hominid was that the impression of the brain on the inner surface was very faint. The inference to the best explanation of these observations was the fragment was part of a *hominid* skull. This plausible hypothesis was a reason for carrying the investigation forward and doing some more excavations, leading to the discovery of a nearly complete *homo erectus* skeleton. Shelley (1996, p. 282) cited this case as illustrating the use of visual abductive reasoning in archeology, because the diagnosis of the bone fragment as *hominid* was based on an explanation of the data provided by a close inspection of the site. From this data a plausible hypothesis was formed that was then tested by further investigations, providing more data that could support or refute the hypothesis.

Two of the examples given by Peirce not only illustrate what he meant by abductive inference but also show he was aware that abduction is common in everyday reasoning as well as in scientific reasoning. The first example quoted below (which I call "The Four Horsemen Example") came apparently from his personal experience and shows how common abductive inferences are in everyday thinking (1965V, p. 375).

THE FOUR HORSEMEN EXAMPLE
I once landed at a seaport in a Turkish province; and, as I was walking up to the house which I was to visit, I met a man upon horseback, surrounded by four horsemen holding a canopy over his head. As the governor of the province was the only personage I could think of who would be so greatly honored, I inferred that this was he. This was an hypothesis.

The second example (p. 375) (which I call "The Fossils Example") illustrates the use of abduction in science, showing that Peirce was aware of its use in scientific fields such as archeology and paleontology.

THE FOSSILS EXAMPLE

Fossils are found; say, remains like those of fishes, but far in the interior of the country. To explain the phenomenon, we suppose the sea once washed over this land. This is another hypothesis.

The abductive inference in both these cases is easily seen to follow the pattern of inference to the best explanation. In the fossils example, Peirce actually used the word "explain." We all know that fish require water to survive. That could be described as a general rule—a normal or familiar way that fish operate. But it could be subject to exceptions. Some fish can survive on land for some time. But how could fish survive this far into the interior where there is now no water? The observed fact calls for an explanation. A best explanation could be that there was water there at one time. In the four horsemen case, the given facts are also "curious." Why would one man be surrounded by four other men holding a canopy over his head? We could hazard a guess by saying that the general rule might be something like the following: only a very important person (such as the governor) would be likely to have a canopy supported by four horsemen. But the "only" here should not be taken to refer to the "for all x" of deductive logic or to warrant a deductively valid inference to the conclusion that this man must necessarily be the governor. It is just a guess, but it is an intelligent guess that offers the best explanation.

Hintikka (1998) expressed disagreement with the view that Peirce consistently equated abduction with inference to the best explanation. Although this view may represent Peirce's earlier perspective on abduction, according to Hintikka (1998, p. 511), it was not his mature view. Hintikka argued that Peirce took abduction to be the only way that a new hypothesis can be introduced in an inquiry (p. 511). He then (p. 511) cited a passage from Peirce where he seemed to claim that a hypothesis can be introduced into an inquiry even if it is not based on previous knowledge. But inference to the best explanation is always, by its nature, based on the given facts, that is, on previous knowledge in an inquiry. Therefore, Hintikka argued, Peirce's mature notion of abduction has to be wider than merely being inference to the best explanation. Hintikka also based his argument on some cases of scientific discovery drawn from the history of science, and some comment on what he took these cases to show will be made in chapter 7.

As well as being important in scientific and legal reasoning, abduction is abundant in everyday argumentation and in everyday goal-directed reasoning of the kind that is currently the subject of so much interest in artificial intelligence. An excellent and highly useful account of the form of abductive inference has been given in the influential work of Josephson and Josephson (1994). Their analysis is quite compatible with the account given by Peirce. They described abduction as equivalent to inference to the best explanation. Josephson and Josephson cited numerous examples of the use of abductive inference in everyday reasoning showing how common this form of inference is. The one quoted below (p. 6), in the form of a brief dialogue, is a good illustration.

> *Joe:* Why are you pulling into this filling station?
> *Tidmarsh:* Because the gas tank is nearly empty.
> *Joe:* What makes you think so?
> *Tidmarsh:* Because the gas gauge indicates nearly empty. Also, I have no reason to think that the gauge is broken, and it has been a long time since I filled the tank.

The reasoning used in this case follows Peirce's pattern of inference to the best explanation. Tidmarsh derives two alternative explanations for the circumstances presented by the gas gauge. The obvious explanation is that the gas in the tank is nearly empty. But there is also a possible alternative explanation. The gas gauge could be broken. But Tidmarsh does remember that it has been a long time since he filled the tank. This additional evidence tends to make the hypothesis that the tank is nearly empty more plausible. On balance, the best explanation of all the known facts is that the gas tank is nearly empty. This conclusion could be wrong, but it is plausible enough to warrant taking action. Tidmarsh should pull into the next gas station.

PEIRCE ON THE THREE TYPES OF REASONING

It is very clear from Peirce's writings that he divided reasoning into three mutually exclusive categories: deductive reasoning, inductive reasoning, and abductive reasoning. "Reasoning is of three types," he wrote, "Deduction, Induction, and Abduction" (1965V, p. 99). The basis of his classification is summed up in the following remark (1965V, p. 106): "Deduction proves that something *must* be; Induction shows that something *actually* is operative; Abduction merely suggests that something *may* be." The distinction as expressed in this quotation suggests that each type of reasoning has a different modality. It suggests that deduction is the strongest form, abduction is the weakest or most conjectural, and induction falls somewhere in between. Deductive reasoning begins "from a hypothetical state of things," paying no attention to "whether or not the hypothesis of our premises conforms more or less to the state of things in the outward world" (1965V, p. 99). For Peirce, deductive reasoning is necessary, and he even claims it is diagrammatic, meaning that it takes place at such a level of abstraction that it can be represented by transformations in a diagram (1965V, p. 100). Peirce's definition of deductive reasoning seems somewhat different from the usual definitions one finds in logic textbooks, but not different enough to raise too many concerns or doubts for the average reader. His definition of induction, however, is more of a departure.

Peirce disagreed so strongly with the theory of induction of John Stuart Mill that he declared, "It would be a waste of time to discuss such a theory" (1965V, p. 103). Dismissing other leading theories of induction as well, Peirce went on (1965V, p. 105) to define inductive reasoning in a way that links it to prediction and to theory. He wrote: "Induction consists in starting from a theory, deducing from it predictions of phenomena, and observing those phenomena in order to see *how nearly* they agree with the theory." This definition of inductive reasoning seems to be an operational one. It is defined in terms of the progress of the process of experimental investigation that would take place in science when a hypothesis is tested. It involves a matching or approximation between two things: theory and observation. The link connecting the two is prediction. The theory makes a prediction, which can then match the observation to a greater or lesser degree.

Peirce defined abduction in terms of explanation and hypothesis. His concise definition (1965V, p. 106) reads: "Abduction is the process of forming an explanatory hypothesis." Peirce even occasionally uses the term "hypothesis" as a synonym for abduction (1965II, p. 374). Thus he saw abduction as prior to induction and deduction in the process of scientific argumentation. Abduction is how the scientist forms the hypothesis that is later tested using deductive or inductive reasoning. This account makes abduction seem vitally important in scientific methodology. Peirce emphasized the central importance of abduction in science, and he saw it as extremely valuable in the process of scientific discovery. He wrote, "Every single item of scientific theory which stands established today has been due to Abduction" (Peirce, 1965V, p. 106, his capital letter A). How is the process of scientific investigation built on abduction? How can scientific truth be discovered by a process of reasoning that does not have logical necessity, or "compulsiveness," as Peirce calls it, and could be wrong? Peirce gave his answer in a resonant passage (1965V, p. 106).

Consider the multitude of theories that might have been suggested. A physicist comes across some new phenomenon in his laboratory. How does he know that the conjunctions of the planets have something to do with that or that it is not perhaps because the dowager empress of China has at the same time a year ago chanced to pronounce some word of mystical power or some invisible jinnee may be present. Think of what trillions and trillions of hypotheses might be made of which one only is true; and yet after two or three at the very most a dozen guesses, the physicist hits pretty nearly on the correct hypothesis. By chance he would have not been likely to do so in the whole time since the earth was solidified.

Several characteristics of abduction are revealed in this passage. First, it is a technique used to narrow down the number of alternatives by picking out one or a few hypotheses from a much larger number of them that are available. Second, it is a process of guessing, or picking the right guess, and thus it is clear that it is a fallible process that can lead to wrong hypotheses as well as to right ones. Third, it comes into play when a new phenomenon is observed, in other words, a phenomenon that has not yet been explained, or explained well enough, in science. The second characteristic seems to add a bit of mystery to abduction. It is guessing of a kind that implies a creative element. Indeed, later (p. 107) Peirce called abduction "insight" of a kind he equated with "the faculty of divining the ways of Nature." He theorized (p. 107) that abduction "resembles the instincts of the animals." These remarks make abduction sound highly intuitive and creative, even instinctive in nature. Thus it can be easily appreciated why it has proved difficult to analyze as an exact technique of scientific reasoning. It is easy to appreciate why abduction has been ignored in the past and brushed aside as "subjective."

Peirce (1965II, pp. 372–75) presented an elaborate but simple example designed to illustrate deduction, induction, and abduction. Suppose we draw a handful of beans at random out of a bag full of beans. We do not know what proportion of white beans are in the bag, but two-thirds of the beans in the handful are white. We conclude that two-thirds of the beans in the bag are white. The inference in this example has the following form (p. 375), representing an even simpler kind of case in which all the beans in the handful were found to be white.

INDUCTION

Premise One: These beans are from this bag.
Premise Two: These beans are white.
Conclusion: All the beans from this bag are white.

According to Peirce's description (p. 374), this inference is inductive because it goes from the case (premise one) and the result (premise two) to the rule. The conclusion is said to represent a "rule" because it is a generalization about all the beans in the bag. By comparison, a deductive inference goes from applying a general rule to a particular case in order to get a result, as in the following example (p. 374).

DEDUCTION

Premise One: All the beans from this bag are white.
Premise Two: These beans are from this bag.
Conclusion: These beans are white.

In presenting this example, Peirce (p. 374) stated the very important thesis that "all deduction is merely the application of general rules to particular cases." I think this thesis is very important because it links deductive reasoning to rules, and rules of a particular kind. Judging from the example above, the kind of rule used to support a deductive inference is one that is absolute in the sense that it does not admit of exceptions when applied to a case. Peirce does not say this, as far as I can see, but it does seem significant that he defines deductive reasoning by linking it to the notions of rule and case, as above.

Finally, we come to Peirce's example of the abductive type of inference using the beans in the bag example (1965II, p. 374).

Suppose I enter a room and there find a number of bags, containing different kinds of beans. On the table there is a handful of white beans; and, after some searching, I find one of the bags contains white beans only. I at once infer as a probability, or as a fair guess, that this handful was taken out of that bag. This sort of inference is called *making an hypothesis.*

The inference in this version of the example is reconstructed (1965II, p. 374) as abductive and as having the following form.

ABDUCTION
Premise One: All the beans from this bag are white.
Premise Two: These beans are white.
Conclusion: These beans are from this bag.

The first premise is the rule, the second is the result, and the conclusion is the case, in Peirce's reconstruction (p. 374). The line of reasoning in the example can also be reconstructed as follows. On the table I see the handful of white beans. On further investigation I find that one bag contains white beans only. These are my findings. They represent the observed facts or empirical data of the case. What could explain these data? Well, a hypothesis that could explain them is that the handful of beans could have come from the bag that was found to contain only white beans. This way the hypothesis works as a best explanation, given what is known and what is not known in the case. A special feature of the abduction example from Peirce is worth noting as well. In this inference, like the deductive one above, the generalization is universal. But the way it applies to the result seems to yield a conclusion by reasoning that is neither deductive nor inductive. It is possible, and for all we know quite probable, that the beans in the other bags are white, too. But until we test that conjecture, it would be reasonable to guess that the beans in the handful came from the bag containing white beans only.

Peirce's beans example and the way he draws the borders around the three types of reasoning are not entirely convincing or satisfactory in certain respects. One problem is that the way he defines induction seems peculiar and controversial. Another is that the beans example and the other examples put forward above are instances of everyday reasoning of the kind with which all of us are deeply familiar. But Peirce had primarily designed his theory of abduction to apply to scientific reasoning, particularly the kind of reasoning used in the process of scientific discovery. In his later work at least, he did see abduction as a way of modeling the logical reasoning that takes place during the process of scientific discovery that begins with a guess or hypothesis and then proceeds through a sequence of testing and refinement. Peirce thought that the three most remarkable "guesses" he knew of were Bacon's guess that heat is a mode of motion; Young's guess that the primary colors were violet, green, and red; and Dalton's guess that there were chemical atoms (Tursman, 1987, p. 18). Several quite detailed examples of how abductive reasoning of the kind described by Peirce are embodied in actual cases of scientific discovery have been presented by Tursman (1987). But for the person who wants to get a more practical grasp of how abductive reasoning is used in thinking and argumentation outside specialized scientific case studies, the details of the scientific context of discovery and verification of hypotheses may obscure the central notion of abductive reasoning. It is easy to get lost in the complexities and controversies in the philosophy of science about how this process works. Scientific discovery is a fascinating and timely topic for research, to be sure, but much light could be thrown on abduction by also analyzing some less technical cases familiar from everyday reasoning. One problem is that the philosophy of science, although very important in its own right, tends to favor examples that are so specific and technically controversial that they do not really serve well to pose basic questions that tend to be overlooked. The extensive scientific examples, although deeply interesting, do not illustrate abductive reasoning in such a compelling way that the reader can say, "Aha, now I know what it is." Thus some reconsideration of other examples could be useful.

Still another problem is that it seems hard to grasp what exactly the defining condition is supposed to be that divides abduction from induction. Peirce seemed to be very much aware of this difficulty. He tried to clarify the problem by making the following general statement (1965II, p. 385).

> The great difference between induction and hypothesis is, that the former infers the existence of phenomena such as we have observed in cases which are similar, while hypothesis supposes something of a different kind from what we have directly observed, and frequently something which it would be impossible for us to observe directly. Accordingly, when we stretch an induction quite beyond the limits of our observation, the inference partakes of the nature of hypothesis.

What Peirce is admitting, and what he concedes explicitly a few lines below (p. 385), is that in some real cases "we have a mixture of induction and hypothesis." This remark reveals the fundamental basis of the Peircian three-way distinction. It is based on the "real world" or set of presumed facts (data) observed in a given case. Deductive inference is abstracted from the data and is independent of them. Inductive inference is based on the data but extrapolates partially beyond them. Abduction extrapolates even further beyond the data. It stretches "quite beyond the limits of our observation," to use Peirce's terms. Thus abductive reasoning "infers very frequently a fact not capable of direct observation" (Peirce, 1965II, p. 386). To prove his point, Peirce (p. 386) used the example of the hypothesis that Napoleon Bonaparte once existed.[7] In his view, an abductive inference of this kind could never be replaced by an inductive inference. It just goes too far beyond the data. This example is quite convincing and helps us grasp what the difference between inductive reasoning and abductive reasoning is supposed to be in the Peircean view. But it also raises many further problems that call for careful consideration and discussion in their own right.

PEIRCE ON THE FORM OF ABDUCTIVE INFERENCE

Although an abductive argument provides a form of support for its conclusion "only problematically or conjecturally" according to Peirce (1965V, p. 117), it is a logical inference "having a perfectly definite logical form." The million-dollar question then is, "What is its logical form?" Peirce gave an answer to this question, as quoted in the important passage below expressing the form of abductive inference (p. 117). In this form of inference, C is a statement or set of statements describing some facts, and A is another statement that supposedly accounts for these facts.

PEIRCE'S FORM OF ABDUCTIVE INFERENCE
The surprising fact, C, is observed.
But if A were true, C would be a matter of course.
Hence, there is reason to suspect that A is true.

Just below (p. 117), Peirce added that he was not sure that this proposed form was the correct account of the matter, but he supported it by going on, in the next few pages, by replying to some objections to it. During the discussion, he tried to probe into this logical form more deeply to reveal more about what abduction is and how it works as a form of logical reasoning. But in a rather opaque passage (1965V, p. 120), he seemed to admit that he could not go further except to say that deductive necessity, inductive probability, and abductive expectability all come from a process of "inhibitory" self-control of thinking. In the final part of the discussion (1965V, pp. 121–23), Peirce argued that the question of abduction is really the question of pragmatism. Perhaps what he is saying is that one has to go beyond the narrow framework of deductive and inductive reasoning to understand abduction. This view seems to be borne out by his own description of how abduction works as a form of reasoning that has instrumental value in the process by which scientific discovery is made possible through the formation and testing of hypotheses. Peirce seemed to be suggesting that we will only be able to model abductive reasoning formally, or by some abstract form of inference, once we get a broader pragmatic picture of how it works in some richer account of the process of scientific thinking. Thus Peirce's view of abductive inference can be seen as genuinely innovative and pioneering. It was on the frontiers of logic when he wrote, and it still is more than a century later.

Peirce's form of abductive inference looks like a kind of reverse *modus ponens* inference. Its form looks like that of the invalid form of inference called affirming the consequent. These appearances make us wonder what relationship there is, if any, between Peirce's form of abductive inference and familiar forms of deductively valid inference. Fann (1970, p. 52) interpreted Peirce as making the claim that any given abductive inference can be reduced to a corresponding deductively valid inference. Fann (p. 52) mounted his argument on the premise that, for Peirce, the only justification for an abductive inference is that it explains the facts. Although this premise accurately represents Peirce's view, the argument Fann (1970, p. 52) based it on is more questionable: "Now to explain a fact is to show that it is a necessary or probable result from another fact, known or supposed. Thus, this part of the problem is simply a question of reducing any given abductive inference to a corresponding deduction. If the latter turns out to be valid, the correctness of the abduction is guaranteed." What Fann appears to be concluding from this argument is that in the Peircian view, there will always be a deductively valid argument matching any correct abductive inference. One might question, then, whether, in Fann's interpretation of the Peircian view of the logical form of abduction, for every correct Peircian abductive inference, there is a corresponding *modus ponens* argument. This question was clearly answered by Fann in the affirmative. He wrote (p. 52) that corresponding to Peirce's form of abductive inference (as quoted above) there is always an argument of the following *modus ponens* form.

MODUS PONENS (MP) COUNTERPART OF PEIRCE'S FORM OF ABDUCTIVE
INFERENCE
If *A* were true, *C* would be a matter of course.
A is true.
Hence, *C* is true.[8]

According to Fann (p. 52), Peirce consistently maintained the view that deduction is the rationale of both induction and abduction. Fann hypothesized that Peirce's view also implies the following thesis: any form of inductive inference is only valid (or structurally correct) because a corresponding deductive inference is (deductively) valid. And in particular, Fann hypothesized that matching any correct abductive inference having Peirce's form of abduction will be a corresponding *modus ponens* inference produced by reversing the antecedent and consequent of the conditional premise.

The view that a *modus ponens* inference of this sort (with antecedent and consequent reversed in the conditional premise) is a correct form of plausible reasoning in scientific argumentation has been maintained by Polya (1954, 18–19). To show how such an inference can be reasonable, he described a common kind of situation that occurs in mathematical research. A mathematician is trying to determine whether a proposition *A* is true or not. The mathematician does not know that but does know that *A* implies *B*. If *B* is false, it would follow deductively by *modus tollens* that *A* must also be false. However, suppose the person finds that *B* is true. What would that suggest? According to Polya (18–19), there is a heuristic inference: "since its consequent *B* turned out to be true, *A* itself seems to deserve more confidence." Polya did not identify this heuristic inference by using the term "abduction." Nevertheless, he did identify it as a form of plausible reasoning and contrasted it with deductive *modus tollens* by placing the two side by side in a display as below (p. 19).

Demonstrative	*Heuristic*
A implies *B*	*A* implies *B*
B false	*B* true
A false	*A* more credible

The form on the right, identified by Polya as a heuristic, appears to have the same structure as the fallacious form of argument called affirming the consequent in deductive logic. It reasons backward from the consequent of a conditional to the antecedent. And yet Polya was putting it forward as a structurally correct form of plausible reasoning.

Polya's remarks on this subject are very interesting in regard to the subject of the analysis of abductive reasoning. They are especially interesting in light of Peirce's theory (or at least Fann's version of it) that the logical form of abductive reasoning is a kind of reverse *modus ponens* inference just like the heuristic inference described by Polya above. A number of questions are raised. Does abductive reasoning of the kind described by Polya occur commonly in mathematical research in the way Polya outlined? And if the kind of mathematical reasoning described by Polya can properly be classified as abductive, can his representation of it as a kind of reverse *modus ponens* form of argument (the heuristic above) be taken generally to represent the form of abductive inference as an identifiable kind of plausible reasoning? These are large questions, and without some better account of abduction than we presently have, there does not seem to be any way to answer them.

I will not go into the question of whether Fann's hypothesis may be taken to accurately represent Peirce's view of abduction. What is more interesting is that Fann's hypothesis itself represents a particular view of abductive inference that is not only comparable to Polya's heuristic above but that has also been put forward by Magnani (2001) as the formal basis of an analysis of abductive reasoning. This view raises the question of the logical form of abductive inference and the question of its relationship to *modus ponens*. In Magnani's view, abductive inference is different from deductive and inductive forms, but is closely tied to both in the process of scientific discovery. These two contentions fit well with both Peirce's and Polya's remarks cited above. All three views seem to agree that abduction is tied to the process of scientific research and inquiry and thus that it has a pragmatic as well as formal logical aspect. We will not attempt to probe more deeply into these issues concerning the precise form of abductive inference yet, reserving this special problem for detailed analysis in chapter 6.

But even at this early point, it is good to notice how much abduction depends on a particular view of explanation. Fann, as quoted above, wrote that "to explain a fact is to show that it is a necessary or probable result from another fact, known or supposed." This view of explanation was popular in philosophy at the time Fann wrote and still is in some circles. It is identifiable with the so-called deductive-nomological model of explanation and its inductive variant associated with Carl Hempel. But once we come to see that this restricted view of explanation represents only one kind of it (in chapter 2), much light can be thrown on abduction. A new way of looking at abduction will be revealed that throws doubt on the kind of tight correspondence between abduction and deduction hypothesized by Fann. For the present, however, it is important to be aware that there is much controversy concerning the relationship between the *modus ponens* form of inference, so familiar in deductive logic, and Peirce's account of the form of abductive inference.

SCIENTIFIC DISCOVERY AND ARTIFICIAL INTELLIGENCE

Norwood Russell Hanson (1958) was an early exponent of abductive reasoning in the philosophy of science, building his analysis along Peircean lines. Hanson's work has been described as "iconoclastic" (Nickles, 1980, p. 22) because he "almost alone" argued the case for an abductive approach to scientific discovery from about 1958 to his death in 1967. His book *Patterns of Discovery* (1958) gave many convincing examples of abductive reasoning in physics and other sciences, but it has not until recently been given adequate credit as a centrally important and highly original work in the philosophy of science and in the study of argumentation. To illustrate abductive reasoning, Hanson used the famous example of Kepler's developing his elliptical orbit hypothesis as an explanation of planetary motion. According to Hanson (1958, p. 85), when Kepler wrote out his reasons for suggesting the ellipse as a hypothesis, these reasons were neither deductive nor inductive. They were reasons based on what Hanson called retroductive inference, or what is more commonly called abductive reasoning. In Hanson's reconstruction of how Kepler reasoned, he drew his conclusion by working from the given celestial observations as facts or empirical findings and then trying to explain these facts by suggesting an explanation (p. 85). Josephson (2001, p. 1622) pointed out that although abduction has been "largely overlooked and underanalyzed by almost 2,400 years of formal logic and philosophy," many examples of it in scientific argumentation can be found, "going back to ancient times." Among examples of best-explanation arguments Josephson cited the following (p. 1622). On the basis of observations of the appearances and phases of the moon, Pythagoras argued that the moon is spherical and lit by the sun. Darwin's hypothesis of natural selection offers a plausible explanation of how well things fit together in nature. Newton's argument for his theory of gravitation is based on his explanation of the motions of the planets and tides.

Hanson regarded Peirce as the discoverer of abduction, and Hanson's own account of the form of abductive inference is based on Peirce's (Curd, 1980). Hanson's account (1958, p. 86) represents the inference as having two premises. *H* is a hypothesis.

Premise 1: some surprising phenomenon *P* is observed.
Premise 2: *P* would be explicable as a matter of course if *H* were true.
Conclusion: hence there is a reason to think that *H* is true.

Hanson argued that Kepler's inference to a hypothesis of elliptical motion was not an inductive inference "from any actuarial or statistical processing of increasingly large numbers of *P*'s" (p. 87). Instead, it was a perceiving of a pattern in the data and then the forming of a hypothesis that enabled what has been observed to be understood. It is important to note that Hanson described abduction as based on a prior process of explanation of observations and that he described this process as one in which the observations come to be understood. Hanson called this process retroduction, as contrasted with prediction. What Kepler did, according to Hanson, was to explain the given data in a way that was different from, and better than, the old hypothesis that had been accepted. Retroduction, in Hanson's view, begins with observation and then moves to explanation of what was observed. Thus Hanson's description of retroduction linked abduction to explanation and linked explanation to understanding.

Hanson did advance beyond Peirce's account of abduction by showing better how the process works in case studies of scientific discovery and by articulating better how abduction works in such cases. Still, critics had problems with interpreting his account. Their criticisms have been summarized by Nickles (1980, pp. 23–25). Some critics were unsure of the difference between the Peirce-Hanson notion of retroductive inference and the model of hypothetical-deductive inference used to analyze the notion of scientific explanation (p. 23). Other critics thought that the Peirce-Hanson model of the logical form of abductive inference failed to account for many contextual factors over and above given observations, such as "previous theoretical results, rational expectations, heuristics, goals, and standards that together direct inquiry" (p. 23). Still others thought that Hanson's "heavy use of Gestalt perceptual metaphors" made his notion of discovery seem psychological (p. 24). This would be disappointing to those who questioned whether logical inference should be based on psychological notions. Another problem, similar to that indicated above about Peirce's own analysis, was the apparent multiplicity of Hanson's notion of abduction. It seemed unclear whether abduction was a notion of hypothesis generation or of argument evaluation (Nickles, 1980, p. 24). Finally, Hanson did not convincingly enough support his claim that there is a special logic of discovery different from deductive and inductive models of reasoning (p. 25). Thus many philosophers, especially those of a positivistic bent, were reluctant to accept the idea that there was a third clear standard of logical reasoning beyond the traditionally accepted deductive and inductive models.

There has been a long tradition of sharply separating justification and discovery. The tradition warns that creative discovery is a psychological notion, whereas justification is a logical notion. This way of drawing the distinction sees discovery as outside the bounds of logic. There has also been an opposed view, expressed from time to time by pragmatists, that discovery does have a logic of its own. For example, Schiller (1917) made a distinction between the logic of proof and the logic of scientific discovery. A pragmatist, Schiller argued that scientific discovery has its own logic, one different from deductive logic. He saw deductive logic as "static" and argued that there should also be a dynamic logic applicable to cases of arguments in which knowledge is growing (Schiller, 1917, p. 273). However, many philosophers doubted that there could be any such thing as a logic of discovery. Popper (1959, pp. 31–32) "sharply" distinguished "between the process of conceiving a new idea, and the methods and results of examining it logically." During Hanson's time of writing, and for some time afterward, the Popperian view was dominant (Curd, 1980). The generally held assumption was that a logic of discovery is simply not possible. Discovery, or any creative process that leads to thinking up new ideas, seems intuitive and unsystematic, and this aspect suggested to many that it lacks any kind of logical structure. During this period, little attention was paid by philosophers to a notion of abductive reasoning different from both deductive and inductive that might be applied to scientific discovery.

A change came with the advent of artificial intelligence. It became apparent to scientists who were engaged in building robots to carry out practical tasks and in creating software that could process information and automate tasks that abductive reasoning is vitally important. The most useful and accessible analysis of abduction, and how it used in AI, is that of Josephson and Josephson (1994). Not only do they give many examples of how abductive reasoning is used in computing and in other fields but also they have presented a model that represents the form of abductive inference. This model goes well beyond Peirce's analysis of abduction and furthermore seems to go in a different direction in several respects. According to Josephson and Josephson (1994, p. 14), abductive inference has the following form, which clearly shows its structure as based on inference to the best explanation. *H* is a hypothesis.

JOSEPHSON AND JOSEPHSON (J&J) FORM OF ABDUCTIVE INFERENCE
D is a collection of data.
H explains *D*.
No other hypothesis can explain *D* as well as *H* does.
Therefore *H* is probably true.

It can easily be seen how the Tidmarsh example from Josephson and Josephson above fits the J&J form of inference. If you reconsider the four horsemen example and the fossils example from Peirce, it is not hard to see how they too fit this model. But how, you might ask, could such a form of inference be evaluated in a given case? How should we evaluate the strength or weakness of a given abductive argument? Peirce would presumably have answered that strength and weakness can be evaluated by testing them out by further observations or experiments. Josephson and Josephson presented an answer that basically agrees with Peirce's theory that abduction needs to be evaluated in light of the process of forming and testing a hypothesis in an inquiry.

The answer presented by the Josephsons is that contextual factors of the given case, of various sorts, need to be taken into account. The multiplicity of these factors suggests that the evaluation of abductive inference is quite different from that of deductive or inductive inference. According to Josephson and Josephson (p. 14), the judgment of likelihood associated with an abductive inference should be taken to depend on six factors.

1. how decisively *H* surpasses the alternatives
2. how good *H* is by itself, independently of considering the alternatives (we should be cautious about accepting a hypothesis, even

if it is clearly the best one we have, if it is not sufficiently plausible
in itself)
3. judgments of the reliability of the data
4. how much confidence there is that all plausible explanations
have been considered (how thorough was the search for alternative
explanations).

Beyond these four factors of "judgment of likelihood," Josephson and
Josephson (p. 14) list two additional considerations required for the
evaluation of an abductive inference.

5. pragmatic considerations, including the costs of being wrong
and the benefits of being right
6. how strong the need is to come to a conclusion at all, especially
considering the possibility of seeking further evidence before deciding.

The process for evaluating abductive inferences presented by Josephson
and Josephson is different from the process of evaluating deductive or
inductive inferences. In a given case, several explanations of the queried
fact are possible. The conclusion to be inferred turns on which is the
"best" explanation at some given point in the collection of data or an
investigation that may continue to move along. But the process of investigation may not be finished. Collection of more facts may suggest a
new explanation that may even be better than the one now accepted.
The conclusion is an intelligent guess based on what is known at some
given point in an investigation that may, or perhaps even should, continue.

The account of abductive inference and inference to the best explanation presented above has emphasized the common elements found in
the analyses given by Peirce, Harman, and the Josephsons. It is necessary to add that this brief account may be misleading in some respects
and that a closer and more detailed explication of the finer points of the
three analyses could reveal important underlying philosophical differences. Inferences to the best explanation, as expounded by Harman and
the Josephsons, can involve deductive and inductive processes of a kind
that would apparently be excluded by Peirce's account of abduction. A
main thesis for Harman, argued at length in his article, is the proposition
that "all warranted inferences which may be described as instances of

enumerative induction must also be described as instances of inference to the best explanation" (Harman, 1965, p. 88). For Peirce, on the other hand, it would seem that deductive and inductive processes are distinct from the abductive proposal of a hypothesis to be tested. It could well be that, when analyzed in more depth, the notion of abduction presented by Peirce is different from the notion of inference to the best explanation presented by Harman and the Josephsons. Indeed, in the theory of Magnani (2001), abduction is not the same as inference to the best explanation. According to Magnani (2001, p. 19), there are two meanings of the word "abduction." In creative abduction, the task is to generate plausible hypotheses. In a second kind of abduction, called inference to the best explanation, the task is to evaluate the hypotheses.

However, the examples presented above, along with the various definitions and characterizations given, suggest the hypothesis that abductive inference and inference to the best explanation can tentatively be taken to be equivalent notions. Peirce's frequent use of explanatory language in his account of abduction certainly suggests the closeness of the two notions in his view. Magnani's account quite rightly distinguished between two components of abduction that represent two different tasks undertaken during the execution of abductive reasoning. Nonetheless, the theory of abductive reasoning set out in chapter 6 will combine these two functions in a single notion of abductive reasoning. In this view, the single notion will be taken to represent abductive reasoning as having a single meaning. According to this meaning, abductive reasoning will be taken to be equivalent to inference to the best explanation.

ABDUCTIVE INFERENCE IN LEGAL EVIDENCE

It might be assumed that because Peirce invented the expression "abductive inference" in the logical meaning we take it to have today, he was also the first exponent of inference to the best explanation as a form of reasoning. However, there is some evidence that the notion of inference to the best explanation has been used as a method of analyzing argumentation in a tradition that may be independent of Peirce's work. Writings in law, especially in the field of evidence, have employed this notion to analyze the kind of inference so common in law in which a conclusion is inferred from a fact by offering an explanation of the fact. John H. Wigmore, in his major work on evidence in law (1940, p. 418), quoted a passage from Alfred Sidgwick's book *Fallacies* (1884) in which

Sidgwick offered a very clear definition of inference to the best explanation. Sidgwick wrote, "By the best explanation is meant . . . that solitary one out of all possible hypotheses which, while explaining all the facts already in view, is narrowed, limited, hedged, or qualified, sufficiently to guard in the best possible way against undiscovered exceptions" (as quoted by Wigmore, p. 418). Sidgwick saw inference to the best explanation as representing a very common form of reasoning that is different from either deductive or inductive reasoning. Wigmore was quick to pick up on the importance of this kind of reasoning in legal evidence judgments, and he applied the idea to the reasoning used in many typical legal cases in a very convincing and helpful way. Wigmore's work has been largely ignored by the logical and philosophical communities who have studied abduction, but much can be learned from it.

Wigmore worked out an elaborately detailed method of weighing the mass of evidence in a legal case by mapping out the argumentation on both sides and then comparing two total networks of argumentation. He constructed a network in the form of an "evidence chart," using an argument reconstruction method similar to what is known today in logic as the method of argument diagramming. The best source of examples of this method as applied to legal cases by Wigmore is his important work titled *The Principles of Judicial Proof* (1913). His evidence charts can be quite massive in some cases. The diagram shows a network of one-step arguments chained together by joining inferential lines. Arrows are used to exhibit single inferences that lead from premises to conclusions in local arguments, and these local arguments are shown as chained to other neighboring ones. The whole diagram, once all the arguments used on one side of a case are connected, represents the mass of evidence on that side in the case. Wigmore (1913, p. 747) used these logical diagrams or so-called evidence charts to "determine rationally the net persuasive effect of a mixed mass of evidence." As Goodwin (2000, p. 229) observed, Wigmore claimed that his method of evidence charts represented more than just the psychological notion of coming to accept a belief. He thought of it as a method for representing the logical process of coming to a correct decision on the basis of evidence in a case.

The actual details of how Wigmore constructed these diagrams and the notation he used are not especially important, although it is worth looking at one of the big ones presented in the *Principles*. What is more interesting for our purpose here is that the single steps of inference in the diagrams are often meant by Wigmore to represent abductive inferences. Wigmore accepted the view that there are only two kinds of inference, deductive and inductive (Goodwin, 2000, p. 234). But an examination of some of the legal examples he used to illustrate the chart method show clearly that he described the inferences in them using the language of inference to the best explanation.

By looking at some examples of how Wigmore treated typical legal arguments of the kind used in court to try to prove something, we can study how Wigmore represented the logical form of the single inferences used by a lawyer. Wigmore (1940, p. 416) offered an analysis of the following common type of example: "*a* planned to kill *b;* therefore *a* probably did kill *b.*" Wigmore began his analysis by commenting that in this kind of case "it is clear that we have here no semblance of a syllogism." So how can one analyze the argumentation in this common form of inference? Wigmore (p. 417) hypothesized that it can be represented as taking the form of argument shown below.

THE FIXED DESIGN ARGUMENT
Major Premise: Men's fixed designs are probably carried out.
Minor Premise: *a* had a fixed design to kill *b.*
Conclusion: *a* probably carried out his design and killed *b.*

This form of argument is highly typical of the kind of argumentation used by the prosecution side in a criminal case. Wigmore saw this argument as a weak one that proceeds by imputing a motive to an individual and then using this motive to argue that this individual killed the victim. But he saw it as an argument that could present legitimate evidence in such a case. What is most interesting is that he used the language of inference to the best explanation when he wrote (p. 418), "There may be other explanations than the desired one for the fact taken as the basis of proof." He also linked this form of argument with argument from sign, using the fictional example of Robinson Crusoe seeing human footprints in the sand (p. 419). This example is one of inference to the best explanation. In the story, Robinson Crusoe was stranded on a deserted island, and the appearance of a set of what looked like human footprints presented him with some evidence for the hypothesis that there was another human being on the island. In the normal classification of argumentation schemes, this argument would be said to have the form of argument from sign.

Another common example of legal argumentation quoted from Wigmore (1940, p. 420) shows perhaps even better how he analyzed cases of arguments used in legal evidence as instances of inference to the best explanation.

THE ROBBERY EXAMPLE

The fact that *a* before a robbery had no money, but after had a large sum, is offered to indicate that he by robbery became possessed of the large sum of money. There are several other possible explanations—the receipt of a legacy, the payment of a debt, the winning of a gambling game, and the like. Nevertheless, the desired explanation rises, among other explanations, to a fair degree of plausibility, and the evidence is received.

The evidence put forward in this example has the form of inference to the best explanation. It shows the conclusion as arrived at by means of a choice among several competing explanations of the given facts. It also shows that the argument is fallible and inconclusive by itself. In a real case, new evidence presented by the other side could show that there was some other explanation for *a*'s coming into possession of the large sum of money. Thus each small item of evidence, in Wigmore's view, needs to take its place within the wider network of inferences that make up the mass of evidence in a case. It is this mass of evidence that can swing the burden of proof to one side or the other in a trial.

Thus we can see that Wigmore's analysis of inference to the best explanation, like Peirce's notion of abduction, is pragmatic in nature. Abduction, or inference to the best explanation, can be understood and evaluated only in relation to the process of investigation in a case. Peirce defined abduction mainly within the framework of the process of scientific discovery and experimental testing of a hypothesis. Wigmore defined inference to the best explanation within the Anglo-American legal framework of evidence law. The paradigm process of legal argumentation is the trial, in which both sides present evidence according to rules of evidence. Wigmore saw using inference to come to accept a conclusion in legal argumentation in a trial as a systematic process in which alternative explanations are considered and then accepted or rejected. His analysis of such arguments continually uses the language of inference to the best explanation, suggesting that at least at the practical level, he was aware of how the model of abductive reasoning can be applied to legal evidence. At any rate, Wigmore's use of abductive inference in his analysis of legal evidence suggests emphatically that the abductive model is highly applicable to legal reasoning. In the past, the notion of abduction has not been widely known to experts on legal logic and legal evidence, and much of their work has centered on deductive and inductive models of rational argument. But even a glimpse of Wigmore's work on evidence shows the enormous potential of abduction as applied to the logical structure of reasoning in legal evidence.

DEFEASIBLE, PLAUSIBLE, AND PRESUMPTIVE REASONING

Defeasible arguments are ones that can be acceptable at the moment even though in the future they may be open to defeat. New evidence may come in later that defeats the argument. Hence a defeasible argument may be defined as one that is now rationally acceptable even though it may fail to retain this status (Pollock, 1987). The canonical example of a defeasible argument, used so often in AI, is the Tweety argument (Reiter, 1980).

THE TWEETY ARGUMENT
Birds fly.
Tweety is a bird.
Therefore Tweety flies.

The Tweety argument may be rationally acceptable assuming that we have no information about Tweety except that he is a bird. But suppose new information comes in telling us that Tweety is a penguin. A penguin is a bird, but it cannot fly. So once we come to know that Tweety is a penguin, the Tweety argument is defeated. Both premises are generally acceptable, and true, as far as we know. But the conclusion is false.

The first premise of the Tweety argument is not a universal generalization of the absolute kind that can be rendered by the universal quantifier of deductive logic. It is not really an inductive generalization, either. It states that birds normally fly or that one can normally expect a bird to fly, subject to exceptions. It is a qualified generalization that implicitly contains a qualifier. If some qualifications are known in advance, they could be stated by listing them and using a term such as "except" to head the list. For example, penguins and ostriches could be listed as exceptions. But suppose Tweety is neither a penguin nor an ostrich, but a bird with a broken wing. Not all possible exceptions can be predicted in advance. Thus a defeasible argument is one that is open ended, whereas a deductively valid argument is closed in that it necessarily implies its conclusion. Pollock's theory brings out this contrast by viewing deductive and defeasible arguments as giving different kinds of reasons to support a claim. In Pollock's theory, defeasible reasons are *prima facie* reasons to support a claim, meaning that these reasons are subject to further considerations. These further considerations are of two types, rebutting defeaters and undercutting defeaters. A rebutting defeater attacks a claim directly and is therefore a reason for denying the claim (Pollock, 1995, 40). An undercutting defeater attacks the connection between the claim and its support rather than attacking the claim directly (p. 41). Thus it is only a reason for doubting the claim, not for denying it.

Defeasible arguments are very important in legal argumentation (Verheij, 1996; Prakken and Sartor, 1996, 1997). For example, if a witness testifies that Bob shot Ed, then that may be a good reason for a jury to accept the statement that Bob shot Ed. But if new evidence comes in showing that Bob has an alibi or that the witness was lying, the argument based on witness testimony may be defeated. Another closely related kind of reasoning that is very important in legal argumentation is presumptive inference. In law, a person may be presumed to be dead, for purposes of settling the estate after a prescribed period, even though it is not known for sure that the person is dead. As long as there has been no evidence that the person is still alive, after a prescribed number of years, the conclusion may be drawn that the person is (for legal purposes) dead. Of course, this conclusion may later be retracted if the person turns up alive. It is merely a presumption, as opposed to a proved fact. A presumption, then, is something you move ahead with, for practical purposes, even though it is not known to be true at the present time. It is a kind of useful assumption that can be justified on practical grounds in order to take action, for example, even though the evidence to support it may be insufficient or inconclusive.[9] Presumption and plausibility are both concerned with the practical need to take action or to accept a hypothesis provisionally, even though the evidence is, at present, not sufficient to prove the hypothesis beyond doubt or show it is known to be true.

Plausibility, according to Rescher (1976, p. 28), evaluates propositions in relation to "the standing and solidity of their cognitive basis," by weighing available alternatives. Rescher (1976, p. 55) sees plausibility as closely related to presumption: "A positive presumption always favors the most plausible contentions among the available alternatives." A proposition stands as a plausible presumption until some alternative is shown to be more plausible. It is a controversial question whether plausibility is different from probability, and it is hard to exclude entirely the possibility that plausibility might turn out to be some special kind of probability. Rescher (1976, pp. 30–31) puts the difference this way. Probability takes a set of exclusive and exhaustive alternative propositions and distributes a fixed amount (unity) across the set, based on the internal contents of each proposition. Plausibility does not assign weights on a basis of internal contents but on a basis of the external support for each proposition being considered. The way plausibility is described in Josephson and Josephson (1994, pp. 265–72) also makes it seem different from probability. As shown there, plausibility has often been measured by coarse-scale "confidence values" that seem to be good enough to decide actions but are different from probability values. According to Josephson and Josephson (p. 266), confidence values are useful in expert medical diagnoses, but it is not helpful to treat them as though they were measures of probability (p. 270). A set of rules for evaluating plausible inferences has been presented in Walton (1992). The rules are based on the distinction between linked and convergent arguments. How the rules work can be roughly explained as follows. In a linked argument, both (or all) premises are functionally related to support the conclusion. In a convergent argument, each premise is an independent line of evidence to support the conclusion.[10] In a linked argument, Theophrastus's rule applies. The plausibility value of the conclusion must be at least as great as that of the least plausible premise. In a convergent argument, the value of the conclusion must be at least as great as that of the most plausible premise.

The notion of plausible inference can best be explained by citing a standard example of it used in the ancient world. Plato attributed this example to Corax and Tisias, two Sophists who lived around the middle of the fifth century BC (Gagarin, 1994, p. 50). Aristotle attributed the example to Corax (*Rhetoric* 1402a17–28). According to the example, there was a fight between two men, and one accused the other of starting it by assaulting him. The man who was alleged to have started the fight was quite a bit smaller and weaker than the other man. His argument to the jury ran as follows. Did it appear plausible that he, the smaller and weaker man, would assault the bigger and stronger man? This hypothesis did seem implausible to the jury. The example illustrates how plausible inference can have the effect of shifting a weight of evidence to one side or the other in a legal case. In such a case, because the event happened in the past and there were no witnesses other than the two principals, a small weight of evidence could shift the balance of considerations to one side or the other. But how does plausible inference work as a kind of evidence in such a case? It is not empirical evidence describing what actually occurred. But it does have to do with appearances. It has to do with how the situation appeared to the jury and how the participants would be likely to react in that kind of situation.

Abduction also relates to hypotheses that are accepted provisionally, often for practical reasons, or to guide an investigation further along. Thus the practical motivation of using abductive inference is comparable to those of presumptive inference and plausible inference. Presumptive inference is easily confused with abductive inference, and the two often tend to be seen as either the same thing or very closely related. The notion of presumptive inference tends to be more prominent in writings on legal argumentation, whereas the term "abductive inference" is much more commonly used in describing scientific argumentation and in computer science. Both types of inference are provisional in nature. Both are also hypothetical and have to do with reasoning that moves forward in the absence of complete evidence. Judging from the account of abductive inference given above, it seems like it can be described as presumptive in nature. But what does that mean? To explore the question, we might find it useful to begin with some account of what presumptive inference is supposed to be.

A dialectical analysis of presumptive inference has been put forward in Walton (1996a), and the main points of the analysis have been nicely summarized in Blair (1999a, p. 56). The analysis presumes a structure of dialogue in which, in the simplest case, there are two participants. They are called the proponent and the respondent, and they take turns asking questions, putting forward arguments, and making other moves. In such a dialogue, when the proponent puts forward an assertion, there is a burden of proof attached to that move. If the respondent asks for justification of the assertion, the proponent is then obliged, at the next move, either to give an argument to justify the assertion or to retract it. This requirement is a rule that applies to the making of assertions in certain types of dialogue. With respect to this rule, assumption may be contrasted with assertion. In a dialogue, a proponent can ask the respondent to accept an assumption at any point, and there is no burden of proof attached. Assumptions are free, so to speak. An assumption is just a hypothesis. It may be proved or disproved when later evidence comes into a dialogue, but you do not have to prove it right away. Presumption can be described as a move in dialogue that is midway between assertion and assumption. According to the dialectical analysis in Walton (1996a), when the proponent puts forward a presumption, the person does not have to back it up with proof but does have to give it up if the respondent can disprove it. As Blair (1999a, p. 56) puts it, "A presumption so conceived has practical value by way of advancing the argumentation, and, in accepting something as a presumption, the interlocutor assumes the burden of rebutting it." As Reiter (1980) and Blair (1999a, p. 56) indicate, presumptive inference comes into play in cases where there is an absence of firm evidence or knowledge. The practical justification of presumptive reasoning, despite its uncertain and inconclusive nature, is that it moves a dialogue forward part way to drawing a final conclusion, even in the absence of such evidence at a given point. Because of its dependence on use in a context of dialogue, it is different in nature from either deductive or inductive inference.

A legal example cited above can be used to illustrate how presumption has an inherently practical justification in moving a dialogue forward. As mentioned above, the presumption that a person is dead is often invoked in legal reasoning in cases where the person has disappeared for a long time and there is no evidence that the individual is still alive. In order to deal with practical problems posed by estates, courts can rule that a person is presumed to be dead as long as there has been no evidence for a fixed period that the person is still alive. For practical purposes, say to execute a will, the conclusion is drawn by presumptive inference that for legal purposes the person will be declared dead. This legal notion of presumptive inference fits the dialectical analysis. There may be insufficient positive evidence to prove that the person is dead. Nevertheless, for legal purposes, a court can conclude by presumptive inference that the person is dead. The justification is the lack of positive evidence that the person is alive. Presumption, according to the dialectical analysis, is comparable to assertion as a move in dialogue except that the burden of proof is reversed. Normally in a dialogue in which the goal is to resolve a conflict of opinions by rational argumentation, when you make an assertion, you are obliged to prove it or give it up (van Eemeren and Grootendorst, 1992). But when you put forward a presumption to be accepted, at least provisionally, by all parties to the dialogue, you are obliged to give it up only if the other party can disprove it. It is this dialectical reversal that characterizes presumptive inference. This type of legal case also illustrates quite well the connection between presumption and the argument from ignorance (*argumentum ad ignorantiam*), a type of argument often taken to be fallacious in logic. Such arguments from lack of evidence (often called *ex silentio* arguments in history) are, however, not always fallacious (Walton, 1996a). Under the right conditions, they can be quite reasonable presumptive arguments. These kinds of arguments are very common in legal reasoning. The most obvious cases are those associated with the so-called presumption of innocence in criminal law.

TENTATIVE DEFINITIONS

So what should be said in answer to the question about the third type of argument, as contrasted to the deductive and inductive kinds? Is this third type of argument best described as abductive, presumptive, or plausible? The best answer, although it will be unsatisfying to those who want a simple answer, is that this type of reasoning is both presumptive and plausibilistic and that it is very often abductive as well. It is perhaps even fair to say that it is typically abductive in nature. Plausible reasoning is like that. What characterizes it as a type of reasoning is that it selects from a set of alternatives, as Rescher's description of it (above) showed, and that it is relativized to a given body of evidence. These two characteristics are also properties of abductive reasoning. But abductive reasoning has the additional characteristic that it is always based on an explanation, or set of explanations, of the given body of evidence, or set of facts in a case. So abductive reasoning also seems to be a special kind of plausible reasoning. But abductive reasoning seems to be inherently presumptive in nature. As Peirce's account makes clear, abduction is a kind of supposition-based reasoning that proceeds by the construction of a hypothesis. A hypothesis is a provisional guess that may have to be given up later, when more experimental evidence comes in. So abductive reasoning is presumptive in nature. The burden of proof is not there. A guess is allowed, even if there is very little or no firm evidence to support it yet. But the hypothesis has to be given up if later evidence to the contrary falsifies it.

When the deductive and inductive categories are contrasted with some third category, what is the basis of the distinction? Is it the strength of the link between the premises and the conclusion? It is this aspect that often seems to be stressed as important. As Blair (1999b, p. 50) pointed out, philosophers interested in the norms that govern argument have focused on the illiative (logical) core rather than on the social practice in which the argument is embedded. But perhaps that way of classifying arguments looks to the wrong place. What should be looked at is how the argument contributes to goals of social practices and how the goals can be interfered with by fallacious arguments. Presumption, abduction, and plausibility have a logical core as types of reasoning. But it is not possible to grasp the important differences between (among) them unless they are viewed dialectically as types of argument. Presumption is best understood dialectically, as indicated above, by seeing how it operates in a dialogue by reversing the obligation to prove. Abduction, as indicated by the analysis above, is also best understood as a dialogue sequence with several distinctive steps. The first step is the existence of a given set of facts (or presumed facts) in a given case. A why question or a how question is then asked about this fact. In other words, an explanation for this fact is requested by one participant in the dialogue. Then the other participant answers the question by offering an explanation. Through a series of questions and answers, several alternative explanations are elicited. There is then an evaluation of these explanations, and the best one is selected.

What should really be emphasized is that plausible reasoning is based only on appearances, on impressions of a case that could turn out to be misleading once the case has been studied in more depth. Plausible reasoning applies to cases where there is some evidence but where there is doubt whether this evidence is conclusive. Something could appear to be true now, but when tested later, it may turn out to have actually been false—or, at any rate, it may now appear to be false, on the balance of the evidence. Plausible reasoning is especially useful in cases where there is some unsettled issue or controversy so that opinions on both sides of the issue are plausible. Plausible reasoning is best judged as relative to the given evidence in a case and even, or especially, when that evidence is yet incomplete. Thus typically, in a kind of case in which plausible reasoning is most useful, there are two opposed theses, both with some weight of evidence behind them, and the total evidential situation is incomplete. As Blair (1999a, p. 56) put it, "In the kind of reasoning characteristic of argumentation schemes, there are both reasons to support a conclusion, and reasons to support the contradictory of the conclusion." The choice between alternatives is made on a balance of considerations. Neither alternative can be proved, but neither can be disproved. It is a decision between either carrying the search for more evidence forward or, because of costs and practical exigencies, making a guess now. Plausible reasoning is steering an evidence-gathering but open-minded dialogue ahead through a mass of uncertainties in a fluid situation by making the presumptive inferences that point to the best path ahead. Thus the context of dialogue is essential to the evaluation.

If this approach is on the right track, then maybe it is better to resist the triadic terminology of deductive, inductive, and abductive (despite the attraction the words have because they go so nicely together phonetically). Instead, we should have a dual classification. On the one side are deductive and inductive arguments. On the other is plausible argument. Plausible argument is a kind of guessing that is especially susceptible to wrong impressions and fallacies. It is not very exact, and it is variable and presumptive in nature. It is vitally important for the user of plausible argument to be open minded, steering a midpath between respecting the facts of a case and asking critical questions. The two main faults of such argumentation are the extremes of being dogmatic and of leaping too quickly or too firmly to a questionable conclusion. Being dogmatic is a failure to be open to further dialogue. Leaping too quickly or too firmly may be a failure to seek more evidence or even being closed to new evidence. Thus plausible reasoning requires different skills from deductive and inductive reasoning. It is less a matter of exact calculation than of steering a dialogue ahead by balancing and weighing many complex considerations on both sides. Abduction is best defined as a special kind of plausibilistic argumentation that has a distinctive argumentation scheme. Many, but not all, plausible arguments are abductive in nature. Abductive arguments, and plausible arguments generally, tend to be presumptive, resulting in conclusions that are hypotheses or partially supported guesses.

Josephson and Josephson (1994) have argued for a new taxonomy of basic inference types, as opposed to Peirce's tripartite taxonomy of deduction, induction, and abduction. They classify inductive generalization as a subspecies of abduction (p. 28). They argue (pp. 19–22) that it is possible to treat every good (that is, reasonable or valid) inductive generalization as a species of abduction. They see abduction not as contrasted with deduction or induction but with prediction. Their arguments for this new taxonomy are impressive and raise many interesting fundamental questions, but in view of the controversial nature of the subject, it is hard to see them as resolving the issue. Perhaps the most significant lesson that can be drawn from their work on abduction, for our purposes here, is their insistence on the importance of plausible reasoning as a fundamental category. What should also be noted is the impressive body of evidence they have presented showing how abduction (and prediction as well) are best treated as species of plausible reasoning.

This chapter will not offer any final word on this controversial issue. As abductive and defeasible reasoning becomes a more and more important topic in artificial intelligence and legal reasoning (Prakken, 1996; Verheij, 1996), the issue will be more and more hotly debated. Instead of trying to offer the final word, this section will conclude by offering tentative definitions of the key concepts featured in the argumentation in the text. These proposed definitions have a partly historical and conventional basis, as outlined above. But they also have a stipulative or persuasive aspect in that they are based on the philosophical considerations given above that indicate how these terms ought properly to be defined in light of recent work in argumentation theory and informal logic. They are only points of departure that give a vocabulary for proceeding more deeply into the analysis of abductive reasoning. They can be called working definitions. They are not meant to be so-called real or essential definitions that are fixed and cannot be altered at future points in the inquiry. The kinds of inferences to be defined are abductive, presumptive, plausible, deductive, inductive, and probable.

Abductive

The word "abductive" is from *ab* and *duco,* leading back. An abductive inference goes backward from a given conclusion to search for the premises that conclusion was based on. Abductive reasoning is familiar in knowledge-based systems in computer science. For example, in an expert system, a user may want to ask what premises were used by the expert system in the chain of reasoning the expert advice-giver used to arrive at a conclusion. Abductive inference is widely taken to be the same as inference to the best explanation.

Presumptive

The prefix *pre* indicates that a presumption is a kind of speech act assuming that something is taken as acceptable in relation to something else later in the line of argumentation. A presumption is something that can be accepted by agreement temporarily as things go forward unless at some future point in the exchange it is shown to be unacceptable. A presumption is a proposition put forward by one party for acceptance by both parties to a discussion, subject to possible retraction of acceptance by the other party at some future point. A presumptive inference enables a conclusion to be drawn provisionally from premises, in the absence of refutation from either party to a discussion, and subject to future refutation by either party.

Plausible

To say something is plausible means that it seems to be true based on appearances. It is even more plausible if it is consistent with other propositions that seem to be true. It can be even more plausible if it is tested by experiment. A plausible inference is one that can be drawn from the given apparent facts in a case suggesting a particular conclusion that seems to be true. Both a proposition and its negation can be plausible, as the ancient legal case of the stronger and the weaker man showed.

Deductive

The notion of deductive inference is the one of this family of terms about which there is the least disagreement. Deductive inference is characterized by the notion of deductive validity, the success criterion at which a deductive inference is aimed. A deductively valid inference is one in which it is (logically) impossible for the premises to be true and the conclusion false. Logic textbooks and scholarly writings in logic widely agree on this way of defining deductive validity.

Inductive

This kind of inference is often defined using the term "probability." Still, there are deep differences of opinion about what this term should be taken to mean (Skyrms, 1966). There is an older meaning of "inductive" coming from Aristotle and Greek philosophy, where it means something such as generalizing from a set of particular cases. In modern terminology, however, inductive inference seems to be equated with probability of the kind characteristic of statistical reasoning.

Probable

Probable inference can be taken to mean many things, but perhaps the clearest definition of it comes from the axioms for the probability calculus. For example, the probability value of not-A (the negation of A) is defined as the probability value of unity minus the probability value of A. There is also an older meaning of "probable," most evident in writings on casuistry, which goes back to Greek philosophy. The term used in Greek philosophy for what is, or should nowadays be translated as "plausible" (*pithanon*), was traditionally translated as "probable." This translation is very confusing since the advent of the probability calculus, because modern readers assume that what is meant is the modern use of the term "probability," referring to statistical inferences of the kind we are so familiar with in statistical polling and collection of data.

In examining the definitions above, we can see an element common to the terms "presumptive" and "plausible." Both are based on the idea of a process of collecting evidence that is moving forward. It could be a process of discussion of an issue, a process of collecting data, or both. The process is not conclusive in the sense that the conclusion arrived at will be known to be true (or false) beyond doubt. But the process may entail that the commitment to a proposition that seems to be true at a given point may be retracted or altered at some future point. For example, at a future point the proposition may seem to be false, or sufficient doubts may arise so that it no longer seems to be true. The common process is one of dynamic collection and use of evidence in which things may go one way or another. Acceptance of a proposition can be contraindicated, leading to its "defeat," or the new evidence may yield additional reasons for its acceptance.

ARGUMENTATION SCHEMES

In a vast preponderance of cases, many kinds of arguments are best evaluated by standards that are neither deductive nor inductive. These types of argumentation are often equated with traditional informal fallacies. In many cases of their use, however, they are not fallacious. In such cases, if seen as presumptive arguments, they do have some weight as rational arguments that could be used to support a claim. They also tend to be defeasible in the most common cases. Pollock (1995, p. 41) offered the following example of a common defeasible argument. Suppose an object looks red to me, but I know that when an object is illuminated by a red light it can look red when it is not. In Pollock's theory, this is an undercutting defeater as opposed to a rebutting defeater. The reason is that red objects look red in red light, too. As Prakken (2003) showed, this example also illustrates the following argumentation scheme.

If something looks like an *x* then it is an *x*.
This object looks like an *x*.
Therefore this object is an *x*.

Prakken cited the legal example, "This object looks like an affidavit, therefore it an affidavit." Prakken's observation is important and interesting and offers several lessons. One is that Pollock implicitly recognized argumentation in his analysis of defeasibility. Another is that defeasible argumentation schemes are very common and important in legal argumentation. A third is that argumentation schemes can be used to fill in missing premises in many common arguments. A fourth is brought out by recalling the example of the discovery of the *hominid* skull described by Leakey and Lewin (1992) and cited by Shelley (1996) as a case of abductive reasoning in archeology (see earlier in this chapter). This case, it will be recalled, was taken by Shelley to illustrate the use of visual reasoning in archeology. Prakken showed that not only is the same kind of visual-based reasoning used in law, but it has an identifiable argumentation scheme. The powerful implications of these lessons become apparent once one begins to see how many of the most common arguments are represented by argumentation schemes of a defeasible sort. Some of the best-known examples are argument from analogy, *ad hominem* argument, argument from ignorance, argument from sign, argument from consequences, appeal to popular opinion, appeal to pity, and appeal to expert opinion. Each of these types of argument does appear to have a recognizable form. But that form is not, at least in the vast range of cases, either a deductively valid form of argument or an inductively strong form of argument. In fact, they all seem to fall into the third category of defeasible arguments having some presumptive (or perhaps abductive) weight of plausibility, offering a tentative reason to accept a claim.

Perelman and Olbrechts-Tyteca (1969), in *The New Rhetoric,* an encyclopedic work originally published in French in 1958, identified many distinctive forms of argument that are often used in everyday conversational argumentation to offer presumptive reasons for tentatively accepting a claim. Many of the most central and common of these forms of argument were modeled using schematic forms called argumentation schemes in Arthur Hastings's Ph.D. thesis (1963). Hastings presented a set of critical questions matching each argumentation scheme. The scheme along with the questions offered a dialogue structure that can be used to analyze and evaluate real arguments of the given type. A more recent book (Kienpointner, 1992) covers many more argumentation schemes, including deductive and inductive forms of argument as well as presumptive forms.[11] Presumptive argumentation schemes have been analyzed in Walton (1996a), including argument from sign, argument from example, argument from commitment, argument from position to know, argument from expert opinion, argument from analogy, argument from precedent, argument from gradualism, and the slippery slope argument. It is also useful to mention the work of van Eemeren and Grootendorst (1984; 1992) in this brief survey. Their work has treated many argumentation schemes commonly used in the type of dialogue called the critical discussion. Many of the kinds of argumentation cited and analyzed by the foregoing researchers were first considered by Aristotle in his writings on informal logic, especially *Topics, On Sophistical Refutations,* and *Rhetoric.* Warnick (2000) has drawn up a table comparing the twenty-eight topics (forms of argument) mentioned in Aristotle's *Rhetoric* with thirteen of the argumentation schemes from *The New Rhetoric* (Perelman and Olbrechts-Tyteca, 1969). Warnick's table shows that there are common forms of argument found in both the ancient and modern accounts. But it also shows why there have been so many difficulties over the years in making sense of the Aristotelian topics. Aristotle, in his usual style, mentions each scheme (topic) briefly, and although he does give examples, the forms of argument are not modeled in the exact manner one would now require in logic. Even modern authors such as Hastings and Perelman and Olbrechts-Tyteca have given only rough and practical accounts of the schemes that are, understandably, not very precise or formally sophisticated. Nevertheless, the usefulness of the schemes, as well as their potential value in studying common argumentation, is very apparent.

The best brief way to introduce schemes is to present a typical example of the ones analyzed in Walton (1996a, pp. 46–110) and Walton (2002, chapter 2). We might start with the argumentation scheme for argument from witness testimony given in Walton (2002).

SCHEME FOR ARGUMENT FROM WITNESS TESTIMONY
Position to Know Premise: Witness *W* is in a position to know whether *A* is true or not.
Truth Telling Premise: Witness *W* is telling the truth (as *W* knows it).
Statement Premise: Witness *W* states that *A* is true (false).
Warrant: If witness *W* is in a position to know whether *A* is true or not, and *W* is telling the truth (as *W* knows it), and *W* states that *A* is true (false), then *A* is true (false).
Conclusion: Therefore (defeasibly) *A* is true (false).

Matching the scheme for argument from witness testimony are five critical questions.

FIVE CRITICAL QUESTIONS MATCHING THE APPEAL TO WITNESS TESTIMONY

CQ1: Is what the witness said internally consistent?

CQ2: Is what the witness said consistent with the known facts of the case (based on evidence apart from what the witness testified to)?

CQ3: Is what the witness said consistent with what other witnesses have (independently) testified to?

CQ4: Is there some kind of bias that can be attributed to the account given by the witness?

CQ5: How plausible is the statement A asserted by the witness?

The set of five critical questions above can be used by a respondent to cast doubt on an argument from witness testimony by probing into its potentially weak points. Argument from witness testimony as defeasible carries probative weight that may be withdrawn if the given argument fails to meet the requirements of the argumentation scheme, if the premises are not plausible enough to carry probative weight as presumptions, or if the right critical questions are asked.

Witness testimony is one of the most important kinds of evidence used in law, and in many cases the witness is an expert. There is a separate scheme representing the form of argument from expert opinion. A more complete and detailed account of this argumentation scheme has been developed in Walton (1997), a book exclusively devoted to the argument from expert opinion (often called the appeal to expert opinion in logic textbooks). Argument from expert opinion has the following argumentation scheme, where E is an expert source and A is a statement (Walton, 1997, p. 210).

ARGUMENT FROM EXPERT OPINION

Major Premise: Source E is an expert in subject domain S containing proposition A.

Minor Premise: E asserts that proposition A (in domain S) is true (false).

Conclusion: A may plausibly be taken to be true (false).

Argument from expert opinion shifts a weight of presumption in a dialogue favoring the acceptance of the statement put forward as true by the expert. If the premises are acceptable to the respondent, then the respondent should also, at least tentatively, accept the conclusion. But this acceptance (or commitment) is subject to retraction depending on the asking of appropriate critical questions by the respondent in the dialogue. Six appropriate critical questions for the appeal to expert opinion are cited in Walton (1997, p. 223).

1. *Expertise Question:* How credible is E as an expert source?
2. *Field Question:* Is E an expert in the field that A is in?
3. *Opinion Question:* What did E assert that implies A?
4. *Trustworthiness Question:* Is E personally reliable as a source?
5. *Consistency Question:* Is A consistent with what other experts assert?
6. *Backup Evidence Question:* Is A's assertion based on evidence?

Some discussion is needed to indicate how question 1 is different from question 4. Question 4, the trustworthiness question, queries the honesty or veracity of the source. This question is about the ethical character of a source. Question 1, the expertise question, queries the competence of the expert. An expert has credibility not only because of the person's knowledge in the field in question but also because that individual has the judgment skills to use that knowledge as applied to a particular problem. When depending on expert opinion, you can go wrong if the expert is lying or incompetent. The relevance of the other critical questions is more obvious, but the analysis of these critical questions in Walton (1997, chapter 7) gives full details. Of note, however, each of the six basic critical questions set out above can admit of critical subquestions used to continue a dialogue in more detail.

The defeasibility of appeal to expert opinion as a type of argument is brought out by the dialectical evaluation of it explained above. Argument from expert opinion has only a weight of presumption favoring one side in a dialogue. When subjected to critical questioning by the other side, the argument defaults, temporarily, until such time as the critical question has been answered satisfactorily. A question about how argumentation schemes should be used to evaluate arguments used in particular cases can now be posed. When has a dialogue reached the stage where all the appropriate critical questions raised by a proponent's argument have been satisfactorily answered so that the respondent must now accept the argument without asking more critical questions? In the case of a deductively valid argument, if the respondent accepts the premises as true, then the respondent must necessarily accept the conclusion. In the case of an inductively strong argument, if the respondent accepts the premises as true, then the respondent must accept the conclusion as probably true. And the degree of probability can be calculated, in many cases, in relation to the degree of the inductive strength of the argument. The addition of new premises can make an inductively strong argument into an inductively weak argument. But an inductively strong argument cannot be made inductively weak simply by asking a relevant question, such as whether the sample is large enough to warrant the generalization. To make the argument less strong, the respondent must give evidence to show that the sample was too small. In the case of an argumentation scheme, the respondent is bound to accept the conclusion tentatively, given that the premises have been accepted, even if the argument is neither deductively valid nor inductively strong. But the acceptance is only tentative depending on further progress of the dialogue. If the respondent just asks the right question, the acceptance of the worth of the argument to determine commitment is suspended. So when is an argument having the form of one of the argumentation schemes binding on the respondent? Even if all the critical questions asked have been answered satisfactorily by the proponent, can the respondent still go on asking critical subquestions? When is the argument finally binding on the respondent? This difficult question probes into the status of argumentation schemes based on a standard of argument evaluation that is different from those properly used to evaluate arguments that are supposed to be deductive and inductive.

The answer to this difficult question is that argumentation schemes represent a different standard of rationality from the one represented by deductive and inductive argument forms. This third class of presumptive (or abductive) arguments results only in plausibility, meaning that if the premises seem to be true, then one is justified in inferring that the conclusion also seems to be true. But seeming to be true can be misleading. You can go wrong with these kinds of arguments. For example, if an expert says that a particular statement is true, but you have direct empirical evidence that it is false, you had better suspend judgment. Or, if you have to act on a presumption one way or the other, go with the empirical evidence. But a presumptive argument based on an argumentation scheme should always be evaluated in a context of the dialogue of which it is a part. When the dialogue has reached the closing stage, and the argumentation in it is complete, only then can an evaluator reach a firm determination on what plausibility the argument has. And this evaluation must always and only be seen as relative to the dialogue as a whole. Typically, one individual argument has only a small weight of plausibility in itself. The significance of the argument is only that it can be combined with a lot of other relevant plausibilistic arguments used in the case. The important factor is the combined mass of evidence in the case. The case will have two sides, and there will be a mass of evidence on both of them. The final outcome of the case should be determined by how the mass of evidence on both sides tilts the burden of proof allocated at the initial stages of the dialogue.

The answer to the completeness question sketched out above is brief. It raises a whole host of related questions. But one central question stands out. Are these kinds of arguments modeled by argumentation schemes abductive in nature? It is easily seen that they are presumptive in nature and that the notion of presumption helps us to understand how they should properly be evaluated. But how does abduction come into it? And what is the difference between presumption and abduction? That was a central question that motivated this investigation. What can be said in answer to it? The first observation to make is that some of the argumentation schemes are very readily identified as modeling abductive arguments. For example, argument from sign is clearly abductive. An example of argument from sign is the following inference: here are some bear tracks in the snow, therefore a bear recently passed this way (Walton, 1996a, p. 47). This argument can be seen as an inference to the best explanation. The bear tracks in the snow are the observed facts or given data. What could explain them? A plausible but not the only possible explanation is that a bear recently passed that way, producing the tracks. If the area is one where bears might be expected to pass, and there is no indication that someone has cleverly faked these imprints, it is reasonable to infer that a bear passed that way. Inference to the best explanation works fine here, but what about other argumentation schemes, such as appeal to expert opinion, for example? If a physician tells me I have measles, using argument from expert opinion, it is a plausible hypothesis that I have measles. But is the argument abductive? Is my having measles the best explanation of what the expert said? Well maybe, but fitting the argument into this format does not seem to throw much light on its structure. The fit seems awkward, at best.

A better way to proceed is to begin with the insight of Blair (1999a, p. 57) that some argumentation schemes seem to be more general, or more abstract, than others. In other words, there may be hierarchies of argumentation schemes. Could it be that some groups of argumentation schemes fall under other argumentation schemes? Following this line of reasoning, it seems possible that some argumentation schemes might fit under abduction whereas others do not.[12] What this hypothesis suggests, in turn, is that abduction could be viewed as a distinctive form of argument in its own right. If this is so, there should be an argumentation scheme for abductive argument. Taking this line of reasoning to its logical conclusion, I propose a new argumentation scheme for abductive argument as shown below.

ARAUCARIA AS A TOOL FOR ARGUMENT DIAGRAMMING

Abductive arguments of the kind typically used in legal argumentation as evidence are typically presumptive and defeasible. They carry weight as evidence only when judged in relation to a larger mass of evidence in a case. This mass of evidence is built up when one single argument is connected to many other arguments. The tool currently used to display such a mass of evidence in a case is the argument diagram. *Araucaria* is a software tool developed by Chris Reed and Glenn Rowe to construct an argument diagram from the text of a given argument (Reed and Rowe, 2002). It is free software released under public license at the University of Dundee in Scotland. An argument diagram can be constructed and used as follows. First you load the text of the argument onto the screen. Then you identify the statements given as premises and conclusions by highlighting them in the text. Then, using *Araucaria,* each statement is represented as a node (point, vertex), and arrows are drawn representing inferences from sets of statements to other statements as lines (arrows, directed lines). By this means, an argument diagram is produced that displays the sequence of argumentation in a text of discourse. *Araucaria* aids a user in reconstructing and diagramming an argument using a simple point-and-click interface. The software also supports argumentation schemes and provides a user-customizable set of schemes with which to analyze arguments. Once arguments have been analyzed, they can be saved in a portable format called AML, the Argument Markup Language, which is based on XML (Reed and Rowe, 2002).

Araucaria has several other features that make it especially useful for analyzing abductive reasoning. It includes a set of presumptive argumentation schemes corresponding to those in Walton (1996a). These argumentation schemes, such as argument from consequences, for example, are very useful for evaluating abductive reasoning of the kind cited in the examples considered in previous sections of this chapter. New schemes can be added, and alternative scheme sets are being made available on the project Web site, which is http://www.computing.dundee.

ac.uk/staff/creed/araucaria/. It is possible to log on to an *Araucaria DB* online repository containing examples of argumentation. You can search for particular forms of argument, and you can contribute your own analyses to the database.

In any argument diagram representing a mass of evidence in a legal case, there will always be a final conclusion, a so-called ultimate *probandum,* the claim that is to be proved or doubted (Twining 1985). Leading into this final conclusion there will be a connected network of argumentation in which premises lead into conclusions. There are two special ways a set of premises can go together to support a conclusion. To explain the distinction, let us assume for simplicity that an argument has only two premises. If it is a linked argument, each premise depends on the other to support the conclusion (Freeman, 1991). Linked premises are often joined to a conclusion by a known argumentation scheme, as in the example of the argument from expert opinion cited above. If one premise is pulled out, the other by itself provides only very little support for the conclusion. In a convergent argument, each premise provides support for the conclusion that is independent of each other premise. In a convergent argument, each premise can be seen as a separate argument for the conclusion, an argument that can stand on its own. If one is pulled out, the other still gives a fairly strong reason that supports the conclusion.

There is one other factor that comes up in argument diagramming that needs to be mentioned. Some arguments as given in a text of discourse are incomplete, and, to be properly stated, one has to insert missing premises or conclusions. Such incomplete arguments are traditionally called enthymemes. The traditional example is the argument, "All men are mortal, therefore Socrates is mortal." The missing premise is "Socrates is a man." This statement, although not explicitly stated in the argument as presented, needs to be added for us to identify the argument properly. Various reasons can be used to justify such an addition. One is that the unstated premise is a matter of commonly accepted knowledge and would not likely be disputed. Another is that adding it in makes the argument valid. Another is that without it, the argument would be invalid. Yet another is that when the missing premise has been inserted, the two premises form a linked argument that supports the conclusion quite strongly. Missing premises or conclusions in an enthymeme can be inserted using *Araucaria*.

Next, we have to see how *Araucaria* can aid a user to construct an argument diagram with argumentation schemes. An example of a real case involving legal evidence brought to trial is quoted below from Wigmore (1935, p. 42).

SALMON'S CASE
Salmon sold medicines in London. M'Kensie bought from him some pills for rheumatism; after numerous doses he died. The medical men, on a postmortem examination, affirmed that certain ingredients of these pills had caused his death; and Salmon was indicted for manslaughter. But on the trial he produced many witnesses, who had taken the same kind of pills with much benefit; one witness affirmed that he had taken twenty thousand of them within the past two years, to his great benefit! If these *circumstances* were true, the inference was inevitable that the pills were not lethal. But was the *testimony* to this circumstance true?

Two kinds of evidence are used in this case, circumstantial and testimonial, combined in a network of argumentation. To show the structure of that argumentation, we put the text of discourse of the case, as quoted above, into a text document. Then we paste that text into the left side of the Araucaria display that appears on the screen. Then, using the mouse, we highlight each statement that is in the text. As each statement is highlighted, a letter of the alphabet will appear on the right representing that statement. To make the example easier for the purposes of illustration, we have already done the key list below.

Key List of Statements in Salmon's Case
(A) The medical men affirmed that certain ingredients of the pills had caused M's death.
(B) The medical men are experts in medicine.
(C) Certain ingredients in the pills had caused M's death.
(D) M's taking the pills caused his death.
(E) Witness W testified that he took the same kind of pills and they caused him no harm.
(F) Witness W is in a position to know about the effects of the pills on him.
(G) If the pills caused no harm to W, it is doubtful that they caused harm to M.
(H) Taking the same pills as M took caused no harm to W.

Now eight circled letters representing the eight statements in the key list will appear in the box on the right side of the Araucaria display. The problem is now to draw arrows from each one that is a premise, or from ones that represent a set of premises, to the other statement that represents a conclusion drawn from that premise or that set of premises. The user does this by clicking on to a statement or set of statements and then clicking on to the conclusion they are supposed to support.

In figure 1.1, all the arrows have been drawn in, showing the premises and conclusion of the argumentation in Salmon's case. The diagram shows an argumentation structure in which the ultimate conclusion of the plaintiff is statement D, and statement H has been put forward by the other side as a refutation, or attempted rebuttal of D. The two-headed arrow represents this refutation relationship. All the other arrows represent evidential support. To make the exposition of what was done easier to follow, one can put the same diagram into a full text form at the click of a button. Here, the result is displayed in figure 1.2. Examining the argumentation in figure 1.2, we can see that there are two main argument structures represented. On the left side, there are two linked arguments supporting H. On the right side, there is a linked argument supporting C, and then C is in turn used as a premise in a single argument supporting D. The double arrow at the top of the diagram once again shows that H is being used as an argument against D (called a "refutation" in Araucaria and represented by the double-headed arrow). Note also that a new statement I has been added as a conclusion drawn from E and F. I is the statement "The pills caused no harm to W." Thus the argument from E and F to I is an enthymeme.

For our purposes here, one of the most interesting things about *Araucaria* is that it can be used to identify and display the argumentation scheme that is the basis of support for a conclusion supplied by the premises. For example, we can see that in the argument on the left for conclusion H, the two premises E and F are linked together as premises supporting I on the basis of an argumentation scheme, namely, *Argument from Witness Testimony* (called "appeal to witness testimony" in the list of schemes). In the argument on the left, the two premises A and B are linked together as premises supporting conclusion C on the basis of the argumentation scheme for *Argument from Expert Opinion*. When the user clicks on "Schemes" in the toolbar, a list of the schemes from Walton (1996a) appears, and the user can select the appropriate scheme and apply it to a given argument. The user can also customize this list by adding new schemes. When the user has done this, the area around the premises

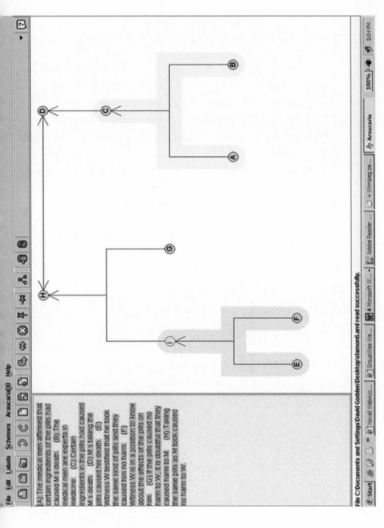

Figure 1.1 Araucaria diagram of Salmon's case. [Note: Normally an argument from expert opinion is to a single expert source, but in Salmon's case the appeal is to "the medical men." This variant of the argument raises some critical questions about who these medical men are (as named sources) and whether they are in agreement about the cause of death.]

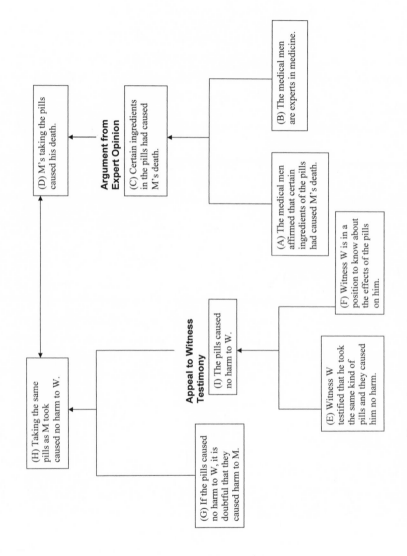

Figure 1.2 Full text diagram of Salmon's case.

and conclusion so designated is displayed with a colored border, and the name of the scheme is displayed just above the conclusion.

The argumentation schemes contained in the list in Walton (1996a) and illustrated in the example of Salmon's case above are presumptive in nature. The premises linked together in the scheme give a reason to support the conclusion, but the reason does not provide conclusive proof of that conclusion. As noted above, such an argument is called defeasible, meaning that it can be defeated later by other arguments even though it is tentatively acceptable as a reasonable argument at this point. Now that it has been shown how such arguments can be represented on an argument diagram, many questions are raised about how they should be analyzed and evaluated. Let us suppose an argument diagram has been constructed showing how all the defeasible arguments in a case are chained to each other to form the mass of evidence collected from the text of discourse in a case. How can an argument evaluator then weigh that evidence? As indicated above, the argumentation approach is holistic. Just one inference by itself, even though it may be in a recognizable form, such as that of *modus ponens* or some other known argumentation scheme, cannot be evaluated just on a basis of knowing the truth-values or confidence values of the component statements. One needs to see how the inference was chained to others and where the chain of reasoning appears to be leading. The argument diagram should show the ultimate conclusion to be proved in the dialogue by the proponent. The chaining of argumentation displayed in the diagram shows how the argumentation as a whole either moves or does not move forward to that single conclusion as its endpoint. Looking at the whole mass of argumentation represented by the diagram, an evaluator can weigh how plausible the argumentation is in support of the conclusion that is supposed to be proved in the dialogue.

The argument diagramming method is very similar to the diagram method used in AI to represent the process of searching for a solution to a problem. A very clear account of how to use the search method for problem solving has been presented by Cawsey (1998, pp. 68–97) with many examples. The method begins by expressing the problem in terms of a goal state and an initial state. In the simplest set of cases, the problem is to get from the initial state to the goal state. The classic example is the blocks problem. There is a pile of numbered blocks on a table in an initial state. The problem is to re-pile them to get them into a different state. For example, the goal state may be to have them in three stacks, where each stack has the numbers in ascending order from bottom to top. There may be more than one solution to such a problem. Each solution can be modeled as a sequence of steps or individual actions leading from the initial state to the goal state. Thus a typical problem-solving diagram would take the form of a tree leading from the root (initial) state to the various outcome states that represent solutions to the problem. In mathematics, such a search tree has the structure called a directed graph or digraph. It is very similar to an argument diagram, except that the argument diagram pictures linked arguments in a different way, as indicated above. The use of graphs as search trees to find solutions to problems is also the basic method of the field in AI called heuristics. Heuristics are techniques for searching through a set of alternative courses of action to decide which is the most effective means of achieving a goal (Pearl, 1984, p. 3). An example (Pearl, p. 3) of problem solving to which heuristics can be applied is that of the chess player who studies the various moves open in a game to judge which one appears best.

Whether such schemes as appeal to witness testimony and appeal to expert opinion that tend to be defeasible as commonly used in law should be classified as abductive forms of argument or not remains a moot point. We will forbear comment on this issue until later, when a better analysis of abductive reasoning has been worked out. For the present it is enough to see that it will be extremely useful for the task of investigating abductive reasoning to understand how an argument diagram can be used to represent a mass of evidence in a case of a kind that typically contains abductive arguments along with other kinds of arguments that are presumptive and defeasible. It will turn out that such arguments can be properly analyzed and evaluated only within a structure such as a search tree, directed graph, or argument diagram that represents its connections with other arguments that make up a given body of evidence in a case.

A Dialogue Model of Explanation

Lipton (1991, p. 2) wondered why inference to the best explanation has been so little developed as a theoretical model of reasoning, given its evident importance and popularity in so many fields. He suggested (p. 2) the following reason: "The model is an attempt to account for inference in terms of explanation, but our understanding of explanation is so patchy that the model seems to account for the obscure in terms of the equally obscure." Hintikka (1998, p. 507) commented that most people who speak of "inference to the best explanation" seem to think they know what an explanation is, but "in reality, the nature of explanation is scarcely any clearer than the nature of abduction." The objective of chapter 2 is to break through this impasse by presenting a new theory of explanation developed from integrating methods from three sources. The first source is work in AI on explanation patterns (Schank, 1986), plan recognition (Carberry, 1990), and explanatory dialogues (Moore, 1995). The second source is the work on simulative reasoning in cognitive science stemming from the experimental findings of Premack and Woodruff (1978). The third source is the recent work on argumentation by van Eemeren and Grootendorst (1984; 1992), including the classification and formal analysis of different types of dialogue frameworks of argumentation (Walton and Krabbe, 1995; Walton, 1998).[1] An account of what explanation is has to be a vitally important first step of any analysis of abductive reasoning as inference to the best explanation.

The new theory of explanation presented in chapter 2 models an explanation as a dialogue between two agents. In the model, one agent is presumed by the other to understand something, and the other agent asks a question meant to enable him to understand it as well. An explanation is successful if it communicates understanding of a sort needed to enable the questioner to make sense of the thing questioned. This model is based on the concept of an agent having understanding of something, meaning that he can make sense of it. The model provides a formal structure for the view of explanation articulated by Scriven (2002, p. 49): "Explanation is literally and logically the process of filling in gaps in understanding, and to do this we must start out with some understanding of something." The formal structure used to analyze explanation in this chapter is a dialogue framework in which one agent is held to be able to communicate understanding to another agent in a dialogue structure of questioning and answering. The dialogue theory of explanation is built on the notion that one party in a dialogue can understand the commitments and the understanding of the other party. It is also built on the notion that the one party can understand what the other party does not understand.

TYPES OF EXPLANATIONS

Is it possible to classify different types of explanations? It is fairly difficult to construct a typology that is very precise, but certain broad categories stand out and are recognized in the literature on explanation. One is the empathetic type of explanation in which one person tries to explain the actions of another person by attributing goals, motives, beliefs, or other kinds of internal states to the other person. Schank (1986, p. 39) called it the "intent explanation" and broke its structure down into one agent's use of empathy to understand the belief-goal-plan-action sequence of another agent. This kind of explanation is very common in history and law. Another is the kind of scientific explanation in which a scientist tries to explain some phenomenon by reducing it to entities and relationships accepted as fundamental in a science. What matters in this reductive type of explanation is not the internal state attributed to a person but what are accepted as the basic units and methods in the science. For example, heat can be explained as molecular motion, or a disease can be explained by relating it to a genetic anomaly. These scientific explanations work because the building blocks in them, such as molecules or genes, are accepted as basic units by a science at a given point in its development. Not all scientific explanations are of this reductive sort. Indeed, as Nettler (1970) noted, the social sciences often use the empathetic type of explanation. According to Nettler (1970, p. 39) the sociologist Max Weber even argued that using explanations of behavior based on understanding of the states of mind of the agent is distinctive of sociology as a science. Still, one can see that reductive and empathetic explanations are basically different in kind. Any classification of types of explanations should take this difference into account.

Another type of explanation that appears to be distinctive is explanation by definition. Definitions have many purposes. Sometimes they are meant to persuade, as in the persuasive definitions studied by Stevenson (1944). Sometimes they are based on scientific knowledge and observation as a basis for taking action, as in medical explanations. Sometimes, for example in law, they are meant to provide a basis for clarification and agreement to help to resolve later disputes, as in drawing up a legal contract or statute. Lexical definitions, of the kind we find in dictionaries, are meant to explain the meaning of a word or phrase to a reader who understands other, perhaps less uncommon words and phrases in a language. Even apart from dictionaries, lexical definitions are commonly used when one person tries to explain the meaning of a term to another person. For example, in teaching another person a language, this pedagogical type of explanation is extremely common. Such an explanation attempt does not always have to take the form of a definition. It can be done, in some instances, by giving an example, pointing to something, drawing an analogy, or telling a story. But in all such cases, the offering of the explanation has a distinctive function. That function is for the proponent to try to get the respondent to understand the meaning of a word, phrase, or any expression in a language. Such explanation can occur in scientific discourse, just as it may occur in everyday conversational exchanges. It may take many forms. But what is common to this type of explanation is that it is closely related to definitions and to the meanings of expressions in a language. To explain, in this sense, is typically to define a term or to otherwise try to convey its meaning to someone who does not understand it.

Still another type of explanation that is very common but cuts across and seems different from the above three categories is the kind that is meant to explain how something works. For example, the proponent may be trying to explain to a respondent how a machine works. Or an expert financial advisor may try to explain to a client how a certain type of investment works. These are not necessarily scientific explanations, and they are generally not empathetic explanations. Usually some sort of orderly process, sequence, or mechanism is involved, and the proponent tries to take the respondent through the steps of the process. For example, suppose I am trying to explain how the office photocopy machine works to someone who is not familiar with it. I assume he is already familiar with photocopy machines and the principles of how they work. He does not need a scientific explanation of how the process works. He just needs to grasp the sequence he has to go through to get the machine to perform the functions necessary to do the jobs for which he will use the machine. In such a case, there will typically be a dialogue. A respondent will ask such questions as "How do I turn it on?" or "How do I get it to copy on both sides of a page?" The proponent will answer by showing a sequence that the user needs to go through by performing operations of various kinds on the controls of the machine. This type of explanation could be called the how-to explanation or maybe the practical type of explanation. It explains how something works, often a mechanical process of some sort that needs to be carried out in order to achieve an outcome.

Finally, there is one type of explanation that is ubiquitous in AI—the type of explanation in the explanation subsystem of an expert system architecture. It allows the program, the expert system, to explain its reasoning to the user. Such a system is based on the components illustrated in figure 2.1. The user interacts with the system through the user interface in a dialogue. How such a system uses a *modus ponens* form of reasoning as the basis of its inference engine can be illustrated by simple medical example (Cawsey, 1998, p. 45).

IF symptom (runny nose) THEN disease (cold).
Symptom (Fred, runny nose).
Therefore, (Fred, cold).

Inferences of this kind chain forward from the knowledge base and case-specific data through the inference engine to provide answers to the questions asked by the user at the user interface. That is how an expert system works. But notice that it is not just the chaining forward of inferences that makes the system work. There also needs to be an explanation system in order for the system to be of practical help to the user. If the user does not understand something the expert has said, the user can ask for an explanation. This explanation could be one of any of the types recognized above. What is important to observe here is how the chaining of reasoning is integrated with the explanation system within the architecture of the expert system.

In an expert system, there is a transfer of knowledge from the expert to the user. This transfer is accomplished via a chain of reasoning that takes premises from the knowledge base and the case-specific data

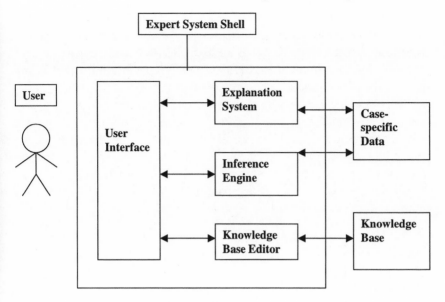

Figure 2.1 Expert system architecture.

and then draws conclusions transferred to the user in response to the user's questions asking for advice or an expert opinion. Thus the structure of the expert system architecture can be seen as one of use of reasoning in an information-seeking dialogue. But that is not the end of the matter. The system has to have an explanation system embedded in the information-seeking dialogue. What is the general purpose or function of the explanation dialogue system? It allows the user to shift from a passive mode of questioning to a more active mode in which that individual can examine the expert and ask for explanations that a non-expert can understand. Thus there is an explanation-seeking dialogue embedded in the wider dialogue in which the expert transfers information to the user from the knowledge base and case-specific data. It is this nesting of the explanation system within the wider framework of the knowledge-based reasoning in the expert system architecture that will prove vital later in this chapter.

Knowledge-based reasoning systems in AI can provide three types of explanations: trace explanations, strategic explanations, and deep explanations (Moulin et al., 2002, pp. 174–76). A trace explanation exhibits the rules and facts used by the system as premises that led to the conclusion put forward. In first-generation expert systems, the system answered how and why questions by examining the so-called execution trace, the sequence of inferences that led to the conclusion of the reasoning (Scott et al., 1977). Trace explanations tend to have a limited usefulness for many users because the user may have limited information about the system's knowledge and goals (Moulin et al., 2002, p. 174). Strategic explanations place an action in context by revealing the problem-solving strategy of the system used to perform a task (Chandrasekaran, 1986). Deep explanations are characterized by a capability to separate the knowledge base of the system from that of the user. In the reconstructive approach to deep explanations (Wick and Thompson, 1992), the knowledge base of the user, rather than that used by the system, is employed in the explanation. Thus such a deep explanation is more comprehensible to the user because it is based on his own knowledge, not that of the system.

MODELS OF SCIENTIFIC EXPLANATION

It was widely accepted in the 1960s that the problem of analyzing scientific explanation had been solved by the model given by Carl G. Hempel.[2] Hempel's model of explanation is called the deductive-nomological model, or DN model, for reasons that are made apparent below. Hempel (1965, p. 174) schematized his model of explanation as a deductive inference based on three variables. $C_1, C_2, \ldots, C_k$ are conditions called "statements of particular occurrences." For example, they could represent positions and movements of celestial bodies such as stars. $L_1, L_2, \ldots, L_r$ represent general laws. Hempel (p. 174) wrote that, for example, they could be laws of Newtonian mechanics. E is a sentence stating what is to be explained. Thus E represents the so-called *explanandum,* or thing to be explained. Hempel presented the following schema to represent the form of an explanation.

$$C_1, C_2, \ldots, C_k$$
$$L_1, L_2, \ldots, L_r$$
$$\overline{}$$
$$E$$

The two components above the line represent the *explanans,* or the part that does the explaining. Hempel's model has also been called the covering law model of explanation. To explain something on this model is to bring it under general laws or show, as in the kind of deductive inference above, that it is covered by general laws. Achinstein (1993, pp. 136–37) presented the following example of the covering law model. Suppose the question is: "Why did this metal expand?" An answer giving an explanation could be cast in the form of an inference according to the covering law model.

This metal was heated.
All metals expand when heated.

This metal expanded.

The second premise in this deductively valid inference is a general law in Hempel's sense, provided the quantifier "all" is taken, as it normally is in deductive logic, to admit of no exceptions. The first premise states the particular conditions of the case. These two statements together can be taken to provide an explanation of the statement that appears under the line. They explain why this metal expanded.

The covering law model was extended to include inductive inferences comparable to the type of deductive inference cited above. Such inferences were called inductive-statistical (I-S) explanations. I-S explanations are inferred inductively from premises that are inductive-statistical laws and premises that describe particular circumstances. Hempel (1965, p. 301) offered the example of a child who was found to have a case of the mumps. What could explain this condition? It could be explained by observing that he had recently been playing with a friend who had the mumps. In this case, the antecedent factors could be the child's exposure to someone with mumps and the fact that he did not previously have mumps. Of course, not every child who meets these two conditions gets the mumps. So the explanation of how the child got the mumps is not based on a deductively valid DN inference. Nevertheless, the child has a high probability of getting the mumps under these two conditions. As Hempel put it (p. 301), "The disease will be transmitted with a high statistical probability." In other words, an I-S explanation has a form similar to that of the deductive variant of the DN model, except that the covering law is inductive or statistical rather than being a universal generalization of the kind that supports a typical deductive inference.

Salmon (1989) has chronicled the generally accepted views of scientific explanation in philosophy in roughly the second half of the twentieth century by citing four decades. The first decade corresponds to the period of the fifties when the DN model came to be accepted as the official view. The second decade was characterized by many critiques of the DN model and expressions of doubt about it. During this decade, Sylvain Bromberger offered a pragmatic account of explanation that viewed an explanation as an answer to a why question. This approach was not widely accepted at the time, however, and the third decade was characterized by the elaboration of an inductive-statistical model that could be seen as widening the scope of the DN model, but at the same time there was an awareness of the deepening difficulties with the received view. During the fourth decade, there was, among other developments (Salmon, 1989, p. 117), an exploration of the role of causation in scientific explanation and a deeper investigation of the pragmatics of explanation.

During those last three decades there had been an active opposition to the DN model, both as a model of explanation in history (Dray, 1964) and as a model of scientific explanation. Von Wright (1971) championed a view of explanation as understanding of human action. Scriven (1962) also argued for the theory that explanation is the reduction of what is not understood to what is understood. Building on this view of explanation as increase in understanding, Finocchiaro (1975; 1980) has used case studies of scientific discovery to argue that scientific explanation is a process of growth of understanding. He argued (1975) that Galileo's achievement of making motion subject to mathematical analysis should be seen as a case of scientific explanation that was successful because it led to a better understanding of motion. He also used Newton's theory of gravitation as a case of a scientific discovery that was a successful explanation because it produced a growth of scientific understanding. This alternative theory of explanation as reduction of what is not understood to what is understood is highly plausible when applied to case studies of scientific and historical explanation.

More recently, it seems to be a trend that more philosophers of science have gone on record as stating that scientific explanation is based on some kind of understanding. Achinstein (1983, p. 16) held that there is a "fundamental relationship between explanation and understanding." Salmon (1998, p. 77) proposed that scientific understanding fits phenomena into a comprehensive world picture, thereby exposing the "inner mechanisms" of a process.[3] Kitcher (1988, p. 168) stated that a theory of a scientific explanation "should show us how scientific explanation advances our understanding." But as Trout (2002, p. 215) pointed out, these statements do not necessarily commit their authors to the view that understanding of what is being explained should be a criterion of a successful explanation. He added another disclaimer as well: "While these declarations associate explanation with understanding, none of these accounts have much to say about the precise nature of understanding." The problem, as Scriven noted above, is that understanding seems too "squishy" a notion on which to build a theory of scientific explanation. What appears to be needed is some clearly definable objective framework in which there can be a transfer where a lack of understanding is replaced by understanding of the thing in question.

One avenue of approach is to define scientific understanding in terms of reduction. In Friedman's view (1974, p. 18), scientific explanations simplify nature by reducing the number of phenomena we have to accept as ultimate. Friedman (1974, p. 5) gave the example of explaining why water turns to steam when heated. The phenomenon can be explained by reducing it to motion of the molecules in the water. This motion increases when the water is heated, and the increase in their motion makes them overcome the force holding them together. Using another example, however, Dieks and de Regt (1998, p. 57) challenged Friedman's view that reduction always fulfills the aim of achieving greater understanding. According to Boyle's law, the pressure of a gas increases when its volume is made smaller. But it is also understandable on the basis of kinetic theory, which gives a more complex explanation. Thus Dieks and de Regt argue that although reduction may sometimes lead to greater understanding, it does not always do so. In their view, reducing something to a deeper level can sometimes make things more complicated and harder to understand (p. 57). They concluded that when scientists probe into deeper layers of reality, their aim is not to achieve greater understanding but to find theories of greater generality. Thus although reduction is important as one way of operationally defining scientific understanding in some way that can be made precise, by itself it does not seem to be sufficient to yield an understanding-based model of scientific explanation.

There is a large body of research in AI devoted to customizing automated explanation systems to be adaptive to the user's knowledge and responsive to the user's needs (Moulin et al., 2002, p. 176). As noted above, deep explanations are based on a separation between the knowledge of the system and that of the user. This approach implies that the system needs to have knowledge about the characteristics and profile of the user and then to base an explanation on that knowledge. This is a lofty aim, however, and there are some problems with it. A distinction needs to be made between individual users and stereotypical, or generic, classes of users (Rich, 1989). Even so, current developments based on such a user-based approach suggest that explanation should be seen as interactive and cooperative, with the system producing explanations based on what it takes the viewpoint of the user to be. Dialogue systems for explanation have in fact been produced (Cawsey, 1992) based on this assumption. Such systems must be able to respond to feedback from the user and must also be based on some way to estimate how the user understands, or fails to understand, some explanation that was offered. In short, it looks very much like recent research in AI is moving beyond the older idea of an explanation as simply a sequence of reasoning from a set of laws or even from a system's knowledge base. It seems to be moving toward a richer notion of explanation as an interactive process between two agents or parties in a dialogue, an explainer and a user, where the explainer must have some understanding of what the user understands.

SIMULATION, UNDERSTANDING, AND MAKING SENSE

Suppose that an explanation can be seen as a transaction in which a proponent answers a question of a respondent in a way that increases or facilitates the understanding of the respondent in a way that fits the question asked. In such a dialogue model, the basic philosophical problem is to try to define what understanding is in a precise way that is useful. In logic textbooks, an explanation is often defined using a metaphor. For example, Hurley (2000, p. 20) defines an explanation as "a group of statements that purports to shed light on some event or phenomenon." This definition is helpful to indicate roughly the function an explanation is supposed to perform and to contrast that function with that of an argument. But it is too metaphorical, psychological, and imprecise to build any theory of explanation on. It reflects the common tendency to see understanding as a psychological notion characterized by an "Aha!" experience (Trout, 2002). The necessity to distinguish between a psychological and a logical analysis of the concept of an explanation has been emphasized by von Wright (1997, p. 1). According to his analysis (p. 1), something can be a reason for an action even though it may turn out that the action was not performed for that reason. Understanding in the psychological sense is based on imputing a motive or intention an agent had as a prior state of mind that led to that agent's action. But understanding in the logical sense is based on the reasons the agent presumably had for carrying out an action, given the presumption that the agent was acting on reasons. This presumption could fail in a given case. The agent could be acting irrationally or otherwise acting without any real reason. Understanding in this logical sense of the term refers to a kind of rationale or coherent account that explains why somebody did something by indicating a sequence of goal-directed reasoning that led presumably to the action. This kind of understanding is often called *verstehen* in the philosophical literature. It is associated with the device called "the rational man" in law. Von Wright (1997) described an "understanding explanation" as a special type of explanation of actions that makes reference to reasons. This concept of understanding can be called reconstructive in a sense defined by Trout (2002, p. 215): "Understanding requires that the individual be able to piece together bits of information in their cognitive possession." As opposed to psychological understanding, based on a feeling that something seems right to you, this notion of understanding is logical in that it is derived by inference from evidence gathered from observing what another agent says and does.

Understanding in this logical sense needs to be modeled in different ways in different kinds of explanations. In law and history, such explanations typically take the form of reconstructing the presumed goals and practical reasoning of an agent into a connected account that makes clear the ends and means in the agent's chain of reasoning. But in many scientific explanations, understanding is shared by a community of experts in a scientific field in virtue of the methods and basic concepts they accept as fundamental to the science. Both types of understanding are based on shared patterns of reasoning and shared assumptions about what is commonly accepted as factual knowledge. Von Wright (1997, p. 2) mentioned two types of scientific explanations of this kind that involve understanding and the giving of reasons. One is medical explanation. In this kind of causal explanation, the phenomenon to be explained is related causally to a physical defect or identifiable disturbance in bodily function. Another is sociological explanation. For example, an explanation of this type might state that a person has failed to carry out an action because of deprived economic circumstances, lack of educational opportunity, or membership in a lower class.

Scientific understanding, according to Salmon (1998, p. 90), involves development of a world picture that is an objective representation of the way the world is. But what is it to fit a phenomenon into a scientific world picture? Friedman (1988, p. 195) sees the essence of scientific explanation as the following sort of increase in understanding: "Science increases our understanding of the world by reducing the total number of independent phenomena that we have to accept as ultimate or given." In other words, one thing can be reduced to another thing that is more basic, and our scientific understanding is thereby increased. Kitcher (1989, p. 432), however, saw understanding the phenomena in science as not simply a matter of reducing "fundamental incomprehensibilities." He portrayed scientific understanding as involving "the internalization of argument patterns" that are found in what initially appear to be different situations. These remarks suggest that argumentation schemes, like causal argumentation schemes for example, may have an important role in scientific understanding.

The kind of explanation most commonly used in law and history, as mentioned above, involves one agent trying to understand the actions of another agent. It can be called an empathetic or simulative type of explanation. One agent does not have direct access to the internal thinking and planning processes of another agent. Where, then, do the data for a simulative explanation of the other party's actions come from? This question is called the problem of other minds in philosophy. The answer is that the explainer must "re-enact" the action, or go through the same process of thinking that the other party went through when that person carried out the action. Many commentators in the past, especially those favoring scientific models of explanations such as the DN model, have found this process highly mysterious. They have doubted that any sense can be made of it.

The most original and articulate exponent of the re-enactment model of explanation, especially as applied to historical explanations, was Robin G. Collingwood. Historians have to rely on eyewitness testimony in order to explain an event that happened in the past. But Collingwood (1946, p. 282) argued that historians cannot stop there. They have to compare the accounts given by different witnesses. These accounts may conflict, and so historians must critically probe into them, sometimes even criticizing them. In Collingwood's view, history is more than just collecting facts. Collingwood (1939, p. 224) called the latter view the "scissors and paste" view of history. He saw the method of history as not just one of drawing inferences from facts, but as a process of question and answer (Dray, 1995). Historians must face the same problem that the historical person they are studying faced, to the extent this is possible given the differences of circumstances. Then historians must try to insert themselves into the mind of the historical person by a process of empathy, or "re-enactment," in order to see how that person tried to solve the problem. Dray (1964, p. 12) explained this re-enactment as a process of vicarious practical reasoning by the historian. The historical person was presumably engaged in a process of deliberation using practical reasoning when acting to solve a problem being faced. Historians must exploit the common understanding of practical reasoning they share with the historical person in order to explain what that person was trying to do. The central characteristic of this process of re-enactment is an ability often called empathy, but also called "attachment" or "simulation" in the social sciences and in AI. Recent studies have gained some insight into how this process works.

In a famous experiment by Premack and Woodruff (1978), reportedly a chimpanzee was shown a video of an actor trying to grab some bananas dangling overhead and just out of reach. The chimp was then shown a series of other videos. Each of them represented the actor carrying out some possible solution to the banana problem. The "correct" or most feasible solution was to move a crate under the bananas and then step on it to reach them. It was found that chimpanzees generally picked this solution. This experiment posed a problem for social scientists who tried to figure out how the chimpanzee arrived at the right solution to the problem just from seeing the actor carry out various alternative actions. What thinking process did the chimpanzee presumably use? The two main hypotheses proposing plausible answers are called the theory-theory and the simulation theory. According to the theory-theory, the chimp used practical reasoning. According to this theory, the chimp is "hard-wired" to engage in goal-directed means-end reasoning and can therefore use this ability to solve the problem. According to the simulation theory (Goldman, 1995, p. 189), the chimp uses simulation (empathy) to pretend it has the same desires, beliefs, or mental states that the actor in the video was presumed to have when he was observed trying to get the bananas. Of course, both theories are (partly) right. The chimp did have to use practical reasoning, but he also had to grasp the practical reasoning supposedly used by the actor whom he observed. Thus it also had to use empathy or simulation.

Taking all these developments into account, we can now put forward a dual hypothesis to explain explanation of the empathetic kind so common in law and history. The first part of the hypothesis is the simulative component. Explanation is first of all based on simulative reasoning in which one agent enters into the thinking of another agent when the first agent sees the other agent carrying out an action or solving a problem. But this simulative reasoning is possible only because of the capability of the two agents to engage in practical reasoning. Thus the second part of the hypothesis is a practical reasoning component. Simulative explanation is possible because both agents involved, the explainer and the explainee, share the capability for practical reasoning. Thus when an explainer sees the actions of the other and hears some things the other says about what the explainer is trying to do, the explainer can fill in the gaps to build up a coherent account that relates all the goals and actions of the other into the account. By means of constructing such an account or "story," one agent can understand the actions of another agent. But what exactly is an account or "story" behind an action? And if this sort of account can be part of the evidence to support or refute an explanation, how should it be questioned, tested, and criticized? These pressing questions remain and are addressed below.[4] Schank (1986, p. 6) clarified these matters by his insightful remark that understanding needs to be understood as a spectrum. At one end is *complete empathy* of the kind found between twins, close siblings, or old friends. At the other end is a minimal form of understanding that Schank called *making sense.* Schank (1986, p. 6) defined it as "the point where events that occur in the world can be interpreted by the understander in terms of a coherent (though probably incomplete) picture of how those events came to pass." Understanding between agents in this minimal sense is made possible because agents share certain ways of acting and thinking in relation to kinds of situations with which they are both familiar.

To understand what understanding is in ordinary conversational discourse, we need to realize that things in everyday life work in fairly predictable patterns that are familiar to all of us by habit and common experience. For example, if you ask me why I broke my favorite sunglasses, I could explain by replying that I accidentally dropped them.[5] You can understand this explanation quite well because you are familiar with dropping objects accidentally and you know exactly how they drop on a hard surface and are broken or damaged unintentionally. Thus my explanation answers your question by helping you to understand that I did not break the sunglasses deliberately but did so accidentally. But you do not have to be a human being to understand the actions or thinking of another party whom you observe engaging in a kind of activity with which you are familiar. From practical experience a chimp can understand very well the problem of getting access to bananas hanging out of reach. The chimp can understand that there can be various ways of trying to reach the bananas and that some ways are likely to work better than others in a given situation. The chimp can make sense of the actor's actions because it is familiar with this kind of problem and with the sorts of actions needed to solve it. This sharing of understanding of ways and means that fall into familiar patterns is based on the twin capabilities of simulation and practical reasoning. Making sense is a minimal kind of understanding, but it is based on what can be called a kind of logical reasoning. The sense of understanding involved in such cases was rightly classified by von Wright as logical rather then psychological because it is based on simulative practical reasoning. The explainer builds up a coherent account representing the practical reasoning structure of the deeds and words of the other agent and then uses practical reasoning and skills of critical questioning to fill in the gaps. In the dual hypothesis regarding explanation proposed above, it is correct to say that a chimpanzee is capable of reasoning. Its capacity to make sense of human actions may be limited, but what it does in the bananas example can correctly be classified as reasoning of a certain sort.

But even if we can grasp what understanding is in a logical as opposed to a purely psychological sense, how can understanding increase or decrease in virtue of an explanation? To approach this question we can postulate that an explanation has a clarifying function in dialogues of various sorts. When a teacher explains something to a student, the teacher is trying to clarify something that was previously obscure to the student. Through this clarifying function the teacher is trying to increase or deepen the understanding of the student. How this function works depends on the kind of conversation the two parties are supposedly engaging in. The conversational postulates or so-called maxims of Grice (1975, pp. 67–68) include the injunction to make your contribution informative (maxim of quantity). They also include the maxim of manner, which includes the injunction to be "perspicuous." Van Eemeren and Grootendorst (1992, p. 50) have a comparable conversational maxim of clarity. It is expressed in the simple injunction "Be clear," which is presumably the same as, or similar to, the Gricean maxim. But as mentioned above, how clarity is determined depends on the nature of the conversation. A scientific explanation in physics may be quite clear to a group of physicists at a conference but terribly obscure if offered to a group of people who have never studied physics. On the other hand, an explanation of some arcane phenomenon in physics presented to readers of a popular magazine may be quite clear and helpful to these readers, yet a group of physicists might find it vague and metaphorical and not very enlightening or satisfactory at all as an explanation. This relativity of explanations to a context of conversation is a huge and intimidating problem for the DN model or other models that are semantic and based on a purely deductive or inductive framework. But is it completely expected by the dialogue approach and suggests to its exponents that they are on the right track.

SCRIPTS, ANCHORED NARRATIVES, AND IMPLICATURES

Witness testimony in court often takes the form of an explanation. The examiner asks the witness a question. Sometimes the question requires a simple yes or no or a factual answer. But sometimes the answer given by a witness takes the form of a "story" or connected account that represents the witness's account of what happened as the person saw it. The examiner can then question parts of the account found to be incomplete or implausible. This notion of the "story" has been put forward by Wagenaar, van Koppen, and Crombag (1993) in their theory of anchored narratives. An anchored narrative is an account of something that allegedly happened that is subject to questioning. If doubts are raised by questions asked, the proponent of the account can then support the account by giving reasons or "anchors" that ground the account in some independent facts or considerations that support it. Wagenaar, van Koppen, and Crombag (1993, p. 33) offered the following illustration of an anchored narrative. In this case, the example is not a legal one but an everyday account made up of five ordered statements.

1. Margie was holding tightly to the string of her beautiful new balloon.
2. Suddenly, a gust of wind caught it.
3. The wind carried it into a tree.
4. The balloon hit a branch and burst.
5. Margie cried and cried.

These five statements make sense not only independently but also as an account that ties them all together. The whole is more than just the sum of its parts. When presented with the five statements in the order above, we are able to fill in a number of gaps. As Wagenaar, van Koppen, and Crombag (1993, p. 33) have indicated, the five statements suggest other statements that are implicit in the account.

For instance, it is suggested that the wind caused the balloon to fly away. But what about the string? Did Margie not hold it tightly? Was the wind so strong that Margie could not have possibly held onto it? Rather unlikely. A lawyer, defending the wind in court, would have argued that the sentences (1) and (2) are contradictory. In fact, Margie let go of the balloon, *after which* the wind caught it. In sentence (4) a causal relationship is suggested: the balloon burst *because* it hit a branch. But there is only a juxtaposition; it is possible that the balloon burst for another reason, e.g. because a boy hit it with his catapult. In sentence (5) it is said that Margie cried, and we assume that this is caused by the loss of her balloon. But it is possible that she cried for a different reason, e.g. because the sudden gust of wind frightened her.

It is possible that Margie might not have let go of the balloon and that she was carried along with it up into the tree. Nothing explicitly said in the five statements rules out that interpretation of what was said to have happened. But this version of the account seems implausible because if Margie had been carried up into the tree and fallen out of it, these consequences would have been dramatic and even dangerous. If this was supposedly what happened, presumably there would be explicit mention of it. Because there was no mention of it at all, we can draw the inference that it did not happen. Such an inference is drawn by default or lack-of-evidence reasoning. This form of reasoning in traditional logic is called the argument from ignorance. It works by drawing a plausible presumption from what is not known, or has not been stated, in a given case. Because there was no mention in the account of Margie's having been carried up into the tree, we can infer that, according to the account, she was not carried up into the tree. It is far more plausible to infer that after the gust of wind caught the balloon, Margie let go of it, and then the wind carried it into the tree while Margie stayed on the ground.

Work in AI has also been built around the idea that much commonsense reasoning is based on unstated assumptions in a text of discourse that can be added in to fill gaps by someone presented with the text. A script, in the sense of the word used in AI (Schank and Abelson, 1977), is a body of commonsense knowledge that enables a language user to understand how things typically happen in stereotypical situations. This knowledge enables a language user to fill in what is not explicitly stated in a given text of discourse. Schank and Abelson used the restaurant example to explain how scripts work. This example, like the case of Margie above, can be presented as a sequence of given statements.

1. John went to a restaurant.
2. The hostess seated John.
3. The waitress gave John a menu.
4. John ordered a lobster.
5. He was served quickly.
6. He left a large tip.
7. He left the restaurant.

When presented with this set of statements, anyone can create an account or "story" out of it, filling in various gaps by drawing plausible inferences. For example, it is plausible to assume that lobster was listed on the menu. It is plausible to assume that John ate the lobster. It is plausible to assume that John paid something for the meal after he ate it and before he left the restaurant. None of these statements was explicitly made, but we can plausibly fill them in because they represent the normal ways of doing things when one goes to a restaurant. They are familiar routines because they are part of a normal sequence of actions.

In both the Margie case and the restaurant case, the statements inserted to fill gaps in the account might be false. But as noted above in the Margie case, they are inserted by default. If there is no reason given to think they are false, then we can infer that they are plausibly meant to be part of the story. You could say that they are suggested by the given statements, along with the script or background knowledge representing normal routines in the typical case of the kind given. Such inferences could be classified under the heading of what was called "implicature" by Grice (1975). An implicature is an inference based on contextual presumptions drawn by one party in a conversation from assumptions about the collaborative goal of the conversation. According to the "Cooperative Principle," a participant in a conversation is expected to make a contribution "such as is required at the stage at which it occurs, by the accepted purpose of the talk exchange in which you are engaged" (Grice, 1975, p. 67). These presumptions can take the form of general postulates or "maxims" of collaborative conversation. For example, Grice (1975, p. 67) has a pair of maxims of quantity telling a speaker to make his contribution as informative as is required, but not more informative than required. These maxims can be applied to the case of Margie and the restaurant above. When someone is trying to explain something to you or presenting a view of what happened, some statements can be taken for granted. To state them explicitly is not informative, because the other party to the conversation can fill them in without any help. If the speaker fails to deny such a normal assumption, the hearer can assume that it is conveyed in the account. The example of the letter of reference related by Grice (1975, p. 71) conveys this idea very well. In a letter of reference for a philosophy job, all the professor wrote was that the student had an excellent command of English and that his attendance at classes had been regular. The reader of the letter would infer by implicature that the speaker is conveying the information that the student is not a good candidate for the job. Once again, the conclusion is drawn by an argument from ignorance. If the candidate had the good qualities that would be important for such a job, such as being diligent, clever, or creative, the reader of the letter would expect the writer to state such things explicitly. Because the writer did not, by default the reader infers that the student lacks these good qualities to any notable degree.

The theory of anchored narratives was constructed to apply to cases of witness testimony in law. In legal cases of witness testimony, the structure is that of a dialogue started by a question. The witness then answers the question. So what we have is a dialogue. The sequence of questions and replies takes the form of a story that is gradually presented as prompted by the questions asked. Each answer fits in with the previous ones, and a connected or coherent account is produced through the dialogue exchanges. The same kind of dialogue framework applies to explanations generally. And the same ideas of scripts and conversational implicatures can be applied to the study of explanations as conversational exchanges. The same kind of simulative practical reasoning model also applies in both instances. A good story presented by a witness in court strings motives, opportunities, and actions together in a coherent order (Hastie, Penrod, and Pennington, 1983, pp. 22–23). Pennington and Hastie gave the example (1993, p. 197) of a person whose motive or goal is blocked by the actions of another person. He becomes frustrated and angry. Then a crime occurs: the second person was attacked. The attack could be presented in court by the prosecuting attorney as a "logical" outcome of prior conditions, as related in a story that supposedly reconstructs the crime. The story could be plausible to a jury, but there will also be a competing story presented by the defense attorney. The jury has to decide which account is the more plausible one.

A comparable dialogue framework can also be applied to explanations generally. An explanation is prompted by a question from a respondent. The proponent then offers an explanation that typically takes the form of a connected account or story or can be reconstructed in this format. The story has all kinds of gaps left by implicit statements that are parts of the story filled in by the questioner and other hearers. The explanation can "hang together" and appear plausible, especially if it is anchored by fitting in with other known facts in the case. Implausible aspects of the story can then be questioned. The resulting dialogue between the questioner and the explainee then provides the textual evidence needed to analyze and evaluate the explanation. The logical reasoning has to do with how the missing parts of the explanation are filled in during the dialogue. As noted above, the inferential structure is one of Gricean implicature and argument from ignorance (default reasoning). This filling in of gaps is typical of how explanations work in practice (Cawsey, 1992). There is also another feature of explanations worthy of comment—a feature that has to do with their contrastive nature.

In a trial, a witness for one side may give an account of what supposedly happened according to how that person saw the events, and a witness for the other side may offer quite a different account, even one that is inconsistent with that of the first witness. The jury has to choose between the two accounts. If one is inconsistent with the other, only one can be a true account of what really happened. One account is a contrast with the other, meaning that although each purports to be a true account of what happened, only one can be right. The attorneys for each side will get a chance to cross-examine the account offered by the witness for the opposing side, and they will try to "pick holes in it," or find parts of it that are not plausible. This characteristic process of dividing a case into two contrasting stories or conflicting accounts is typical of how legal reasoning works in a trial. McCarty (1995) found similar characteristics in an AI system he devised for reconstructing the argumentation in a Supreme Court decision. His analysis was based on the notions of prototype and deformation. A set of facts describing a case can be classified in one way or in a contrasting way, using a different prototype. The example offered by McCarty (1995) concerns a dispute about whether a dividend distributed in the form of stock was taxable or not. One side in the trial begins with a standard account, or prototype, of taxable gains, whereas the other begins with a standard account of nontaxable gains. Each side uses previous cases to try to show how the stock distribution at issue fits its prototype. Thus the notion of two opposed accounts being given of what appear to be the same facts is quite familiar in law.

THE DIALOGUE MODEL OF EXPLANATION

The thesis that explanations arise from why questions has been advocated in the literature of analytical philosophy from time to time. For example, van Fraassen (1993) postulated the theory that an explanation should be seen as an answer to a question of the form "Why A?" where A represents a fact to be explained. In this sort of approach, an explanation is viewed as a dialogue made up of a question along with the answer to it. Van Fraassen's pragmatic theory of explanation (1980, pp. 97–157) is based on a theory of why questions and how such questions are used in dialogue. His theory seems to go beyond the positivistic theories that have dominated the scene for so long in analytical philosophy. According to his theory, a why question asking for an explanation is always based on a contrast class. For example, the question, "Why did the sample burn green?" should be taken to pose the contrastive question, "Why did the sample burn green as opposed to some other color?" (van Fraassen, 1980, p. 127). In van Fraassen's theory, an explanation must establish a contrast between the fact in question and a series of other facts. In his theory (1980, p. 143), a response to a why question should be judged in terms of three dialogical factors: the topic, the contrast class, and the relevance relation. His approach is encouraging because it is dialogue based. But the approach goes only so far. It will help to look at an example to see where to go next.

Lipton (1991, p. 35) used the following simple example to show how natural the contrastive analysis of explanation is: "When I asked my 3-year-old son why he threw his food on the floor, he told me that he was full. This may explain why he threw it on the floor rather than eating it, but I wanted to know why he threw it rather than leaving it on his plate." As van Fraassen (1980, 126–29) observed, the why question generally does not simply ask for an explanation of a fact, but asks for it is a contrastive way, as in the question, "Why this rather than that?" Hempel (1965, 421–23) had earlier observed that we do not explain events, but only aspects of them. For example, we do not explain an eclipse tout court, but we may explain why it lasted as long as it did or why it was visible from a certain location. Lipton (1991, p. 35) also put the point by saying that the kinds of explanations that we typically give depend on our interests. I believe that the case studies of realistic conversational examples of explanations in AI by Cawsey (1992) demonstrate the same point. When someone asks for an explanation of why the photocopy machine does something in a certain way that may seem peculiar to him or her, the person is asking why it does the task in this unusual way, as opposed to the normal way the person is familiar with, having used other such machines like it in the past. The person assumes that the other party in the conversation is familiar with this contrast already and will base an explanation on it, rather than going into abstruse details of the mechanisms of the photocopy machine and how it was designed or the abstract engineering principles behind the mechanism.

This contrastive feature of the typical why question of the kind requesting an explanation reveals the pragmatic and dialectical aspect of explanations. An explanation of the typical sort needs to be viewed as a why question embedded in a dialogue (conversational exchange) that is ongoing between two parties. The question needs to be interpreted in light of the type of dialogue, its original topic or subject matter, other statements that can be taken by the hearer as presuppositions of the question, and the prior questions that have been asked and replied to before the question at issue is being considered. For example, in the case where the parent asked the child why the child threw food on the floor, the contrast is with the normal case where, when you have had enough to eat, you leave the rest on the plate. The parent's question, "Why did you throw the food on the floor?" asks for an explanation of why the child's action diverged from this norm. Of course, the child may not grasp any of this, but if the conversation were to take place between two adults, the one asking the question would presume that such an unusual action in place of the usual or expected one might have some special circumstances behind it that would serve to explain the action.

In Hempel's case of the eclipse, the kind of explanation wanted, which may be indicated by the why question asking for it, would depend on the hearer's presumed understanding and perhaps as well on the previous conversation. If the conversation was about how long eclipses last, for example, then an explanation of this eclipse would pertain to its length, perhaps as contrasted with other eclipses that were longer or shorter. If the questioner just asked, flat out, for an explanation of the eclipse, it might indicate that the person does not understand that the moon passes between the earth and sun occasionally. However, if there is reason to think the questioner understands this, perhaps as indicated by the previous conversation, then the question needs to be interpreted by contrasting it with some other factor, which the respondent needs to try to figure out. Much of the problem with explanations lies in understanding the question and trying to figure out, in light of what the questioner already knows or understands, what the questioner seeks to understand. The problem with analyzing any given explanation is to situate it in a context of dialogue.

What form should such a dialogue take? The literature in *AI* is helpful in providing a more detailed answer to this question, because researchers in computing have tried to devise software systems that can actually be used for computers to communicate and for users to communicate with computerized knowledge-based systems. Moore (1995, p. 1) outlined six main characteristics of the dialogue model of explanation. First, explanation takes the form of a sequence of moves between two parties in such a dialogue. It is "an inherently incremental and interactive process, requiring a dialogue between the advice giver and the advice seeker." It is incremental in the sense that each exchange in the dialogue sequence is built on previous exchanges in the sequence. Second, an explanation evolves as new information comes in during a sequence of dialogue. The new information facilitates understanding and learning during the dialogue process. Third, each party to an explanation must understand ways of thinking and beliefs shared by both parties. The process of explanation requires each party to make assumptions about the other party's beliefs, plans, and goals. Fourth, understanding of an explanation can be tested through feedback (Moore, 1991). The respondent, or advice seeker, can indicate verbally by responses whether an explanation offered by the proponent, or advice giver, has been understood correctly or not. Fifth, when the proponent presents an explanation to the respondent, the proponent expects the respondent "to ask further questions, request clarification, or provide some kind of indication when something is not understood." Thus the respondent also has obligations to meet in order to help make an explanation successful. Sixth, what constitutes a successful explanation is defined in dialogue terms. A successful explanation is reached through questioning in response to which the proponent continues to supply information or clarification until the respondent is satisfied. The dialogue model views an explanation as going through various stages of being asked for, being presented, being questioned, being improved, and so forth, as the dialogue proceeds. Thus both the notions of an explanation attempt and of a successful explanation are defined in relation to the stages of such a sequence and the moves made by both parties at a given stage of the dialogue.

Hamblin (1970, chapter 8) showed how to use systems of formal dialogue to distinguish between argument and explanation in a dialogue model. The method is to distinguish between different kinds of why questions. The way to do this is to indicate the function of why questions as a type of speech act in a dialogue structure. Hamblin (1970, p. 273) argued that why questions are ambiguous in at least three ways. One meaning of a why question is to request an argument. For example, when the proponent asks the respondent, "Why A?" for statement A, he or she may be requesting that the respondent produce an argument. In Hamblin's theory, this request asks for a premissary base, say a statement B, and a conditional or linking statement of the form, "If B then A." A second meaning of a why question is to request a justification for the act of having made a prior statement. For example, when a respondent has made a statement A earlier in a dialogue, the proponent of a why question may then ask, "Why did you say that?" The proponent might then answer, "In order to impress X" (p. 273). A third meaning of a why question (p. 274) is to request an explanation. This could be a request for a causal explanation or a teleological explanation, according to Hamblin (1970, p. 274). An example of a causal explanation would be the following dialogue sequence. The respondent asks the proponent why it is cold in here, and the proponent replies, "Because the heat is off." An example of a teleological explanation would be the following dialogue sequence. The respondent asks why John is in the library, and the proponent answers, "Because he has an essay to finish." Thus Hamblin has shown that asking a why question can be ambiguous in three ways, and he has showed how each meaning can be represented as having a distinctive function in a dialogue structure.

Several important lessons can be learned from Hamblin's analysis. One is that the difference between an explanation and an argument needs to be conceived in relation to the dialogue structure of each of the two types of speech acts. The key is that both need to be defined in relation to a certain type of question asked by one party in a dialogue and in relation to the answer that needs to be given in order to fulfill the request put by the question. Hamblin was mainly concerned with argument in dialogue in his chapter on formal dialectic (chapter 8 of Hamblin, 1970), and he did not attempt to use the dialogue structure to define what an explanation is. Nevertheless, he did set out rules of dialogue that define conditions for the success of an argument and that can perhaps be extended to encompass the notion of explanation as well. Several of the rules of dialogue he discussed (pp. 270–71) apply to the asking of questions, and to the asking of why questions in particular. The rules are commitment based. That is, they are based on the idea that a participant in a dialogue has a set of statements designated as that person's commitments at the beginning of a dialogue and that statements can be added to this set or deleted from it as the dialogue proceeds. Could the same sort of dialogue framework be extended to the notion of explanation? It seems that it could.

The first step would surely be to distinguish between different types of questions that give rise to explanations. One, as Hamblin noted, is the why question. Another would be the how question. As Hamblin noted, some why questions request a causal explanation, whereas others request a teleological or means-end goal-oriented explanation. The how questions request information about the process by which something came about or how it works. For example, I might ask a colleague, "How does this photocopy machine work?" Or I might ask someone, "How did John injure his foot?" Given the parallel drawn by Hamblin between explanation and argument, we might then try to set up rules for different types of explanations in different types of dialogue. But how could we carry out such a research project? Hamblin devised his rules governing argumentation in dialogue based on the notion of an arguer's commitment. This was his main tool and what made his dialogue-based analysis of argumentation possible. But when it comes to explanation, we seem to be left in the dark. The notion of an arguer's commitment is not all that helpful in relation to analyzing explanation. We seem to need some notion comparable to commitment that can be defined clearly and precisely in the dialogue structure. Explanations are supposed to throw light on something obscure or puzzling to a questioner. But what does that mean, in exact terms, for functions of formal dialogue theory? Here we seem to face an abyss, and it is hard to know how to proceed.

The answer to the puzzle is that we need to expand the notion of commitment in dialogue beyond the point that Hamblin took it and beyond the point to which it has been taken in Walton and Krabbe (1995). A participant in a dialogue begins with a designated commitment set, and that set then expands or contracts according to the rules of a dialogue and according to how the participant makes moves governed by these rules. That is the dialectical framework that has been used to analyze and evaluate argumentation so far. What is now being added to Hamblin's dialogue framework is that the arguer who has a commitment set is seen as an agent. But when an agent has a set of commitments, this set will have a certain structure that helps the agent to organize the individual's thinking and make it instrumentally useful. Suppose the agent is capable of practical reasoning. The agent's commitment set will be composed of statements that can be linked to each other by means of practical reasoning. For example, one statement might represent an outcome that can be brought about by making another statement in the set true. Or to put it another way, one item in the agent's commitment set might be a means to an end represented by another item in the commitment set. Suppose I am committed to making a copy of this sheet of paper. I may know that the only way to do this is to push a button on the photocopy machine. Therefore, by practical reasoning, I am also committed to pushing the button on the photocopy machine. One commitment leads to another and is connected to another in an agent's commitment set just because the agent is an agent and is assumed to be capable of practical reasoning. Because there will be many such connections in an agent's commitment set, even in the most ordinary and simple case of everyday reasoning and thinking, the commitment set will have a structure. It will be more than just a set of statements. It will be a connected set of them joined to each other by inference links. It will be a web or interlocked set of statements knit together by threads of inference. So if an agent is committed to one particular statement, that agent will automatically be committed to many neighboring ones as well, unless the person retracts commitment to each of them individually. Of course, we already know from the study of commitment in argumentation in Walton and Krabbe (1995) that commitments are "sticky" in this way and that they come in groups for an arguer. What does this tell us, if anything, about explanations and how they work in a dialogue format?

The answer is that the commitment set of a participant in a dialogue needs to be seen as an organized network of statements that has a structure imposed by sets of logical relationships between statements in the set. It is this logical structure that was so important in dealing with the key problem of retraction of commitment in Walton and Krabbe (1995). For example, suppose a participant in a persuasion dialogue is committed to statement A and that statement A implies statement B. Is that participant then automatically committed to B at the next move of the dialogue? And suppose that participant is committed to A, but will not commit to B, so that now the commitment is to a logical inconsistency.

What should happen next in the dialogue, according to the commitment rules? Should the participant have to remove the inconsistency from the commitment set by retracting one or other of the commitments that produced it? These are hard questions, and it was said in Walton and Krabbe (1995) that there are no easy answers. There are many different systems of dialogue reflecting different levels of rationality or kinds of rationality that the argumentation in them is supposed to represent. The formal dialogue is only a model. But it can represent not one, but several different kinds of structure as normative models of rational argumentation. If so, how could the dialogue structures represent models of explanation? The answer is similar to the way commitment was used in Walton and Krabbe (1995) to represent normative models of argumentation that can be used, for example, to analyze logical fallacies. An agent in a dialogue will have a set of commitments that lock together into a structure formed by logical inferences connecting each commitment to other commitments. The whole network hangs together. It does not have to be logically consistent. That would be too strong a rule to apply universally to dialogues that can contain all sorts of mistakes and fallacies. But if a proponent's commitment set can be shown by a respondent's questioning to be logically inconsistent or to lead to other commitments that are dubious from a point of view of practical reasoning, then the proponent should be obliged to at least deal with the putative inconsistency or practical problem by replying appropriately to the questions posed.

The final step is to see that this structure, imposed by the network of an agent's commitment set in a dialogue, can be used to define what can be called the agent's "understanding" of the issue or subject being discussed in the dialogue. Understanding is not meant here in a purely psychological sense, but rather in the normative sense of rational understanding. It is a kind of understanding that, ideally, should be shared by the proponent and the respondent in a dialogue. When the two parties fail to have a satisfactory mutual understanding of something they are discussing there is a puzzlement or lack of understanding that leads to the appropriateness of a request for an explanation. To be successful, the explanation must answer the question by removing the inconsistency or failure of the commitment set to make sense to the questioner. The putative inconsistency of commitments, or apparent failure of practical reasoning to square with commitments taken to represent known facts of a case, must at least be dealt with in a way that meets the concern or breakdown of understanding expressed by the question. Here, then, is a general method or research program for providing a dialogue-based theory of explanation. How well does this commitment-style approach work? The problem is that the notion of understanding, like the notion of commitment, is so fundamental to everyday human reasoning that, paradoxically, it almost seems hard for us to understand it. The paradox is posed by the bothersome question, "How can we understand understanding?" The project of coming to understand understanding involves circularity. But the circularity is not a vicious one, provided the question and the answer to it are approached in the right way. Just as we can come to understand commitment as a normative notion through setting up systems of formal dialogue with rules and clearly defined moves, so we can come to understand understanding as a normative notion that is based on clearly defined standards of rationality by using the same kinds of dialogue structures. The basic point is that the target notion of understanding is not one of complete or total understanding of everything, but a reconstructive one that enables us to put a given explanation in a given text of discourse into a certain rational perspective. Of course, rationality is not everything. Some would say it is nothing at all. However, it would be an error to try to engage in rational argumentation with such a person, other than by pointing out that the argument is self-refuting.

THE SPEECH ACT OF EXPLANATION

In contrast to the DN model, a dialogue model of explanation can be constructed. In the dialogue model, an explanation is seen as a kind of inference, or at least as based on an inference or chain of reasoning. But there is much more to explanation than just this central inference, according to the dialogue model. An explanation is an inference used by one party as part of a dialogue with another party. Introducing the term "dialogue" might suggest a loss of precision that can be preserved by sticking to the simpler model of explanation as a deductively valid inference (something philosophers are comfortable with). But precision need not be given up, because formal conditions for such a dialogue can be stated. A dialogue can be seen after the style of Hamblin (1970; 1971) as having a formal structure governed by rules that define the kinds of moves allowed, the roles and obligations of the two participants, how making a move affects a participant's commitments, and what constitutes a successful sequence of moves. Up to the present, formal systems of dialogue have mainly been applied to argumentation and logical fallacies as they occur in argumentation. But the same kinds of dialogue structures can also be applied to explanations.

The first point that needs to be understood is that explanation needs to be defined in the dialogue structure as a distinctive type of speech act. The idea of speech acts derives from the work of Austin (1962) and Searle (1969). Austin observed that certain natural language utterances, such as "I now pronounce you man and wife" (uttered during the wedding ceremony), are like actions in that they have effects that change the world. Searle identified and classified a number of these so-called speech acts by stating formal conditions that define their success or failure in a dialogue format. Speech acts have now become very important in computing because it has become vital to formulate communication policies that define how one system can communicate with another in an orderly conversation. Such policies will enable software entities to engage in joint exchanges of information and deliberations necessary to carry out tasks requiring collaboration. Various formal communication languages of this sort have been devised and are currently being improved while they are in use (Wooldridge, 2000, pp. 131–34). Singh (1993, p. 55) has presented a table of the basic kinds of speech acts that are most central to these recent developments in computing and has included examples. The column on the left represents the force of the utterance. The column on the right gives an example.

Assertive	The door is shut.
Directive	Shut the door.
Commissive	I will shut the door.
Permissive	You may shut the door.
Prohibitive	You may not shut the door.
Declarative	I name this door the Golden Gate.

Other types of speech acts that are of basic importance are *request* and *inform*. The speech act approach can also be applied to the concept of an explanation. In the literature on argumentation, the speech act approach has been used to specify the conditions that define *argument* as an identifiable kind of speech act within a dialogue framework (van Eemeren and Grootendorst, 1992, pp. 30–33; Walton, 1996a, pp. 37–41). Argument can be contrasted with explanation using a speech act analysis that identifies the different functions that each speech act has in a framework of goal-directed dialogue. Basically an argument is used when there is an unsettled issue, and the purpose of using an argument is to try to settle the issue one way or the other. An unsettled issue is characterized by a particular proposition or designated statement and one of two attitudes toward it expressed by two participants in a dialogue. In one type of case, the one party has expressed doubt that the proposition is true or acceptable, and the other party tries to use rational argumentation to try to get the first party to accept it by removing this doubt. In the other type of case, the two participants have opposed opinions about the proposition at issue. One thinks it is true, and the other thinks it is false. Explanation contrasts with argumentation. In a case of explanation, both parties accept the designated proposition as true or factual. Neither doubts it is true. Both accept it as a given fact that is presumed to be true. But there is something about it that one party fails to understand. The purpose of the other party's giving an explanation is to try to get the first party to come to understand the proposition. Thus the difference between argument and explanation does not reside in the use of inference or reasoning. Both do so. But they use reasoning for different purposes in a dialogue. In other words, each represents a different kind of speech act.

The speech act conditions for an explanation can be set out as follows. This form of speech act is somewhat simplistic. Different kinds of explanations need to be analyzed by making conditions more specific or by adding new conditions. But this model gives a general basis, much as Hempel's DN model gave a general basis for his view of explanation. This model could be called the dialogue model for obvious reasons or the inferential-pragmatic model because it combines inferential conditions with pragmatic conditions that define how an explanation should be used in a dialogue. In the dialogue model, the one party, called the respondent (or explainee), asks a question. The question is a request for something. Thus the speech act of explanation comes, at least partly, under the general category of a request. But the request is not a request for information. It is a request for the proponent (or explainer) to provide the respondent with understanding.

Speech Act Conditions for Explanation: The Dialogue Model
Dialogue Conditions
Dialogue Precondition: the speaker and the hearer are engaged in some type of dialogue that has collaborative rules and some collective goal as a type of dialogue.
Question Condition: The speaker asks a question of a specific form, such as a why question or a how question, containing a key presumption.

Presumption Condition: The presumption in the question can be expressed in the form of a proposition that is assumed to be true. The presumption is taken to be "given" or datum that is not in question, as far as the dialogue between the speaker and hearer is concerned.

Understanding Conditions

Speaker's Understanding Condition: the speaker has some kind of special knowledge, understanding, or information about the presumption that the hearer lacks.

Hearer's Understanding Condition: the hearer lacks this special knowledge, understanding, or information.

Empathy Condition: the speaker understands how the hearer understands the presumption, premises, and inferences and understands how the hearer expects things to normally go and what can be taken for granted in these respects, according to the understanding of the hearer.

Language Clarity Condition: in special cases, the speaker may be an expert in a domain of knowledge or skill in which the hearer is not an expert and must therefore use language only of a kind that the hearer can be expected to be familiar with and can understand.

Success Conditions

Inference Condition: the speaker is supposed to supply an inference, or chain of inferences (reasoning), in which the ultimate conclusion is the key presumption.

Premise Understanding Condition: the hearer is supposed to understand all the premises in the chain of reasoning used according to the inference condition.

Inference Understanding Condition: the hearer is supposed to understand each inference in the chain of reasoning.

Transfer Condition: by using the inference or chain of reasoning, the speaker is supposed to transfer understanding to the hearer so that the hearer now understands what was previously not understood (as indicated by the question).

The first problem with the dialogue model that needs to be discussed is how it differentiates between an explanation attempt and a successful explanation. If a speaker and a hearer engage in a conversational exchange that meets some of these conditions, it will be recognized that an explanation attempt is being made. If all of the requirements are met, including the transfer condition, then the explanation has been successful. But an important question is how the degree to which an explanation has been successful should be judged. This should especially depend on how well understanding is transferred from the speaker to the hearer. How can that be ascertained in a given case?

The answer is that each case needs to be judged on its merits, depending on the evidence that can be gathered from the details of the case as known. In some cases, very little may be known. An explanation may have been offered, but we may not have any or much information about the state of the respondent's understanding either before or after the explanation was presented. In other cases, we may have a lot of evidence from the given text of discourse of the dialogue. The respondent may have asked for further clarifications or may have replied that the explanation has provided understanding. In some cases, it may be evident that the gap in understanding between the two parties is wide. One may be an expert on a highly technical subject whereas the other knows almost nothing about it. In this kind of case, one has to look very closely at the explanation itself and at the questions and replies in the dialogue leading up to it and following from it. In the dialogue model of explanation, the text of discourse of the dialogue exchange between the two parties is the basis of evidence enabling an observer or critic to judge how successful the explanation was.

DIALOGUE MODELS OF SCIENTIFIC ARGUMENTATION AND EXPLANATION

Six basic types of dialogue have been recognized as centrally important in argumentation theory. In a persuasion dialogue, one party tries to persuade the other to accept a particular proposition. Persuasion can be defined as a speech act in which the proponent of a thesis "persuades" a respondent to come to accept that thesis by presenting an argument. The argument has to meet two main requirements. First, the premises have to be propositions that the respondent is committed to in a dialogue, or at least propositions that the respondent may later be persuaded to accept and become committed to. Second, the conclusion of the argument has to be the proponent's thesis. We could sum up these two characteristics by saying that the argumentation in a persuasion dialogue is other based. Of course you are trying to prove your own conclusion, but you must do it by basing your argument on the commitments of the other party. This summary represents the essence of persuasion dialogue in a simple formula. It is not common to think of computer programs as having a capability for persuasion, but recent research in knowledge-based systems, and especially in multiagent systems, have acknowledged such a function. For example, the system as an agent must make another artificial or human agent accept a piece of advice or adopt or abandon a goal (Moulin et al., 2002, p. 170). Thus AI is developing systems that are based on a notion of rational persuasion (Bench-Capon, 1997).

The inquiry is a type of dialogue in which an investigating group tries to prove some designated proposition, to disprove it, or to show that it cannot be either proved or disproved. The term "prove" is meant here in a much stricter sense than in a persuasion dialogue. In an inquiry the aim is to verify a mass of facts as data and then use these facts to establish a conclusion very firmly in place as a "finding." The main characteristic of the chain of argumentation in the inquiry is cumulativeness. To say a chain of argumentation is cumulative means that each proposition in the chain has been established so firmly that it will never need to be retracted at any future point in the dialogue. At its early stages, an inquiry can go through a discovery stage in which questions are asked about the evidence collected at a given point. The making of imaginative efforts to generate hypotheses to explain the data is characteristic of the argumentation at this stage. But as Schum (1994, p. 451) noted, some of these efforts are more productive than others. In his view (p. 451), "Efficient means for both *search* and *inquiry* are necessary in productive discovery-related activities." The argumentation in the searching undertaken at this discovery stage of an inquiry is not cumulative. It is a free-ranging kind of argumentation in which questions are asked, often of a causal nature, and then a hypothesis that can explain the data at that point in the search is tentatively put forward as a commitment. But as further data come in, the hypothesis may need to be retracted if it fails to explain the newly enlarged body of data. It is this discovery stage in which abductive reasoning is so typically used in scientific argumentation.

The other types of dialogue that have been analyzed in the literature are negotiation, information-seeking dialogue, eristic (quarrelsome) dialogue, and deliberation. A very useful formal model of deliberation dialogue as a normative framework of argumentation has been devised by Hitchcock, McBurney, and Parsons (2001). In this model, a deliberation dialogue begins by posing a "governing question" that formulates the problem to be solved. This governing question is asked at the opening stage of the deliberation. During the argumentation stage, both participants make moves by recommending actions or policies that will supposedly solve the problem set by the governing question. As the sequence of argumentation proceeds, the proposal made by one party is revised, considered, rejected, recommended, or confirmed by the other party. Once the argumentation has examined all the relevant proposals and the reasons for and against them, the dialogue reaches a closing stage. Each type of dialogue has four stages: a confrontation stage, an opening stage, an argumentation stage, and a closing stage. There is no space here to examine further the types of dialogue and their characteristics. The reader is referred to Walton (1998) for further details.

At a later stage, scientific argumentation, it can be argued, takes the form of an inquiry. Before it is accepted, a statement must be verified so that, as the inquiry proceeds, there will be no need to go back and retract that statement. This is the property of cumulativeness. Of course, cumulativeness is only an ideal in a scientific inquiry. In practice, retractions often have to be made as new data come in. But as a scientific inquiry proceeds, it strives in the end to be complete by eventually collecting and processing all the relevant data.

It was argued above that although reduction is a useful concept for defining scientific understanding, it is not sufficient to fully define understanding of the kind aimed at in scientific explanations. Perhaps it is an ideal of a certain kind of scientific explanation that it reduces the thing to be explained to some units already accepted as fundamental in a science, such as genes or molecular motions. This ideal may represent what is aimed for at the end of an investigation. However, along the way, at earlier stages such as the discovery stage, the tentative scientific explanations that are offered may be useful even though they are not yet this deep. Salmon (1992, p. 37) distinguished between a deep explanation and a request for an ideal of what he calls an explanatory text and a request for explanatory information. At an early stage of an investigation, trace explanations and strategic explanations might be useful to move the investigation forward, even though they do not represent the ideal kind of explanation that is aimed at as the ultimate aim of the investigation. This kind of explanation may trace a line of reasoning from something better understood to something not so well understood, indicating a direction in which the investigation should proceed. This kind of explanation is based on reasoning that can increase the questioner's understanding of where to go next by using defeasible forms of reasoning represented by argumentation schemes. Kitcher (1989, p. 432) has offered a hint of this connection by defining scientific understanding as "the internalization of argument patterns" found in what initially appear to be different situations.

How is increase of understanding to be defined in the earlier discovery stage of scientific argumentation, where very little is yet known? What kind of dialogue structure does the argumentation in this stage have? In Kuhn's analysis, it is a persuasion dialogue (Kuhn, 1970). Opposed scientific theories based on differing paradigms offer conflicting explanations of the same data. They use argumentation to try to cast doubt on the opposed theory and to give convincing reasons to accept their own viewpoint. But what about cases where the investigation is at an even earlier stage, where theories have not yet been well enough formulated to give rise to conflicting paradigms? In these cases, a scientist may simply be trying to give some sort of scientifically acceptable explanation for a finding that is puzzling or that raises interesting questions. In still other cases, the scientific researcher may be trying to solve a practical or technical problem, for example, trying to design some new software or a new pesticide that will not pollute the environment or harm humans. In these cases, the process of discovery may be better modeled as deliberation dialogue than as persuasion dialogue. The scientist has a goal for the research project, and the goal is to produce some technique, device, or product that will be an acceptable means to that end.

It may seem strange at first to think of scientific argumentation as taking place within a so-called framework of dialogue. The term "dialogue" suggests a conversation between two persons, and it sounds subjective and personal. Scientific reasoning, most of us think, is objective and impersonal. Scientific theories, hypotheses, and results are supposedly objective. They are propositions that are true or false and are proved to be so by factual investigations that eliminate the personal element. What matters are the "facts," and the theories that explain the facts are expressed in objective mathematical equations and quantitative laws. But it has to be remembered that the participants in a dialogue, according to the view of argumentation as dialectical, need not be actual human beings. They are agents, entities that can make moves in dialogues and that have commitments inserted into or removed from commitment sets based on these moves. Agents can be software entities, for example. They do have the capacity for making speech acts of well-defined kinds and thereby for communicating with other agents. But they can only do so in a way that is structured by the rules for the type of dialogue in which they are taking part. Thus it is possible, and indeed very useful, to think of various kinds of scientific argumentation not only as logical reasoning but also as logical reasoning used for some purpose in a framework of dialogue representing some kind of scientific activity. The problem is that there are many philosophies of science, ranging from positivism and foundationalism, which see scientific argumentation as rigidly structured, to other views, such as that of Kuhn and Feyerabend, that see it as looser, more like a persuasion dialogue.

The problem is that deductive and inductive logic have been taken in the past to be the models of scientific argumentation. These are context-free models of rational argument that do not seem to require the study of any pragmatic framework of argumentation use. It is only more recently that the advent of interest in abduction has made Peirce's pragmatic approach begin to seem a plausible contender against these earlier theories. Thus the project of viewing scientific argumentation as proceeding through different stages in a goal-directed sequence, and as having different characteristics during different stages of the sequence, still seems highly problematic and questionable to many. It seems to make science too subjective. Certainly it is against positivistic views of science, which have been widely accepted in recent times. It may be accepted as a sociological view of how scientific argumentation actually proceeds, as can be illustrated by case studies of scientific discovery. But it seems to go against the grain as a normative or logical model of the rationality of scientific argumentation. Nevertheless, taking this step is very useful, and indeed it is necessary if we are to gain any grasp of how abductive reasoning works in scientific discovery.

Scientific investigation can be seen dialectically in two main ways, using the nature model or the community model. In the nature model, the scientific community can be seen as engaging in an information-seeking dialogue with nature. The scientific community asks questions, and nature provides information in answer to the questions. In the community model, the investigator is seen as an agent who engages in dialogue with other members of the scientific community. Thus the investigator is seen as the proponent of an argument who presents a new hypothesis, theory, or argument. The other scientists who take part in the dialogue express doubts about this argument. In order to reply to these doubts, the proponent has to present evidence of a kind that can properly be used to support the claim. Thus the scientific community will be divided into two camps in any given case, according to this model. Some will make the case for a new finding or hypothesis, and some will be skeptical about it and require proof before they come to accept it.

Both models can be applied at various stages of the process of a scientific investigation. The nature model may be most useful at the discovery stage and the testing stage. The community model may be more useful at the stage where a scientist has already collected data, carried out testing, and written up arguments for publication or presentation to colleagues.

Starting from the generally accepted opinion that there is growth of knowledge in the history of science, Finocchiaro (1975; 1980) has argued for the much less widely accepted thesis that scientific discoveries are instances of the growth of understanding. As noted in the second section above, he supported and developed Scriven's thesis (1962, 2002) that a successful explanation is one that increases understanding. Finocchiaro supported this thesis by presenting case studies of scientific discovery. In the case of Galileo's theory of planetary motion, Finocchiaro (1975, p. 119) argued that Galileo mathematically described those aspects of the motion of bodies he did not understand and then explained them by proposing laws as hypotheses. Thus according to Finocchiaro's account, this process of scientific explanation involved laws and hence the DN model. This much is evident from the account Galileo gave in *Two New Sciences,* where he gave an exposition of his results (Finocchiaro, 1975, p. 122). But Finocchiaro (p. 122) drew attention to a passage where Galileo cites considerations of simplicity that show he considered certain aspects of motion as difficulties or things that are incomprehensible. He took this passage as evidence that, for Galileo, the transition from lack of understanding to understanding is an essential part of a successful scientific explanation. Finocchiaro (1980) also studied the case of Newton's discovery of gravitation. Using Newton's texts and letters, he argued that an important objective for Newton was to give "conceptual intelligibility" to the notion (p. 246). According to Finocchiaro's analysis of the case, Newton's attempt to solve the problem he saw himself as addressing needs to be expressed in relation to his attempts to make it intelligible as a scientific concept. In both cases, scientific discovery is based on a notion of explanation that moves from a perception of a problem that poses a difficulty because it cannot be understood to a new theory or to an explanation that gives the understanding needed to solve the problem.

The DN model and the dialogue model may not really be opposed to each other as analyses of what a successful scientific explanation is. They may rather complement each other or may fit in together as providing criteria for certain respects in which an explanation can be judged successful. It is too soon to tell what the outcome of such studies will be. Still, the dialogue theory is more comprehensive than the DN theory, and thus the latter may turn out to fit in as one aspect of the former.

EXAMINATION DIALOGUE AND
SHARED UNDERSTANDING

Explanation, like argumentation, can take place in many different conversational settings. Explanation is especially important in certain types of dialogue, however. It is vitally important in teaching, or what might be called pedagogical dialogue. Presumably, education is not just the passing on of information. It should include explanation, and the student should ask questions about any part of an explanation that is not understood. This process of asking for explanations is a very important part of advice-seeking dialogue and is acknowledged in AI as an important component in an expert system. As we have noted many times, explanation is central in science and in the methodology of experimental science. It is also basic to history as a discipline. And, finally, explanation is an important part of law at all levels. For example, it is often an important part of witness testimony and examination in court. Although a scientific explanation may represent an ideal of unification, the explanations in pedagogy, expert systems, history, and law may be successful (in context) even though they fall short of this ideal.

There is one type of dialogue that is especially basic to understanding how explanation works in all these contexts. Examination is a probing kind of dialogue in which one party tests out the answer previously put forward by the other party. For example, suppose you are getting some advice from your financial adviser, and this expert tells you that investing in a certain stock would be a good idea. But you have heard that this stock is overvalued. You might then probe more deeply into the advice by saying that you have heard this stock is overvalued and ask why you should invest in a stock that may be overvalued. You yourself are not an expert on financial matters, but you can still ask critical questions about what this expert says, based on information you may have or on what you may have heard other experts say. This sort of probing into expert advice is a type of examination dialogue. Another type of examination dialogue is the kind that occurs in court when an expert witness is examined. For example, a medical expert may testify regarding the cause of death of a victim in a homicide case. The attorney who questions the physician is probably not an expert in medical matters. Even so, the attorney must examine the expert by critically probing into the details of what was said. Sometimes the attorney must ask the physician on what evidence the opinion was based. This type of verbal exchange is an examination dialogue.

The study of expert systems in AI has been much concerned with explanations precisely because of the need to question an expert if the user is to take maximal advantage of expert advice. The dialogue framework in such cases is a human-computer interaction in which the computer system (expert software) and the human user ask and reply to questions. An aspect of the dialogue that is vital to the success of such a system is what Silverman (1992, p. 4) calls the critiquing process.

> Critiquing involves a two-way communication, a mutual search for truth. Both the originator and recipient of the initial criticism can grow and improve from the interaction. The criticism recipient benefits either from improving his task result or from increasing his credibility in the eyes of the originator. In the latter case, the criticism originator learns of his own erroneous judgment and grows through the exchange.

The critiquing process can be seen as an examination dialogue in which the human user questions the expert system not only to get the expert's pronouncements but also to understand them. This process of gradual understanding is modeled by Silverman in the form of a dialogue sequence of questions and answers that go in a cycle (p. 4). The expert produces a so-called task result that answers the question of how to carry out some task. Next, the critic analyzes the task result and asks questions, criticizing any apparent errors or problems that are found in it. When the critic fails to find any more apparent errors, the cycle ends. The dialogue continues as long as the critic continues to ask appropriate questions. Whenever the critic asks such a question, the system must respond by offering an explanation or some appropriate sign of recognition of error. Through this process of dialogue, revisions of the task result are accomplished, leading to a better plan for action. As Silverman indicated in the quote above, the process benefits both parties.

Another type of examination dialogue is also distinctive and noteworthy. It occurs as part of pedagogical dialogue. It is the testing part. In this type of dialogue, the teacher asks questions of a student in order to test the student's knowledge. The student is supposed to give an answer. This kind of testing can be informal in class. Students can also ask questions to test out how well the teacher knows the field. Then there are the official kinds of examinations we are all so familiar with, those in the form of written tests, essays, and other assignments. In examination dialogue the questioner is seeking information, but is seeking information about the information possessed by the other party. So you could say that in examination dialogue the questioner seeks information about information. The questioner seeks information about whether the respondent has information.

A typical problem in examination dialogue is that one party cannot understand why the other fails to understand something because there is too much of a gap between the background, commitments, and shared understanding of the two parties. Explanation by transfer of understanding may be impossible if the one party has an insufficient basis of shared knowledge to simulate the thinking in the other. Thus it may be that the one party does not understand why the other party does not understand something. The purpose of explanation, in the dialogue theory, is for the explainer to transfer understanding to fill a gap in the questioner's understanding of something so that the questioner can make sense of it. But making this notion of explanation workable presumes that the questioner already has some understanding that is roughly of the same kind as the explainer's, by which the questioner can make sense of the explanation. In some cases, however, the explanation attempt is bound to fail, because the shared understanding is simply not there. This problem could be a serious criticism of the dialogue theory explanation.

In fact, this problem is not only theoretical. It has been noticed in the development of software systems that deal with explanations in dialogues in which one party is an expert and the other is not. Cawsey (1992, p. 115) has called the phenomenon "guessing at the user's problem," which occurs in a dialogue when the questioner cannot articulate why something is not understood. The solution in the EDGE software for expert systems dialogues developed by Cawsey is to have a menu option for the user to click on—a "what?" icon—to indicate that the last reply has not been understood. The expert system can then try to diagnose the failure and remedy it. AI systems have learned to deal with this common phenomenon. It is dealt with by expanding the explanation to fill in gaps and extend the questioner's understanding. It should be realized, however, that explanation attempts of this sort are not always successful. Sometimes the gap between the understanding of the questioner and that of the explainer is simply too wide.

Suppose, for example, that the explainer is a scientist in some special field of expertise and tries to express an explanation in terms that only another expert in the same field would understand. The explanation may be a good one if directed to a respondent who is an expert in that field. Yet it may fail, because the questioner is not such an expert. This observation reveals many things about explanation, understanding, and abduction. In the dialogue theory, an explanation attempt, in order to be successful, needs to fill in a fairly narrow gap in the questioner's understanding. If the gap is too broad, and the two parties do not share sufficient common knowledge for transfer of understanding, the explanation may fail. What is shown is that there can be different kinds of understanding. Scientific understanding can only be shared by two parties who already have quite a broad basis for agreement and understanding. They must share certain methods and agree in advance that an explanation can only be successful if it reduces the thing to be explained to basic concepts or units accepted in science or in that field of scientific expertise. For example, an explanation may only be regarded as acceptable if it reduces the thing to be explained to atomic particles that are known and recognized or to genes, genetic structures, or other elements or structures that are regarded as understandable in science. Thus ordinary explanations, legal explanations, and scientific explanations may be quite different. Basically, in the dialogue theory, it is recognized that what is accepted as shared understanding is quite different in different cases. The requirements for what is accepted as "understood" vary with the type of dialogue. How commitment and understanding are defined, and what the criteria of success are, will also vary according to the type of dialogue.

As shown above, one of the most common types of dialogue in which explanations are attempted is examination dialogue. In such a dialogue, there may be quite a wide gap between the understanding of the explainer, an expert in a scientific field, and the understanding of the questioner, who may not be an expert in that field and who lacks specialized knowledge of it. Despite such a gap, however, the explanation can be successful if the two parties can bridge the gap. The questioner can persist when the explanation is simply not understood. The explainer can be responsive by filling in the gap in a way that is sensitive to the understanding of the questioner. What is shown is that understanding is a reflexive notion. One party in a dialogue must try to understand the understanding of the other party. That party must also try to understand what the other party fails to understand and why it is not understood.

What lesson can be derived from these observations? Magnani (2001) derives the lesson that two distinct types of abduction should be recognized: (1) theoretical abduction characteristic of scientific explanations and scientific theory formation and (2) manipulative abduction. The latter type is a more practical kind that one might find in explanations outside science or prior to the formation of a scientific theory. Certainly it is right that scientific explanation needs to be based on a special notion of shared understanding. In contrast, examination dialogue in the expert advice kind of case dwelt on by AI research involves a different dialogue framework, one of examination dialogue in which one party is an expert and the other is not. The lesson I would draw is that it is necessary to have a dialogue theory of explanation in which these phenomena can be dealt with by means of a dialogue between the two parties. In the dialogue, one party tries to understand why the other does not understand something by continuing a line of questioning and answering.

DIALECTICAL SHIFTS AND EMBEDDINGS

In this chapter a dialogue model of the speech act of explanation has been constructed. It is based on two primitive notions, those of understanding and of dialogue. The notion of simulative reasoning was used to build up a model of understanding in the minimal sense of "making sense" explained by Schank. Making sense represents a minimal kind of empathy between agents through which one agent is able to use means-end or practical reasoning to reconstruct an anchored narrative representing the commitments of the other agent. It is this connected network of commitments that, when put together as a coherent account, is the vehicle whereby one agent understands the actions or goals of another agent. This model of understanding may seem so radical to some readers that it may seem to postulate or require a new notion of rationality. It will be the purpose of chapter 4 to investigate the dialogue model of explanation further by asking what rationality is and by proposing a new view of it that fits with the notion of making sense that will be presented in chapter 3.

The other notion that needs further analysis and clarification is that of the dialogue as a model of both argumentation and explanation. The main problem here is to figure out how examination dialogue works. We especially need to give some clear account of the examination type of dialogue, in line with modern formal dialogue theory. The key problem here is that of dialectical shifts and embeddings. As the study of explanation dialogues in expert systems has shown, there is a kind of dialectical shift involved in the typical way an expert system works. Basically, the expert advice dialogue is an information-seeking type in which the user tries to get advice or information from the expert source. But because domains of expert knowledge tend to be technical, the user often needs to ask the expert to explain what has just been said. In order for the user to really understand the advice being given and to test its worth, the user will often have to initiate a shift to an examination type of dialogue. This kind of shift is both familiar and necessary in expert systems and is common in any kind of dialogue where explanations and advice are being given. When the second type of dialogue kicks in, the user will critically probe and question the expert's statements, explanations, and arguments. The user will have to ask, "What are your reasons for that statement?" The dialogue, in such an instance, has more of a critical edge. It is no longer purely an information-seeking type of dialogue.

But for the reader who is not familiar with dialectical shifts and embeddings, it may be helpful to see how they can be formally represented in dialogue theory. Reed (1998) has presented a way of formalizing argumentation in a manner that allows dialectical shifts and embeddings to be taken into account. A dialogue frame is defined (Reed, 1998, p. 248) as a four-tuple composed of a type of dialogue, a topic, a pair of participants, and a sequence of utterances. The type of dialogue, t, can be any one of five: persuasion, negotiation, inquiry, deliberation, or information seeking. The topic, τ, is defined as the unsettled issue that is supposed to be settled by the dialogue if it is successful. The proponent and the respondent are designated as xi and yi. Each speech act (utterance) made by one party to the other as a move in the dialogue is numbered. So $u^i x_i \rightarrow y_i$ refers to the ith utterance in which the proponent made a statement and the respondent offered some support for that statement. Using this notation, Reed then defines the notion of a dialogue frame F in the following way (p. 248).

$$F = \langle\langle t, \Delta\rangle \in D, \ \tau \in \Delta, \ (u^0 x_0 \rightarrow y_0, ..., u^n x_n \rightarrow y_n)\rangle$$

The formula tells us that when two parties are engaged in a dialogue of a certain type, each time one makes a move, the other must reply by making an appropriate move for that type of dialogue. The dialogue frame represents a sequence of such moves in any type of dialogue in which the participants take turns making moves appropriate for that type of dialogue. For example, one kind of frame could be that for a negotiation dialogue. In this type of dialogue, the proponent can, say, make a proposal, and the respondent has the option of accepting that proposal or of engaging in further argumentation. To illustrate a dialectical shift of the kind that would be considered an embedding, Reed used an example familiar in the AI literature. In this example, a proponent and respondent are engaged in deliberation dialogue about how to go about hanging a painting on the wall. They both accept that they need a hammer to hang the picture. The proponent says that he knows where there is a hammer they can get. But who should get it? To answer this question, the two start a process of negotiation. At this point, there has been a shift from deliberation to negotiation dialogue. Following Reed's formalization of the notion of a dialogue frame, the initial sequence of moves in the discussion about hanging the painting can all be marked as speech acts in the deliberation dialogue. But then, from the point of the shift, all the following moves in the sequence of argumentation can be marked as part of the process of negotiation that has just begun.

Using this formal model allows us to represent a sequence of argumentation in which there is a shift from one type of dialogue to another. In the example above regarding hanging the painting, the shift represents an embedding of the one type of dialogue into the other. This is so because the shift to the negotiation dialogue is a constructive step that helps the original deliberation dialogue to move forward. But not all cases of shifts are cases where one dialogue is embedded in another. It has been shown by Walton and Krabbe (1995) that there are many cases where dialectical shifts underlie fallacies and other problematic failures of reasoned communication. In such cases, the shift actually moves the original dialogue away from achieving its goal or even blocks the progress of the dialogue altogether.

Having introduced formal modeling of shifts and embeddings, how can such notions help to solve the problem about examination dialogue posed at the beginning of this section? What precisely is the nature of the examination type of dialogue? One hypothesis is that examination dialogue can be modeled as a type of persuasion dialogue that is embedded into an information-seeking dialogue. Its purpose is to increase the understanding of the information receiver (and possibly that of the information giver as well). The proponent in an information-seeking dialogue basically just wants to get information. But to get that information in a form that can be used, the proponent has to understand it. In some cases, such as that of an expert consultation dialogue, understanding something you have been told may not be all that easy. The only way you can really make sense of it is to probe into it critically so that you can produce for your own satisfaction some kind of coherent account of the subject matter that makes sense to you. Let us say, for example, that you go to your doctor after having a heart attack, and the doctor advises you that you have a congested artery and should immediately have coronary bypass surgery. This may be very good advice, but to be satisfied with it, you may need to ask the doctor a lot of questions. It may help if the doctor explains the nature of the operation and why it is needed, preferably without using a lot of specialized medical terminology that you do not understand. But at some point in the explanation, you may ask some critical questions about why the doctor thinks it necessary for you, in particular, to have this quite serious operation right away. You may have heard that it might be possible to have a line inserted that can be manipulated robotically and used to break up the blockage. You may be doubtful that your condition is so serious or life threatening that you really need to have your chest cut open immediately when a less invasive technique could possibly be used. At the beginning, the physician may do a lot of explaining of the facts concerning what technology is available or best for what condition and what was found in your case about the arterial blockage. When the dialogue reaches a later interlude, more argumentation than explanation may be going on. For example, the doctor may defend the recommendation by giving medical reasons to support it. You may question these reasons not only because you may not understand them but also because you want to be sure they are right. So there has been a shift from explanation to argument.

In a case such as this one, the dialogue has shifted from an information-seeking mode to a mode that is much more like a critical discussion. True, you, as the patient, are not yourself an expert. You may not be a physician. But still, you need to be convinced that the physician is doing the right thing. Thus even though you are not equals, you need to engage in a sort of critical discussion with the doctor in order to probe into the reasons lying behind the recommendation. That is why, in this sort of case, the second type of dialogue in the shift is best described as a critical discussion or persuasion dialogue of a certain type. It is not the straightforward type of critical discussion in which both parties agree to abide by rules and to resolve a conflict of opinions by rational argumentation. Rather it is a kind of persuasion dialogue that is prompted by a need to understand something that is part of an information-seeking dialogue. The need for the persuasion dialogue derives from doubts of the one party evoked by the failure to understand a recommendation that the other party concludes is warranted. This type of examination dialogue is thus best seen as a form of persuasion dialogue that is embedded in, and arises from, a prior information-seeking dialogue. But because of its critical and reason-seeking nature, it is best classified as being a type of persuasion dialogue.

3

A Procedural Model of Rationality

Any attempt to analyze abductive reasoning and to define it as a distinctive type of reasoning to be contrasted with deductive and inductive reasoning raises fundamental questions for logic as a discipline. In chapter 1, we saw that AI systems use forward chaining of reasoning from a given database or set of "facts" using a set of rules to generate conclusions derived from the facts. Reasoning is here seen as a forward chaining of inferences, and in some instances it could also be a sequence of backward inferences. But backward chaining proceeds by explanation from the given data as conclusion to the premises on which it was supposedly based. This model of rationality, which is very common in AI (Prakken and Sartor, 2003, p. 505), is called the inference-based model. But Prakken and Sartor (2003, p. 505) cited another model of rationality they called the procedural view, which embeds a chain of reasoning into a dialogue game, or formal dialogue structure. In this model, a rational argument takes into account "the very possibility of counter-arguments." This procedural notion of rationality, associated with the new field of computational dialectics that is growing in AI, offers some useful tools that can be used in conjunction with the dialogue model of explanation. Chapter 3 introduces the reader to these useful tools.

COMPUTATIONAL DIALECTICS

Among the new developments that prove to be very useful are the new techniques of multiagent reasoning that are now used in artificial intelligence research in computer science (Wooldridge and Jennings, 1995; Boman and Van de Velde, 1997). What these developments will be taken to indicate is that rationality should not be seen in the model of an agent acting alone in nature. A better approach is to see rationality in a framework in which two or more agents act in a coordinated way by communicating with each other as they act. The other development that proves useful for understanding such communication as part of rationality is the recent research on informal fallacies (van Eemeren and Grootendorst, 1992; Walton, 1995). Still another is the use of dialogue-based models of argumentation of the kind applied to the speech act of explanation in the last chapter. This branch of study is called the new dialectic (Walton, 1998) in argumentation theory and has been called computational dialectics in the field of computing. One of the most promising areas of application for computational dialectics is to legal argumentation and especially to evidence law.

Bench–Capon (1997) has shown that artificial intelligence must concern itself with rationality and that legal argumentation can be studied from a viewpoint of rational argumentation that has a dialogue structure. In his view, "An understanding of argument is central to an understanding of rationality" (p. 249), and an understanding of the kind of arguments found in law is best achieved by studying defeasible arguments of the kind typified by the Toulmin schema (p. 254). In this schema, an argument is seen as an inference drawn from data to a claim by reason of a warrant, a kind of defeasible generalization that is subject to exceptions. Formal logic has its place in legal argumentation, according to Bench–Capon (1997, p. 256), but the most common kind of argumentation used in law is defeasible. Such argumentation, as shown by Bench–Capon, can only be properly analyzed as rational argumentation if viewed in the context of a process of investigation or dialogue in which evidence is collected and assessed at each stage of the process. Accordingly, current research in the field of law and artificial intelligence has shifted to a dialogue model in which argumentation is analyzed not only with regard to its logical form but also by taking pragmatic factors into account. Such pragmatic factors concern the point at which the argument was used for some conversational purpose in a dialogue or investigation in which evidence is gathered and evaluated at each move.

Scientific argumentation has often been taken to represent the leading ideal of rationality and of rational thinking based on evidence. But is evidence of the kind gathered in a criminal investigation or put forward and examined in a trial based on some underlying notion of rationality or justifiable reasoning? Legal reasoning is more problematic, because it is defeasible, and as recent events have shown, wrongful convictions are a lot more common than once was thought. Thus the project of trying to reveal how legal evidence and argumentation can be based on some underlying notion of rationality has proved to be very difficult. Evidence in court is brought in through such forms of argument as argument from expert opinion, a kind of argumentation that is notoriously tricky and can be used to mislead a jury. Such forms of argumentation have, in the past, even been seen in logic as fallacious. They can be rational under the right conditions of use, however, and we could hardly get by without them, either in law or in everyday life.

Hage (2000) has shown how computational dialectics, the use of dialogue-based models to analyze and evaluate rational argumentation, especially as applied to legal argumentation, has grown and flourished in recent work in artificial intelligence. Dialogues (Hage, 2000, p. 138) have provided a means to "overcome the foundational difficulties that plague legal justification." Gordon (1995) has constructed a formal model of legal argumentation called the pleadings game, based on the insights of Alexy (1989), who devised discourse norms of rational argumentation to apply to legal discourse of the kind one would find in a trial. This model can be called procedural in the sense of Lodder (1999, p. 24), meaning that it does not concentrate just on the structure of reasoning schemes but also on the procedure in which statements are justified. Such a procedure is nondeterministic, meaning that there is no predetermined outcome. An argument is typically evaluated at some point in a dialogue as a move in that dialogue, and it could be defeated or more strongly supported at subsequent moves. For example, in a trial, expert testimony may be introduced as a kind of evidence, but then it will be subject to reappraisal when the cross-examining attorney asks questions about it. The trier (judge or jury) can, at the end of the trial, arrive at a decision by looking at both sides of the dialogue and weighing the evidence.

The typical forensic and testimonial evidence used in a trial is based on abductive reasoning in which attempts are made to offer competing explanations of what the law calls the facts (the accepted findings) of a case. Typically, such facts come from previous investigations by the police, for example in a crime investigation. Keppens and Zeleznikow (2002) have presented a model of crime investigation in which plausible reasoning is used abductively to draw inferences by hypotheses used to explain data. For example, suppose investigators are confronted by a dead body along with accompanying evidence found at the scene. The standard hypotheses are "homicide," "suicide," "accident," or "natural causes" (p. 2). The method of investigation typically employed is one in which there is an alternative set of "scenarios" or possible explanatory accounts that appear to fit the facts. Further evidence, such as DNA evidence for example, may be collected and tested as the investigation proceeds if any sort of crime is suspected to be involved. An account given by a witness may appear to be the best explanation of the facts at one point in the investigation, but then the DNA evidence collected at a later point may offer a competing account that points to quite a different explanation of what happened. In this model, an abductive inference can be a best explanation of the facts collected at one point in an ongoing investigation pointing to a particular hypothesis among the competing hypotheses that could be suspected. But then later, as the dialogue continues and more facts are collected, through questioning expert witnesses for example, a different hypothesis seems to provide the best explanation. Thus it is not just in trials but also in other contexts of investigation and evaluation of evidence that the dialogue model of rationality shows much promise. A piece of evidence might be evaluated differently in one context, such as that of a police investigation, than it would be in another context of dialogue, such as that of a criminal trial. It might be evaluated quite differently once again in the context of scientific discovery, where different standards of evidence would apply.

The procedural model of rationality is dialectical. It can be used to show not only how legal arguments should be judged acceptable in some cases but also how such arguments can fail, or even be fallacious, as used in other cases. According to the dialectical model used to analyze informal fallacies, an argument is defined not only as reasoning but also as the use of reasoning by two parties in a collaborative goal-directed dialogue of the kind envisaged by Grice (1975). Fallacies are not only errors of reasoning but also in many cases deceptive tactics used to try to get the better of a speech partner in a supposedly collaborative dialogue. Thus, as shown in the last chapter, explanation and argument can be contrasted in the dialogue model as having different functions. The purpose of an argument is to remove one party's doubts about some thesis or statement that is unsettled or doubtful. The purpose of an explanation is to remove one party's lack of understanding of some statement that is presumed to represent an existing fact. Within the dialogue framework these two functions can be seen as quite distinct.

Adopting this procedural approach, we can see how rational arguments and rational explanations both contain reasoning. Yet despite this common element, they can also be distinguished quite clearly from each other at the dialectical level. At this level, the reasoning is used for a different conversational purpose. Thus the same form of argument might be rational as used in law (in a court, for example) but quite weak or inappropriate, even fallacious perhaps, if used in scientific research.

It has now become widely accepted in AI and law that dialogue-based models of argumentation, or so-called dialectical models, are useful for analyzing and evaluating legal argumentation (Bench-Capon, 1997; Hage, 2000) and especially for studying defeasibility of legal argumentation (Prakken and Sartor, 2003). The term being used more often to refer to the new field composed of applying such dialogue models to computing is computational dialectics. The term "dialectic" is meant here not in the Marxist-Hegelian sense but as Aristotle used it, that is, to refer to the use of argumentation in a conversational framework. The standard framework is one of orderly disputation in which one participant makes a claim and the other participant casts doubt on the claim by using arguments that defeat or undercut it or by putting forward opposed arguments that purport to refute it. The participants take turns making moves such as asking questions of the other or putting forward arguments opposed to those of the other.

Lodder (2000, p. 255) reported that the term "computational dialectics" first appeared, to his knowledge, when Ron Loui and Tom Gordon organized an American Association for Artificial Intelligence workshop by that name in Seattle in 1994. On the Web page for that workshop (http://www.aaai.org/Conferences/National/1994/aaai94.html), the following explanation of the term "computational dialectics" was given under the call for participation in the workshop.

> Dialectic is an idea that simply will not disappear. It is the idea of structured linguistic interactions proceeding according to a largely adversarial protocol. Beginning with the ancients, dialectic appears to be synonymous with rationality. Today, computation informs the study and use of such structured dialogues. The term "Computational Dialectics" is meant to describe an area of activity in AI, which considers the language and protocol of systems that mediate the flow of messages between agents constructing judgment, agreement, or other social choice, to recognize or achieve an outcome in a fair and effective way.

According to Prakken and Sartor (2003, p. 506), computational dialectics is a promising research line that originated in the seventies when logicians such as Hamblin (1970; 1971), Mackenzie (1981; 1990), and Walton (1984) embedded propositional logics in dialogue game models for argumentation. In such games there are speech acts for moves such as claiming, questioning, and disputing. The proponent wins if the proponent succeeds in making the respondent accept the initial claim, whereas the respondent wins if the respondent succeeds in making the proponent withdraw the initial claim (Prakken and Sartor, 2003, p. 506). In the nineties, AI and law researchers such as Gordon (1995), Loui (1998), and Lodder (1999) applied these dialogue games to legal disputes. Two survey articles (Bench-Capon, 1997; Hage, 2000) outlined the literature on the development of dialectical models in AI and law from the historical roots to the current systems that are evolving.

Rationality, in this view, should not be confined just to things you can know or prove beyond doubt. It should be a broad enough concept to include rational opinions that can be supported by good reasons that are, nonetheless, inconclusive (Prakken and Sartor, 2003). In this view, a defeasible argument can be a rational argument if there is enough support behind it in a dialogue to shift the burden of proof or refutation to the critic who opposes it. Many of the same remarks can be applied to the dialectical theory of rational explanation proposed in the last chapter. The success of an explanation needs to be evaluated, according to that theory, in light of the question asked and how the one who tried to explain something reacted to it. The dialogue sequence of questions and replies needs to be examined as a whole. The important points here are how the answer is related to the question and whether the respondent was open to requests for further clarifications that could help the questioner make sense of what was asked about.

REASONING AS CHAINING OF INFERENCES

So far the discussion has mainly been about arguments and explanations, but sometimes the word "reasoning" was used. Surely this is the term we need to turn to in order to understand how the term "rationality" should best be used in applied logic. What is the connection between reasoning and rationality? And what is reasoning? It seems to me that there is a useful sort of reply to these questions that would enable an inquiry about abductive reasoning to move ahead. This reply can be expressed in the form of a set of ten propositions that offer provisional definitions and clarifications compatible with current methods of applied logic.

1. Rationality is based on reasoning.
2. Reasoning is a chaining together of inferences.
3. Practical reasoning is means–end goal-directed reasoning of agents, leading to actions.
4. Theoretical reasoning is some kind of reasoning different from practical reasoning.
5. Reasoning is used in arguments and explanations.
6. Reasoning is not the same as arguing (or as an argument).
7. Reasoning can be evaluated as correct or not by various logical standards.
8. Deductive reasoning can be evaluated as valid or not by standards of deductive logic.
9. Formal fallacies are faults in reasoning.
10. Informal fallacies are dialectical faults in argumentation.

These propositions have all been advanced and defended in the literature on argumentation and AI. Some require special comment. The notion of forward chaining of reasoning has been introduced via the simple examples of rule-based systems in chapter 1. But this notion needs to be more precisely defined for logic, even though it is a familiar tool in artificial intelligence. To see how the essential structure works in a simple case, let us consider an inference of the *modus ponens* form.

(*I1*) If A then B
A
_____

B

This inference can be chained forward by connecting it with another inference. The second inference can also be of the *modus ponens* form. The conclusion of the first inference can then be reused as a premise in a next one thus.

(*I2*) If B then C
B
_____

C

The two single-step inferences, thus chained together, form a longer sequence of reasoning. The second step could then be chained to a third inference. The conclusion of the second inference then becomes a premise in the third inference. The sequence of reasoning can be expanded into a lengthy chain in some cases. The kind of chaining represented above is called "chaining with *modus ponens*" (Russell and Norvig, 1995, p. 280). In traditional syllogistic logic, it was called a *sorites* argument, constructed by using a conclusion of one syllogism as a premise in a next one. This kind of chaining, as indicated in chapter 1, is also called *forward chaining* or reasoning from premises to a conclusion. Backward chaining, or reasoning from a given conclusion back to the premises it was based on, is also a common device in AI, but it raises other issues. The concept of the chain of reasoning is easy to grasp and is a familiar notion in knowledge-based reasoning of the kind so familiar in AI (Hage, 2000, p. 148). I am less sure how controversial the other points in the above list are. They seem pretty harmless to me, but I am sure there are many who will disagree with some or perhaps even all of them. The last two are probably the most controversial. But if these ten points are regarded as provisional assumptions, they can be used as a basis for exploring abductive reasoning.

Defining procedural rationality needs to begin with a definition of "reasoning." As indicated in the previous chapter, both arguments and explanations are based on reasoning. It is at least partly in virtue of this dependence that we can properly speak of explanations and arguments as being rational. Fortunately, such a notion of reasoning based on chaining reasons together in a sequence to form support for a claim has become widely accepted and used in AI (Loui, 1998). According to Loui, each step of inference in such a chain of reasoning can be based on premises that represent general policies that may apply to a given case, but then may be shown at some later stage of a dialogue, once new information has been collected in the case, to no longer be applicable. Thus a chain of reasoning that looked to be a convincing argument at one stage of a dialogue may turn out to be shown to be less convincing later on. Loui (1998) calls this kind of reasoning resource-bounded nondemonstrative reasoning based on policies. Such a notion of bounded rationality has now become widely accepted in computer science, as the theory of computational dialectics has become more and more widely accepted in such areas of computing as multiagent systems. According to this approach, argument is seen as a process (Bench-Capon, 1997, p. 258) made up of a chain of inferences used for some purpose in a dialogue game (Gordon, 1995). The dialogue game has a formal structure in that it allows for certain kinds of moves to be made by either party. These moves typically include the asking of questions and the put-ting forward of arguments to support a claim. As applied to legal argu-mentation, the dialogue game can be adversarial (Lodder, 1999). But the same chain of reasoning could need to be evaluated quite differently in a different dialectical context—for example in a scientific investigation meant to prove or disprove a hypothesis by collecting all the relevant facts by scientific methods.

An argument is an exchange between two parties in a goal-directed context of dialogue. So conceived, it always involves two parties, a pro-ponent and a respondent. They do not have to be two people—you can argue with yourself by first advocating one side of an issue and then advocating the other side. Reasoning, by contrast, does not have to in-volve two participants. In fact, I am not even sure it needs to be done by an agent or reasoner. A chaining together of a sequence of syllogisms, for example, could quite rightly be called reasoning even though it is just a sequence of propositions. But of course practical reasoning always requires an agent. To summarize this view of argument and reasoning, I will express the relationship as follows (Walton, 1990). Reasoning is a chaining together of steps of inference. An argument is a conversational exchange between two parties in which the two parties reason with each other. So argumentation uses reasoning and is based on reasoning. But reasoning is a context-free notion. It only involves a chaining of propositions. Argument is a dialectical notion. It is a matter of how rea-soning is used for some purpose in a conversational exchange between two parties.

FORWARD AND BACKWARD CHAINING RULE-BASED SYSTEMS IN ARTIFICIAL INTELLIGENCE

Although some light has been thrown in this chapter on the question of whether there is a third category of logical reasoning other than deduc-tive and inductive, some key questions have merely been posed with more urgency. In particular, basic questions about abductive reasoning remain unanswered. But some problems have at least been posed that suggest directions to carry the inquiry further. The first problem is that although inference to the best explanation does seem to involve a back-ward kind of reasoning, it also seems that there can be examples of backward reasoning that are not cases of inferences to the best explana-tion. In AI, it is known that it is sometimes useful to chain backward from a given conclusion in order to determine what statements in a given knowledge base were the premises on which the conclusion was (or could be) based (Russell and Norvig, 1995). And in the definition of abductive reasoning tentatively proposed in chapter 1, it was this backward chaining notion that defined abduction. But what is meant by backward and forward chaining? In AI, forward chaining is reasoning from a given database of premises to a conclusion. The best way to proceed is to examine a simple example of forward chaining of a typical kind in AI in a knowledge-based system. The best type to begin with is a rule-based system, which operates using a set of rules to derive a conclusion from a set of premises called "facts," representing data in a knowledge base.

A simple example of how a forward chaining rule-based system works has been presented by Cawsey (1998, pp. 30–31). This example illustrates all the components of a knowledge-based system and shows how they combine together in a rule-based system. A sprinkler system is programmed to go off only if the smoke alarm goes off and it is hot in the area. In the system, there are three rules and two facts.

SIMPLE FORWARD CHAINING EXAMPLE
R1: IF *hot* AND *smoky* THEN ADD *fire*
R2: IF *alarm*_beeps THEN ADD *smoky*
R3: IF *fire* THEN ADD *switch*_on_sprinklers
F1: *alarm*_beeps
F2: *hot*

The system searches to find rules where the antecedent of a conditional (called the condition of the rule in AI) matches with a set of facts. F1 matches with the antecedent of R2. By *modus ponens* a new fact is produced.

F3: *smoky*

But once this new fact is produced, the newly enlarged set of facts "fires" (to use the AI term) R1. Because both *smoky* and *hot* are now in the database, R1 is fired, producing yet another fact that needs to be added to the database.

F4: *fire*

But then, of course, once fire is in the set of facts, R3 is fired by means of yet another *modus ponens* inference. The system then performs the action *switch_on_sprinklers*. This simple example illustrates a forward chaining system. There is a given set of facts and rules, and the system fits facts to rules. As each rule is fired in a *modus ponens* type of inference, new facts are generated.

One thing to notice is that the if-then rules in the system do not really look like the conditionals of deductive logic that we are familiar with in logic, such as the material conditional. The antecedent describes a condition that may or may not be met in the given case. The consequent describes an action. If the condition is met, the action is supposed to be carried out. If the condition is not met, the action is not supposed to be carried out. Thus the rule in a knowledge-based system is more like a biconditional of the kind that is familiar in deductive logic. For two propositions *A* and *C,* the biconditional can be equated with the two conditionals "if *C* then *A*" and "if *not-C* then *not-A.*" The type of rule used in computing says, in effect: if *C* then *A,* and if *not-C* then *not-A.* Thus the kind of rule so familiar in AI does not seem to be adequately modeled by the kind of conditional used in deductive logic. It seems more like a biconditional. And it also seems different because the consequent of the conditional is an action, whereas the antecedent is a so-called fact, or some item that is part of a database. It is evident from the example that the forward chaining reasoning is based on some sort of *modus ponens* type of inference at each step, where a set of facts fitting the antecedent of a conditional then triggers an inference, or fires a rule, in AI language, in which the conclusion derived is the consequent of the conditional. This new fact is then added to the database. But the inference does not seem to be the deductive version of *modus ponens* so central to classic propositional logic. How to model the computer type of conditional from condition to action is an unsolved problem for logic.

To explain a little more how forward chaining in a rule-based system in AI works, Cawsey (1998, p. 31) has extended the simple example given above by adding a few more facts and rules in the slightly more complex example below. The problem posed by this extended example is to figure out what happens if more than one rule has its condition met by the facts. Which rule should be fired first?

COMPLEX FORWARD CHAINING EXAMPLE
R1: IF *hot* AND *smoky* THEN ADD *fire*

R2: IF *alarm_beeps* THEN ADD *smoky*
R3: IF *fire* THEN ADD *switch_on*_sprinklers
R4: IF *dry* THEN ADD *switch_on*_humidifier
R5: IF *sprinklers_on* THEN DELETE *dry*
F1: *alarm_beeps*
F2: *hot*
F3: *dry*

In this more complex example, there are two rules that could be fired: R2 and R4. If R2 is chosen, *smoky* will be added to the set of facts, and then R1 will be fired. That will add *fire* to the facts, firing R3 and leading to the action of firing the sprinklers. Once the item *sprinklers_on* is put into the set of facts, that will fire R5, which will delete *dry* from memory. As long as *dry* is deleted, R4 will not be fired. This is a good outcome because there is no need to have the humidifier on while the sprinklers are on. But suppose R4 were to be fired first, instead of R2. Once R4 is selected, F3 (*dry*) matches the condition, and the humidifier is turned on. But then the same sequence as above is set into motion as well, leading to the turning on of the sprinklers. This is a bad outcome because both the sprinklers and the humidifier are now on at the same time.

Thus the general problem for forward chaining systems is to have a system for deciding which rule should be applied first. One outcome might conflict with another, and AI has developed what are called conflict resolution strategies to try to deal with such problems. As indicated in the complex example above, such strategies may involve deletion of some of the given data in a set of facts. Another approach is to allow the user to prioritize the rules (Cawsey, 1998, p. 32). One approach that immediately suggests itself is to apply formal models of argumentation in dialogue (Hamblin, 1970; 1971) to complex cases of this sort, because this problem is very reminiscent of typical problems of adding and deleting propositions from an arguer's commitment set in formal dialogues (Walton and Krabbe, 1995). If a participant in a regulated dialogue puts forward an argument that leads to a conclusion that conflicts with one of the prior commitments, for example, the inconsistency must somehow be resolved before the dialogue can proceed further. Like the problem posed by forward chaining systems in AI, this problem requires different strategies or rules for the resolution of inconsistencies and typically for the retraction or deletion of propositions in a commitment set or a database.

Now the reader has a clear idea of what forward chaining reasoning is in a rule-based system in AI. Abduction is some kind of backward chaining—but what kind? Suppose, for example, that the sprinklers are observed to have been turned on in a given case. We could reason backward and infer that it must have been hot before the sprinklers went off and that there must have been smoke in the building. In such a case, we would be reasoning backward, or abductively, from the data that was observed, the sprinklers being on, to some previous events or states that caused that outcome or that explain how it occurred. This would be an abductive inference from the data to an explanation of that data. But how would we get from the observed fact to the cause by abduction? Was it simply by chaining backward from the conclusion to the premises it was based on, following the forward chaining path of reasoning backward? There are a number of problems with this suggestion.

One is that in an artificial system such as the ones in the examples presented above, presumably the system is closed, meaning that no new data are allowed in. This rule is sometimes called the closed world assumption (Reiter, 1980). It means that the database is closed or fixed by presuming that any statement not in it is false. This assumption in effect corresponds to the type of argumentation called *argumentum ad ignorantiam* in logic: if a proposition is not known to be true, then it is assumed to be false. Sometimes it is also called a lack-of-knowledge inference or simply inference by default. In real life, however, such an assumption very often cannot be realistically made, because a decision must be made under uncertainty and in a situation of incomplete knowledge. The problem is that many cases of abductive reasoning, such as the examples presented in chapter 1, are cases of just this sort. They are guesses or hypotheses at the discovery stage in science, or in cases of legal argumentation they are based on evidence that is, by its nature, not completely known. For example, suppose that in a real case, the sprinklers went off. Would this mean that there was heat and smoke, or might it just mean that the sprinkler system malfunctioned or that someone turned it on manually? We could not say that we had really established the cause in a legal case unless each of these possibilities had been examined and assessed very carefully.

It would seem that abduction is more than just backward chaining of reasoning; it is a kind of backward chaining from given data, by some form of plausible reasoning that is open to the collection of new data, to some prior state or premise that supposedly explains the data. Thus the pressing problem to be solved in order to get a more adequate account of abduction is how to define the notion of an explanation on which it is built. If abduction should be defined as inference to the best explanation, as all indications above suggest, then we are confronted with the huge problem of developing a theory of explanation. Any theory of abduction built on the notion of explanation will therefore inevitably be quite wide in scope as well as controversial. It will have to be at least capable of dealing with explanations not only of the kind found in science but also of the kind found in legal argumentation and in everyday argumentation not bounded by any discipline or special framework. This problem seems to be a large and most intimidating one. But, as stated above, it also seems to be the most central and pressing one if we are to come to grips with realistic cases in which abduction seems to be most useful. The problem needs to be at least confronted before any further real progress on analyzing and evaluating abductive reasoning can be made. This problem is addressed in chapter 2, preparing the way to the treatment of two other problems in chapter 6.

One of these problems is posed by the fact that, in cases of everyday argumentation where abduction is used as a process of reasoning based on backward chaining, there are gaps in the chain of reasoning. Of course in an AI system such as the examples presented above, the system is closed and the data are all there, by assumption. Thus the whole chain of reasoning is also there. In real cases of abduction, it is not so simple. Many premises in the chain of reasoning are based on "common knowledge" and are not stated explicitly. In logic, this is the traditional problem of enthymemes. An argument may sometimes be based on unstated premises, and the problem of enthymemes is to find or determine these missing premises. This very hard problem is considered in more detail in a later section of this chapter, but better steps toward a solution cannot be taken until the new theory of abductive reasoning has been worked out in chapter 6.

The third and most fundamental problem is that of the logical form of abductive reasoning. Is it really a kind of backward *modus ponens* reasoning, as Peirce's form of abductive inference seems to suggest? Or should the form of inference be modeled along the apparently different lines of the Josephson and Josephson account? It would seem that somehow the two accounts ought to be combined, or at least it should be shown how each relates to the other structurally. But carrying out this project seems to call for a pragmatic investigation yielding a framework in which an inquiry is carried out through the process of forming and testing a hypothesis. But here the acute problem is one of multiplicity.

Peirce's analysis of abduction is set in some rough and undeveloped pragmatic framework of the process of scientific discovery, hypothesis formation and testing, and scientific theory formation. His account is not purely descriptive, and it is clear from his remarks, as noted in chapter 1, that he means it to represent a logical model of how scientific argument ought to proceed, ideally or normatively. Not all of the examples of abductive inference cited above are scientific in nature, however. Some of them are arguments from everyday conversational contexts. Others are from such disciplines as law and medicine. The examples of abductive reasoning in evidence law, especially, represent a context of argumentation that is quite different from that of scientific argumentation. Something that is acceptable as scientific evidence is not necessarily acceptable as legal evidence and vice versa. The standards for these two types of evidence are quite different, even though scientific evidence has an ever-growing role as legal evidence—expert testimony of scientists in courts, for example. The huge problem posed here is that abduction is partly a matter of the form of reasoning the abductive inference takes, but it is also a matter of grasping how that kind of inference is used for various purposes in various contexts. Awareness of the importance of this contextual aspect of abduction would seem to lie behind Peirce's memorable slogan that abduction is pragmatism.

THE PROBLEM OF ENTHYMEMES

As illustrated in using *Araucaria* to diagram the knife case in chapter 1, enthymemes are incompletely stated arguments that need to have one or more statements added before they can be properly evaluated. The missing statement(s) can be a premise, several premises, or a conclusion. An example of an enthymeme is the following argument: "Jones is not allowed to drive, because she does not have a valid driver's license." The nonexplicit premise in this argument can be expressed as a conditional: if a person does not have a valid driver's license, then that person is not allowed to drive. Or it could be put in the form of a generalization: no persons who do not have a valid driver's license are allowed to drive. In either case, the question is whether the conditional or the generalization should be seen as absolute or defeasible. In this case, the best interpretation is to see it as an absolute conditional or generalization. The reason is that one can reasonably assume that the prohibition against driving without a license is an absolute one. No exceptions to it are allowed. The basis of this assumption could be called "common knowledge" or something of the sort. This is a reasonable way to interpret the argument because it is plausible, based on what might be seen as common presumptions. An example of an enthymeme found in a logic textbook (Hurley, 2000, p. 289) is as follows: "The corporate income tax should be abolished; it encourages waste and high prices." In this argument, the missing premise is the generalization, "Anything that encourages waste and high prices should be abolished." Once this premise is supplied, the following complete (or more complete) argument is produced.

> Anything that encourages waste and high prices should be abolished.
> The corporate income tax encourages waste and high prices.
> Therefore the corporate income tax should be abolished.

This argument appears to be deductively valid, assuming the first premise is supposed to be a universal generalization that is not subject to exceptions. Indeed, Hurley (2000, p. 289) tells his readers that all enthymemes, once completed, are deductively valid. This claim is a common one in current and traditional logic textbooks. Let us call it, as stated by Hurley (p. 289), the deductive validity thesis about enthymemes: "An enthymeme is an argument that is expressible as a categorical syllogism but that is missing a premise or a conclusion." The corporate income tax example is a typical case of an enthymeme, and Hurley's analysis of it is typical of the sort found in logic textbooks. Several features of his analysis fit with some of the methods outlined above. In the corporate income tax example, one must chain the reasoning backward from the conclusion in order to try to determine what statements it was based on as premises, using the given premise(s) as further guides. Is Hurley right that this backward chaining method is part of a purely deductive task that can be carried out with syllogistic logic? This claim appears highly dubious. In fact, it seems much more plausible to say that the argument in the corporate income tax example is based on a defeasible generalization that is not an absolutely universal one.[1] Indeed, it looks like the argument is not based on deductive reasoning at all, but on the argumentation scheme of the argument from consequences that will be considered in chapter 4. These observations raise a hornet's nest of difficulties for the traditional doctrine of enthymemes. It will not be until we achieve a better analysis of abductive reasoning in chapter 6 that we can really begin to deal with them effectively, providing a more satisfactory solution to the problem of enthymemes in chapter 7.

Another example of an enthymeme is the following argument: "Eating oatmeal lowers cholesterol, because Smith said so, and he is a physician." The nonexplicit premises are that Smith is an expert in a domain of knowledge (medicine) and that if an expert says something is so, then it is so. But now consider the second nonexplicit premise. If you take it in an absolute way, it is false. And as suggested in chapter 1 in the discussion of the argumentation scheme for appeal to expert opinion, to take it as such comes close to committing the fallacy of appeal to authority, because it suggests that experts cannot be wrong. A much better way to interpret it is as a defeasible conditional that puts a presumption in place but is subject to exceptions.

There are many open questions and problems concerning the traditional doctrine of enthymemes. The longstanding tradition stemming from Aristotle is that an enthymeme is an incomplete syllogism.[2] This view favors deductive logic and is therefore an interpretation that has seemed highly plausible to logicians, given the dominance of deductive logic after Aristotle invented the theory of the syllogism. The problem is that as soon as it is applied to common arguments such as the corporate income tax example above, it starts to fall apart.[3] This argument is not deductively valid once it is completed by filling in the missing premise. Instead, the generalization that functions as the warrant of the inference is subject to exceptions. It is defeasible. Thus the structure needed to supply the missing part and display the complete argument is not that of a syllogism or any form of deductive logic. It is a defeasible argumentation scheme. Such forms of argument resemble syllogisms. They often seem to have the kinds of forms we are familiar with in deductive logic, such as *modus ponens,* but they are based on generalizations that are not universal and that hold only for the most part.[4] Thus the traditional notion of enthymeme needs to be expanded to encompass not just deductively valid arguments such as syllogisms but also cases where a missing part of an incomplete argument is indicated by a defeasible argumentation scheme.

It might seem that, once suitably expanded to include argumentation schemes, the doctrine of enthymemes provides an automated method or "enthymeme machine" that can be used to fill in missing parts of any argument. Unfortunately, the problem cannot be solved so easily. As Burke (1985), Gough and Tindale (1985), and Hitchcock (1985) showed, inserting missing assumptions into a text of discourse to make an argument in it valid may not always represent what the arguer really meant to say. The problem, then, is to know what an arguer really meant to commit to as a statement if the arguer did not explicitly state it. Maybe the argument really intended to be put forward is invalid, even though the arguer was not aware of it. The same cautionary remarks apply even when defeasible argumentation schemes are considered. Whenever an argument analyst attributes missing premises or conclusions to an arguer on the basis of an inferential structure that makes the missing part explicit, there is always the danger of the straw man fallacy. This fallacy is the tactic of exaggerating or distorting an interpretation of an opponent's argument in order to make it look more extreme and more vulnerable than it is, thereby making it easier for the proponent to attack or refute it (Scriven, 1976, pp. 85–86). Formulating the problem of incomplete arguments in this way shows how difficult it is. Simply adopting the traditional view that an incomplete argument is a syllogism or argumentation scheme with a missing premise or conclusion does not, by itself, provide a complete solution to the problem. The arguer's commitments also need to be taken into account.

A dialogue-based tool often invoked to deal with enthymemes is the so-called principle of charity. This principle offers a way of solving the problem of having to choose between competing interpretations of an argument, both of which would make it come out valid. The principle of charity rules that one should choose the interpretation that makes the original argument come out as strongest, most plausible, or most sensible (Gough and Tindale, 1985, p. 102). Johnson (2000, p. 127) formulated another version of the principle of charity thus: "When interpreting a text, make the best possible sense of it." A problem posed by both of these versions of the principle is how to apply it to real examples of incomplete arguments. Of course, the obvious way is to interpret the principle as meaning that an argument that makes the most sense, or is most plausible, is the one that makes the argument strongest. But the same objection as the one applied above to the traditional Aristotelian interpretation of the enthymeme applies to this new version, too. The principle of charity, interpreted as above, seems to be fulfilled by inserting missing premises or conclusions until the "best possible" argument is produced (Gough and Tindale, 1985, pp. 102–3). The same problem then arises. The original argument may have really been weak, and by artificially making it stronger, the user of the principle of charity may be distorting it. The user of the principle of charity may be committing a reverse version of the straw man fallacy by applying the principle to a given argument in a mechanical way. The user makes a bad argument look good by getting the arguer's position wrong. Such a misinterpretation is surely a kind of error.

The notion of the enthymeme, or incompletely expressed argument, is important, despite its problematic nature, for constructing a notion of abductive reasoning that can be applied to real cases in, say, legal argumentation or scientific discovery. Abduction, in such cases, depends on backward and forward chaining of a sequence of reasoning. In many instances, the chain of reasoning can only be identified by filling in missing links in the chain that were not explicitly stated in the discourse. Such missing statements are often commonsense empirical generalizations in the form of defeasible generalizations, as illustrated in the corporate income tax example above.

MULTIAGENT PRACTICAL REASONING

Practical reasoning is a goal-directed, knowledge-based, action-guiding species of reasoning that meshes goals with possible alternative courses of action in relation to an agent's knowledge of its given circumstances in a particular situation. Practical reasoning is carried out by an *agent,* an entity that is capable of intelligent action on the basis of observing its circumstances, including its own actions, and using this information to guide its actions. The assumption is that an agent will normally have some information on the consequences of its actions, as these are observed to occur, and can adjust its subsequent actions accordingly. This capability is called feedback.

The notion of practical inference is the basis of the structure of practical reasoning worked out in the accounts of Clarke (1985), Bratman (1987), Audi (1989), and Walton (1990). Practical reasoning now has an important role to play in multiagent technology in AI (Wooldridge, 2000, p. 21). In this account, a practical inference has two premises—one states that the agent has a goal, and the other cites a means that the agent could use, in its given circumstances, to carry out its goal. Because agents can be machines in some cases, the requirements for the use of nonsexist language are met by letting the agent be "it," as opposed to "she" or "he." Practical reasoning is the chaining together of a sequence of practical inferences. According to the account in Walton (1990, p. 85), a practical inference has the following general form. The letters $A, B, C, \ldots$, stand for things brought about by agents, which may be thought of as contingent propositions and are usually called "states of affairs." For ease of exposition, the agent will be referred to using the first-person pro-nouns "I," "my," and so forth.

> (*PI*) *A* is my goal.
>   To bring about *A*, I must first bring about *B*.
>   Therefore I must bring about *B*.

The "must" is not taken to express logical necessity. It is taken to express a so-called practical ought, meaning that the agent should become com-mitted to bringing about *B* once it realizes that it is committed to bringing about *A* by some means or other, and it realizes that bringing about *B* is a necessary means for bringing about *A*. The accounts given by Clarke (1985), Bratman (1987), and Audi (1989) are comparable to (*PI*). The accounts of Clarke and Audi express the "wants" or "inten-tions" of the agent as the major premise and the beliefs of the agent as the minor premise. In contrast—and this is a significant difference—the analysis of practical reasoning in Bratman and in Walton is commitment based (or acceptance based). The commitment-based type of analysis does not refer to the actual intentions or wants of the agent, but only to the agent's goals, as far as these can be determined from what the agent has gone on record as saying in a given case.

The scheme (*PI*) only represents a necessary condition scheme for practical inference. A corresponding sufficient condition scheme is the same as (*PI*), except that the second premise expresses a sufficient con-dition relation, rather than the necessary condition relation expressed in (*PI*). In a chain of practical reasoning, some of the inferences will be of the necessary condition type, and others will be of the sufficient condi-tion type. Up to this point, practical reasoning does not seem to require a dialectical framework. But according to the account given in Walton (1990), practical reasoning should be evaluated in any given case by ask-ing critical questions. Although a single agent can pose these questions alone, taking into account the viewpoint of the questioner as well as that of the respondent agent implies a dialectical framework. Corresponding to the form of inference *(PI)* is the following set of five appropriate critical questions.

1. Are there alternative possible courses of action to *B*?
2. Is *B* the best (or most acceptable) of the alternatives?
3. Do I have goals other than *A* that ought to be considered?
4. Is it possible to bring about *B* in the given circumstance?

5. Does *B* have known bad consequences that ought to be considered?

As practical reasoning, an inference of the form *(PI)* shifts a weight of plausibility to the conclusion that the agent ought to go ahead with the designated course of action. So conceived, a practical inference is a defeasible kind of argument that makes its conclusion plausible, given that the premises are plausible. But a practical inference only supports its conclusion subject to further relevant information coming in that might call for its retraction. Asking any one of the appropriate critical questions shifts the issue of acceptability back onto the proponent. Until the question is answered adequately in the dialogue, the weight of plausibility in favor of acceptance of the conclusion is retracted.

Many enthymemes are based on nonexplicit assumptions about means and ends in goal-directed practical reasoning. Consider the following argument: "I am thirsty, therefore I am going to drink this glass of water." The nonexplicit premise is that drinking the glass of water is a means to satisfy my thirst. It is easily seen that this argument is defeasible. Suppose that I obtain an additional piece of evidence. I learn that the water in the glass contains cyanide. This new information prompts the asking of the critical question whether drinking the water might have harmful side effects, given that health is also a goal for me. A negative answer to the critical question will then defeat the original argument. My thirst may be a good reason for drinking the water, other factors being equal. But once this new factor is taken into account, it is no longer a good enough reason. There is now a stronger reason for not drinking the water.

Practical reasoning is used in various types of conversational exchanges between two parties; such exchanges are called dialogues, or types of dialogue, of the kinds cited in chapter 2. The examples of empathetic explanations in chapter 2 were clearly based on practical reasoning. For example, one agent might ask a second agent to explain an action of the second agent as observed by the first agent. The second agent might achieve a successful explanation by offering an account of the goal or intention of the action. The first agent can then use plan recognition to make sense of the account offered by the second agent. What connects the reasoning together in the given account, and what enables the first agent to make sense of it, is the capacity for practical reasoning shared by the agents. As indicated in chapter 2, a dialogue that provides the framework for this shared use of practical reasoning is a conventional goal-directed conversation, which may be of various types. The type of dialogue in which practical reasoning is most typically used in everyday conversations is that of deliberation. As shown in chapter 2, deliberation arises out of a need to take action in a given situation, and its purpose is to determine the right, or the most prudent, course of action in that situation. Deliberation is often seen as a solitary procedure, but it can also be seen as a type of dialogue where an agent (or two or several agents) looks at two (or several) sides of an issue or problem about what to do.

Franklin and Graesser (1996) have surveyed a number of proposed definitions offered by scientists working in artificial intelligence research. Among the characteristics they cite as central in these definitions are the abilities of agents to perform autonomous execution of actions (p. 22); to "perform domain oriented reasoning" (p. 22); to "perceive its environment through sensors" (p. 22); to act on its environment (p. 22); to "realize a set of goals and tasks" (p. 22); to "act autonomously" (p. 22); to perceive, affect, and interpret "dynamic conditions in the environment" (p. 22); to "employ knowledge of the user's goals or desires" in carrying out some set of operations (p. 23); to "engage in dialogs and negotiate and coordinate transfers of information" (p. 23); to have "some degree of independence and autonomy" (p. 23); to carry out "autonomous, purposeful action in the real world" (p. 24); and to be "autonomous, goal-oriented, collaborative, flexible, self-starting, and to have character, adaptiveness, mobility and communicative skill" (p. 24). The dialectical aspect of practical reasoning becomes apparent in this definition of what an agent is. An agent bases its actions not just on its observations of its external circumstances and its own actions but also on the communications it receives from other agents.

To support the various characteristics cited above, Wooldridge and Jennings (1995, pp. 116–17) distinguish between two usages of the term "agent"—a stronger and a weaker one. According to the weaker use of the term, an agent is defined as a computer system that has the following four properties (p. 116). *Autonomy* means that an agent has control over its actions and internal states. *Social ability* means that an agent can interact linguistically with other agents. *Reactivity* means that an agent perceives its environment and reacts to changes in it. *Proactiveness* means that an agent can take the initiative in its goal-directed actions, instead of passively responding to these changes in its environment. Even this weaker use of the term "agent" is dialectical because of the second property. But the stronger usage adds additional properties. According to the stronger usage, an agent has the first four properties comprised by the weaker usage and also has the following four properties (p. 117). *Mobility* means that an agent can move around an electronic network. *Veracity* means that an agent will not knowingly communicate false information. *Benevolence* means that an agent will do what is asked and not have conflicting goals. *Rationality* means that an agent will act in order to achieve its goals and not prevent its goals from being achieved (in line with its beliefs about these matters). According to Wooldridge and Jennings (1995, p. 117), this weak usage of the term "agent" is "relatively uncontentious" in computer science. In other words, it comprises the central characteristics that a majority in the field would agree on. The strong usage they see as "potentially more contentious." Nevertheless, the properties in the strong usage are very important, they think, for modeling multiagent reasoning in the kinds of agent software systems currently being designed.

To study how the notion of agent relates to conceptions of practical rationality, we could regroup the above characteristics of an agent under two different categories. The first category includes the properties of autonomy, reactivity, proactiveness, and mobility. This category excludes the long-term qualities of the character of the agent and its social properties. It stresses the relation of an agent to its external circumstances, where the circumstances do not include the actions of other agents. This first notion of an agent comprises the practical reasoning carried out by the agent as it perceives its external circumstances and its ability to use these perceptions as a basis for carrying out intelligent actions. This notion of how the agent reasons could be called single-agent reasoning. The agent is working alone, so to speak, in a natural set of circumstances that it acts on. The only actions it has to take account of are its own.

The second group of characteristics has to do with observing the actions of other agents and, more particularly, the speech acts of those other agents. This aspect is made up of the process of intelligent communication with other agents. This second notion of an agent includes social ability, veracity, benevolence, and what Wooldridge and Jennings call rationality. The kind of reasoning characteristic of this second notion of agent can be called multiagent reasoning. Two or more agents are reasoning together. The first group of abilities is used, but instead of just acting on the perceived circumstances of its environment, the agent is also acting in light of the perceived actions of other agents, who respond in dialogues to the prior actions of this agent. There has to be communication back and forth, where all parties to the dialogue can grasp the import of a message from another agent and react in an appropriate way so that the other party can react to that reaction. The dialogue that moves between the two (in the simplest case) parties must make sense, based on the assumption that each grasps the message output of the other. Also important in this second notion of an agent is the idea that it has long-term qualities of character of the kind Wooldridge and Jennings call veracity and benevolence.

BOUNDED RATIONALITY

The view advocated in this chapter is that rationality is at least partly a dialectical concept, instead of being a narrowly logical concept having to do only with truth and falsity and with inferences drawn from them or with consistency of sets of statements. What matters in judging irrationality, according to the procedural view, is how these statements were put forward, defended, and elaborated in response to questioning in a conversational exchange with a speech partner. This view is a dialectical one from the point of view of traditional logic, because it implies that the evaluation of argumentation needs to be partly a function of the use of a statement or argument in a conversational context. Judging an argument to be logically acceptable or deficient as a cognitive entity can no longer be regarded as just a function of the truth-values of the propositions in it or whether the conclusion follows by logical entailment from the premises of the argument. It needs to be considered a pragmatic and contextual matter of how the argument was supposedly used for some purpose in a conversational exchange. Rationality, in other words, needs to be defined as a dialectical concept. The dialectical view of rationality follows in the footsteps of the unjustifiably neglected account of it in Bartley (1962), one that also sees reaction to criticism as an important criterion of rationality.

The procedural view has already been defended; the fallaciousness of arguments needs to be judged on the basis of how well an argument, or other move in argumentation, contributes to a goal-directed conversation between two (or more) parties (van Eemeren and Grootendorst, 1992; Walton, 1995). This thesis is not new and has been widely argued for by a growing international and interdisciplinary group of scholars in the field of argumentation studies. What is new here is the attempt to extend this dialectical view of argumentation to the analysis of the concepts of rationality and irrationality. The hope is that by doing so, new resources for defending rationality can be made available. The fuel that seems to have fired so many of the recent attacks on rationality is that the abstract structures of traditional deductive logic, and its inductive ally, do not give a rich enough framework to deal effectively with all of the problems of rationality suggested by the critics. The much-touted problems are that you can deconstruct a text of discourse many different ways, depending on assumptions you as critic bring to the task and that critics and intellectuals generally bring their own positions and interests into their criticisms of an argument, importing a subjective element. The conclusion often drawn is that rationality is subjective and that therefore one argument is as rational as another. It is not a long leap to the conclusion that there is no such thing as rationality at all. Thus there is a sharp challenge posed here to logic as the field supposedly representing rational thinking. The response that needs to be made to the challenge is that we need to move to new models of rationality. As shown in chapter 2, this shift to new models is already well under way in AI. For example, Hage (2000, p. 149) has shown how dialectical models in AI and law work with a notion of bounded rationality in which the set of premises held to be acceptable for an argument can be assumed to change over time as an argument proceeds. The fact that such assumptions can change at a later point in the dialogue and that the argument then based on them can now lead to a different conclusion does not necessarily imply that the former argument was irrational. It may have been rational within the bounds of what was known or accepted earlier and what is not known or accepted yet.

4

Defeasible *Modus Ponens* Arguments

In chapter 3, it was shown how reasoning typically takes the form of a forward chaining of defeasible *modus ponens* inferences that are not deductively valid. It is argued in chapter 4 that many common arguments used in everyday reasoning have the form *modus ponens* or a form similar to *modus ponens* but are not deductively valid. Once this new view of the matter is developed, it can be shown how there are two argumentation schemes involved. One is the deductively valid form of *modus ponens,* and the other is a defeasible form of *modus ponens* that is not deductively valid. Thus in constructing a set of argumentation schemes that can be used to analyze and evaluate argumentation, we need to have a scheme for deductive *modus ponens.* But we also need to have a scheme for defeasible *modus ponens.* And indeed, the latter form of argument is fundamentally important, because many of the most common defeasible argumentation schemes can be classified under this general type. They are extremely common arguments of the most mundane kind. True, they have been sadly neglected by logic until recently, when concerns about defeasible arguments have attained a high visibility, especially in computer science (Reiter, 1985).[1] Adopting this approach to argumentation schemes has to be based on a new way of classifying types of generalizations. The implications of the nonstandard approach to generalizations and conditionals presented in this chapter will turn out to be especially striking in legal and scientific argumentation, but they are broadly applicable to argumentation in everyday conversational discourse as well.

A TYPICAL CASE OF ABDUCTIVE REASONING IN EVIDENCE LAW

Abductive reasoning of the most common sort is found in reasoning about evidence of the kind used in police investigations and trials. The abductive model applies most obviously to legal cases of circumstantial evidence that comes under the category called trace evidence. Wigmore (1935, p. 82) presented a simple example to illustrate this kind of evidence.

THE BROKEN KNIFE CASE

On a charge of burglary, the window having been raised by a knife, and a fragment of the blade being left in the window, the accused's later possession of such a knife is evidential. He may explain that he found it in the street after the burglary, and the question of the identity of the fragment with his knife may arise.

Wigmore's use of the word "explain" tips us off to how natural the abductive model is when applied to the evidence in this case. It is a case of competing explanations of the same set of facts. The facts are that the fragment of blade found in the window matches the knife found in the possession of the accused. How can such facts be accounted for? The explanation offered by the accused is that he found the knife in the street after the burglary. But there is an alternative explanation. According to this explanation, the accused used the knife to break in, and during this activity, a fragment of the knife blade broke off and embedded itself in the window.

Viewing the evidence in this case in the abductive model, we can look at the facts of the case of admitting of two possible explanations. If one is the correct explanation, the other is not. If the first explanation is correct, it can be inferred that the suspect is guilty of having committed the burglary. To complete the explanation, we need to fill in some commonsense assumptions about the way actions are normally carried out. One is the assumption that the normal way to use a knife to gain entry to a house through a window is to pry the window open by levering the edge of the window against the frame. Another is the assumption that when such an action is carried out, it might well damage the knife blade, leaving fragments of it in part of the window, such as the frame. Once such plausible assumptions are filled in, however, the explanation hangs together as an account that is based on a chain of plausible reasoning. The same process is needed to fill out the competing explanation offered by the accused. For example, it is a plausible assumption that if a person were to find something on the street that was seen as useful or valuable, the person might well pick it up and take it home. If this competing explanation offered by the accused is plausible enough, it raises doubt about drawing the conclusion that he is guilty or at least that the former argument for guilt is undercut or shown to be questionable. Further evidence could support the one line of argumentation or the other. For example, a witness might testify to seeing the suspect using the knife to pry the window open, or a witness might testify to seeing the suspect pick up the knife on the street. If one of these items of new evidence were found, it would tend to show that one of the competing explanations is more plausible than the other. Thus it is fairly clear how the abductive model would apply to this sort of simple case of legal evidence.

It is also possible to reconstruct the evidence in the broken knife case as a sequence of argumentation made up of the following propositions. First, we start with the facts of the case, or the things that were found, and then it is necessary to fill in some implicit assumptions needed to draw inferences from these facts. The so-called facts are things that were found, in the form of propositions that are initially accepted as true, and are not in question, as far as the argumentation at that point is concerned. The statements *A, B,* and C are classified as facts, in this sense of the term. The statement *H* is the ultimate conclusion drawn from premises *A* through *G*. Each of the statements in the argument is assigned a letter in the key list below.

KEY LIST FOR THE BROKEN KNIFE CASE
(A) It was determined that the window was forced open by a knife.
(B) Fragments of the blade of a knife were found in the window.
(C) The fragments of the blade found in the window were found to match the knife found in the possession of the accused.

To these facts we need to add certain commonsense generalizations (as they might be called by Anderson and Twining [1991, p. 87]) that can be expressed in the form of conditionals. These are expressed in the form of the conditionals *D, E, F,* and *G*.

(D) If the window was forced open by a knife, and fragments of the blade of a knife were found in the window, it is plausible that the fragments found came from the knife used to force the window open.
(E) If the fragments of the blade discovered in the window were found to match the knife found in the possession of the accused, then the fragments of the blade found in the window came from

the knife possessed by the accused.

(F) If the fragments of the blade found in the window came from the knife used to force the window open, and these fragments matched the knife found in the possession of the accused, then the accused used the knife found in his possession to force open the window.

(G) If the accused used the knife found in his possession to force open the window, it is highly plausible that he is guilty of the charge of burglary.

All these premises are used in a chain of argumentation to support the conclusion *H*, the ultimate *probandum* of the prosecution side of the case.

(H) The accused is guilty of the charge of burglary.

How can the conclusion *H* be drawn by a chain of reasoning from the premises *A* through *G*? To show how it is possible, we have to show how three interim conclusions are drawn from subsets of the statements above used as premises.

(I) The fragments of the blade found in the window came from the knife used to force the window open.

(J) The fragments of the blade found in the window came from the knife possessed by the accused.

(K) The accused used the knife in his possession to force open the window.

These three interim conclusions are then used as premises of further arguments. To see how all these statements are chained together in a sequence of argumentation that leads to the ultimate conclusion to be proved in the case, let us proceed one step at a time.

In the first step of the chain of argumentation, *I* is derived as a conclusion from *A*, *B*, and *D*. This argument has the following form. *D* has the form of a conditional: "If *A* and *B* then *I*." *A* and *B*, however, are both facts as the case is outlined above. Thus the following inference can be drawn.

If *A* and *B* then *I*
A
B
Therefore *I*

The second step in the reasoning is that E and C are used as premises in a *modus ponens* argument that leads to statement J as a conclusion. E is a conditional of the form "If C then J." But because C is true (factual) in the broken knife case as described above, the following inference can be drawn.

> If C then J
> C
> Therefore J

At this point, the two conclusions I and J have each been shown to follow as conclusions derived from factual statements and conditional statements that would be accepted as plausible in the case.

The next step is that I and J can now be used as premises, along with the conditional F, to draw K as a conclusion. F is a conditional that I and J as the two statements conjoined as the antecedent. F is the conditional "If I and J then K." Thus the following inference can be drawn.

> If I and J then K
> I
> J
> Therefore K

In the final step of the argument, G is used as a premise along with K as an argument for inferring K. This works because G is a conditional of the form "If K then H," and K has already been derived as a conclusion in the argument above. Thus we have the following *modus ponens* argument.

> If K then H
> K
> Therefore H

The chain of argument from the given facts and generalizations is now complete, leading to the ultimate *probandum* H.

The broken knife case appears to be a most simple and ordinary example of the use of abductive reasoning as evidence of the kind commonly found in police investigations of crimes and in criminal trials. Once analyzed as above, the reasoning is seen as a chain of *modus ponens* inferences linked to each other and leading to the ultimate conclusion to be proved by one side in the case. Next, let us see how *Araucaria* can be used to draw a diagram that represents the whole sequence of argumentation. In figure 4.1, the set of statements in the key list for the broken knife case has been inserted as a text document on the left, and the argument diagram for the case has been drawn on the right.

Figure 4.1 does not show all the statements in the list represented in the box on the left. To see them all in *Araucaria* you would have to scroll down. Nevertheless, as shown by figure 4.1, each statement in the key list has been represented in the set of nodes in the diagram in the right box. Each set of premises in each subargument forms a linked argument leading to its conclusion. For example, the premises C and E lead by an argument (indicated by the arrow) to the conclusion J. In the next subargument, J functions as a premise, along with premises I and F, leading to conclusion K. This structure represents a chaining of argumentation. J is a conclusion in the first subargument but then functions as a premise in the next subargument. What is shown in figure 4.1 is that there are four linked arguments making up the mass of evidence as a whole chain of argumentation leading to H, the ultimate conclusion. Each linked argument represented in the diagram looks like an instance of *modus ponens*—but are they really instances of *modus ponens*?

The commonsense generalizations formulated as conditionals licensing the *modus ponens* inferences in the broken knife case are defeasible. They state that if one statement is true then another is generally true, but subject to exceptions. Thus if the first statement is taken as a hypothesis, it follows by plausible reasoning that the second can tentatively be accepted as true. The problem posed by the case is whether an argument of this form, as used in the knife case and many other typical cases of legal evidence of the same sort, should be treated as deductively valid. In a deductively valid inference, if the premises are true it follows necessarily that the conclusion has to be true. These linked inferences in the knife case, apparently of the *modus ponens* type, do not appear to be deductively valid. This problem is a central issue for abduction, and the rest of this chapter will be taken up with trying to resolve or at least clarify it.

The same problem is posed by the argumentation schemes introduced in chapter 1. Appeal to witness testimony and appeal to expert opinion are also forms of argument that are important in legal evidence and that do not appear to be deductively valid even though they do appear to have a *modus ponens* form. This was shown clearly in the case of appeal to witness testimony, once the warrant underlying the argument was

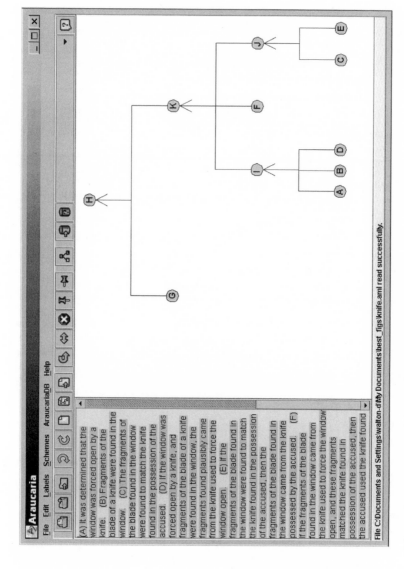

Figure 4.1 Araucaria diagram of broken knife case.

formulated as a conditional, that is: if witness *W* is in a position to know whether *A* is true or not, and *W* is telling the truth (as *W* knows it), and *W* states that *A* is true (false), then *A* is true (false). The same *modus ponens* structure is evident in the case of the argumentation scheme for appeal to expert opinion, once the underlying warrant has been stated: if an expert *E* says that statement *A* is true, then *A* is true. It would be mistake to see this conditional as expressing an absolute generalization stating that all instances where an expert *E* says that *A* is true are instances where *A* is true. This would make the expert omniscient, and it is just this kind of unrealistic viewpoint that is characteristic of an unconditional respect for authority that is behind the view that *ad verecundiam* arguments are fallacious. It would seem that although appeal to expert opinion has a sort of *modus ponens* form, it is not a form of argument that should be seen as deductively valid. The same observation can be applied to many of the most common argumentation schemes.

ARGUMENTATION FROM CONSEQUENCES

Presumptive argumentation schemes, as indicated in chapter 1, involve forms of argument that are neither deductive nor inductive. They represent arguments that are subject to defeat but can be tentatively acceptable to form a hypothesis that enables an investigation to move forward. Typical of them are causal arguments that make predictions in cases of uncertain reasoning where not all the conditions of the case can be known. Hastings (1963, pp. 65–77) postulated an argumentation scheme he called argument from cause to effect (or prediction). In his account (p. 65), cause-to-effect reasoning can take two forms: "The first is a prediction on the basis of existing conditions, saying that certain events will occur in the future. The second form is that of a conditional or hypothetical structure, in which the results of hypothetical conditions are predicted: *if* we adopt your proposal, *then* the budget will be overdrawn and we will lose members." The first form does not seem, by itself, to be an argument. It is a prediction. It could be part of an argument, but by itself it does not have a conclusion or premises. It is merely a statement, which is true or false. The second or hypothetical form does not seem to be an argument by itself, either. It is a conditional statement. Again, it is true or false. But if you put the two statements together and fill in some missing assumptions, you can get an argument of the following form.

THE BUDGET PROPOSAL ARGUMENT

First Conditional Premise: If we adopt your proposal, then the budget will be overdrawn.

Second Conditional Premise: If the budget is overdrawn, we will lose members.

Missing Premise: Losing members is a bad thing, i.e., we do not want it.

Conclusion: We should not adopt your proposal.

The form of reasoning exhibited in this argument is a chaining together of two single arguments, each of which has a *modus tollens* form: if *A* then *B*; not-*B*; therefore not-*A*.

The argumentation structure can be revealed as a backward chaining sequence that is abductive in nature. First, we start with the missing premise. Using it and the second conditional premise, we can infer by *modus tollens* that the budget's being overdrawn is a bad thing. Then, using this interim conclusion and the first conditional premise, we can infer, again by *modus tollens,* that adopting your proposal would be a bad thing. Then we need to rely on an additional assumption.

> *Additional Assumption:* If an action is a bad thing, then it should not be carried out.

This assumption is nearly tautological in practical reasoning. If something is a bad thing—that is, if we do not want it—then it should not be carried out by a rational agent engaging in practical reasoning because practical reasoning is based on the goals an agent is committed to regarding as "good things" for that agent. These are the goals the agent is committed to carrying out.[2]

Now that the argumentation in Hastings's example has been reconstructed, the *modus tollens* form of argument on which it is based is revealed. But this analysis now presents a bit of mystery. *Modus tollens* is a deductively valid form of inference. As used above in the budget proposal argument, however, it is not deductively valid. The reasoning is that both the first and the second conditionals are causal rules that are abductive and defeasible in nature. This mystery cannot be fully solved until chapter 6 when the question of whether *modus ponens,* and *modus tollens* as well, can have forms that are not deductive in nature. This question is very controversial, and it will take a whole chapter to address it properly and to propose a well-supported solution.[3]

In the meantime, another problem needs to be considered. The budget proposal argument, as analyzed above, has a form that is very well represented by an argumentation scheme already known in the literature as argumentation from consequences. It is an extremely common form of argument that can take two basic subsidiary forms. In a positive form, it is argued that an action should be carried out because carrying it out will have good consequences. This form is called argument from positive consequences. In the negative form of argument from consequences, it is argued that an action should not be carried out because carrying it out will have bad consequences. This form is called argument from negative consequences. Aristotle defined argumentation from consequences as a distinct form of argument, or what he called a "topic" in *Topics* 117a7–15. The following translation of the passage where he identified this form of argument is quoted from the Loeb Classical Library edition (p. 391): "When two things are very similar to one another and we cannot detect any superiority in the one over the other, we must judge from their consequences; for that of which the consequence is a greater good is more worthy of choice, and, if the consequences are evil, that is more worthy of choice which is followed by the lesser evil." This passage shows how argument from consequences takes account of a balance of considerations when making a decision between two courses of action. If things are otherwise balanced for and against, we should choose according to the consequences. If an action has good consequences, that is a reason for choosing it. If an action has bad consequences, that is reason for not choosing it (or for choosing an alternative). The general rule suggested by Aristotle's formulation is as follows: all else being equal in a case, choose the action that has the greater preponderance of good consequences as far as one knows from the information given.

Hastings's budget proposal argument presented above seems to be an instance of argument from negative consequences. At least in the analysis offered, it seems to fit this argumentation scheme. It is a little complicated, however, by its being an argument that combines two instances of argument from negative consequences in a chain of reasoning. This way of presenting argumentation, however, is extremely common, as can be shown by considering another example. The following example is a comparable instance showing how argumentation from negative consequences is used.

The Cigarette Tax Example

The federal government's decision to lower taxes on cigarettes will have bad consequences, because there is evidence to show that cigarette consumption increases as prices decrease, and increase in consumption leads to smoking-related illnesses that shorten lives and consume millions of health-care dollars. Therefore, we should be against the government policy expressed by this decision.

This type of argumentation, whether in the positive or negative form, may be defined as argument for accepting the truth (or falsity) of a proposition that recommends a course of action by citing the consequences of accepting (or rejecting) that proposition. In the cigarette tax example, the negative consequences cited are smoking-related illnesses along with the shortening of lives and the loss of health-care dollars. All three are generally regarded as bad outcomes. Thus you could analyze this example as containing three instances of argument from negative consequences. The use of argumentation from consequences in this case seems highly reasonable. We do regard all these outcomes as negative, and therefore, because they are consequences of smoking, we should conclude that smoking is a bad practice. If lowering taxes on cigarettes will increase smoking, the argument gives a reason for not lowering taxes on cigarettes.

The basic argumentation scheme representing these forms of argument has been set out in Walton (1996a, p. 76). In this analysis, A is a proposition that can be made true (brought about) by an agent. The argumentation scheme below includes both the positive and negative forms in one general scheme.

ARGUMENT FROM CONSEQUENCES
Premise: If A is brought about, then good (bad) consequences will (may plausibly) occur.
Conclusion: A should (not) be brought about.

This argumentation scheme can be reformulated in such a way that it is seen to be based on an implicit premise that has the form of a generalization. This premise functions as a warrant in the sense used by Toulmin (1958). It could be called the major premise of the inference.

MP FORM OF ARGUMENT FROM CONSEQUENCES
Major Premise: If bringing about A has good (bad) consequences, then A should (not) be brought about.
Minor Premise: Bringing about A has good (bad) consequences.
Conclusion: A should (not) be brought about.

The *modus ponens* form of argument from consequences brings out how this type of argument is normally used in a typical case of deliberation. Clearly it is a form of practical reasoning. It is a normal, and indeed a very important, kind of argumentation used in deliberation. It tends not to be deductively valid, however. It is a kind of practical reasoning typically used under conditions of uncertainty and lack of complete knowledge. It is a presumptive form of inference that leads to a conclusion that represents a hypothesis postulating the best or "least worst" choice among a set of alternative possible courses of action.

Just like the example of the argumentation schemes described in chapter 1, the scheme for argument from consequences needs to be evaluated on a balance of considerations. Corresponding to the argumentation schemes for argument from consequences are the following three critical questions (Walton, 1996a, pp. 76–77).

CQ1: How strong is the likelihood that these cited consequences will (may, must, and so forth) occur?
CQ2: If A is brought about, will (or might) these consequences occur, and what evidence supports this claim?
CQ3: Are there other consequences of opposite value that should be taken into account?

The idea put forward in Walton (1996a, pp. 75–77) is that if an argument in a given case has a form corresponding to argument from consequences, and if the premise is acceptable, then a weight of presumption is thrown onto the conclusion by the argument. Thus if such an argument is put forward by a proponent in a dialogue, and the respondent accepts the premise, then the respondent should, on a balance of considerations, also accept the conclusion. This form of argument, however, is not absolute, or closed, like a deductively valid argument. It is open to critical questioning. If the respondent asks one of the above critical questions, then the weight of presumption attached to the argument is temporarily suspended until the question has been answered satisfactorily. In other words, argument from consequences is defeasible in a dialogue.

The examples of argumentation from consequences given above show that this form of argument does seem to have the *modus ponens* form, or at least a form similar to *modus ponens.* But it has also been made clear why seeing argument from consequences as having a deductively valid form would not really do justice to the way this kind of argument works and how it should be evaluated. Hence we are led to the more general issue posed by the paradox stated above, because it does seem, judging by current and past logic textbooks, as well as other writings on logic, that arguments quite similar in structure to these examples are classified as having the *modus ponens* form. Are some *modus ponens* arguments deductively invalid?

It will be shown below that there are many ordinary cases of arguments having the form of *modus ponens* that are deductively invalid. In recent work on argumentation schemes (Hastings, 1963; Perelman and Olbrechts-Tyteca, 1969; Kienpointner, 1992; Walton, 1996a), many examples are presented that show that such arguments are not rare or unusual. In fact, they are extremely common. In Walton (1996a) the thesis is propounded that many common arguments that have the *modus ponens* form (or what appears to be that form) are presumptive arguments that can be judged structurally correct or incorrect by standards appropriate for presumptive arguments. These arguments can be structurally correct from a presumptive point of view, although not deductively valid. The forms of such arguments are called argumentation schemes. Many would classify these types of arguments as abductive or as species of abductive arguments. The first premise, in many cases, is a conditional. But it is not the "tight" kind of conditional that is falsified or defeated by finding one instance where the antecedent is true and the consequent is false. It is a loose kind of conditional that asserts that if the antecedent is true, then generally the consequent is true, subject to exceptions. In current usage, it is a defeasible or default type of conditional.

DEFEASIBLE INFERENCES AND *MODUS PONENS*

Of course there is a question here of how to define the *modus ponens* form of inference. As noted above, the typical argumentation scheme links a conditional warrant with another statement that fits the antecedent of the conditional. The conclusion then states the consequent of the conditional. But some might say that such a type of inference does not have the form of *modus ponens*. They might argue that the first premise is not really a conditional. Why not? It has the form "If *A* then *B*." But the defenders of this view might counter that it is not a material conditional, the kind appropriate for logic, because it is not the kind represented by the truth-functional connective called the hook (horseshoe). On the other side, many would say that there are a lot of conditionals, such as counterfactuals and probabilistic conditionals for example, that do not have the form of the hook, either. In this view, which is my own view of the matter, the if-then statement in the argument from consequences can rightly be classified as a species of conditional, even though it is not well represented by the truth-functional hook. In this view, the argument from consequences does have the *modus ponens* form. What needs to be appreciated is that whether an inference counts as having the *modus ponens* form or not depends on what counts as a conditional (that fits into the conditional premise). Thus in this section, some relevant aspects of the subject of conditionals are discussed.

There are some problems of usage in describing conditionals and inferences arising out of them. The way conditionals are described is not standardized between logic and computer science. In computer science, abductive conditionals of this sort, or sometimes even all conditionals used in inferences, are typically called "rules." This usage is somewhat comparable to Toulmin's terminology, in which a conditional of the sort cited above would be called a "warrant" (Toulmin, 1958). An example of how an artificial intelligence system uses types of inferences that are similar to *modus ponens* inferences is the ArguMed System constructed by Bart Verheij to provide argument assistance for lawyers. The ArguMed System uses what are called "step warrants" that express how particular statements can be used as reasons to support another statement. According to the account given by Verheij (1999, p. 44), a step warrant is similar to a Toulmin warrant, but also "plays a role analogous to the classic rule of inference *modus ponens*." How the system models an argument can be illustrated by the example of defeasible reasoning presented by Verheij (1999, p. 45): "Peter has violated a property right. As a result, at first sight, he has committed a tort. However, there is a ground of justification for Peter's act. As a result, on second thoughts, Peter's violation of a property right does not justify that he has committed a tort." In the ArguMed System, as in many AI systems, conditionals are based on so-called rules. An example of a rule in the ArguMed System is: "As a rule, if Peter has violated a property right, then he has committed a tort" (Verheij, 1999, p. 45). But the key feature of rules, and of the kinds of inferences commonly based on them, is that they are defeasible. What this means is that the rules are subject to exceptions, so if the case proves to be an exception, the inference will default, or fail. This property of defeasibility is illustrated in the case cited above. As a general rule of law, if Peter has violated a property right, then he has committed a tort. But in this particular case, there is a ground of justification for Peter's act. In this case, therefore, there is an exception to the rule, and the inference defaults (is defeated). It does not follow that Peter committed a tort, as it seemed at first.

This process of basing an AI system on the model of defeasible reasoning is very common in AI systems. In fact, it is quite typical of how rule-based systems work. But the question posed here is how the model of reasoning in such systems is based on *modus ponens* or some form of inference that appears, at least, to be quite similar to it. The kind of reasoning used in ArguMed does seem to depend on a type of central inference that is similar to *modus ponens*. For example, from the account above, it can be seen that the following kind of inference would be used in ArguMed.

> If Peter has violated a property right, then Peter has committed a tort.
> Peter has violated a property right.
> Therefore Peter has committed a tort.

This inference looks for all the world like an instance of *modus ponens*. And it seems to function in somewhat the same way as an inference. If both premises are true, then that is a reason for accepting the conclusion as true. Yet it is also different from *modus ponens,* or at least the kind of *modus ponens* we are familiar with in deductive logic. In that kind of *modus ponens,* it is impossible for the premises to be true and the conclusion false. In ArguMed, that feature does not characterize the *modus ponens*–like inference just above. In that inference, it is possible for the premises to be true and the conclusion false in certain cases. These are the cases that defeat (or "undercut," in Verheij's terms) the inference. In this respect, the inference above is different from *modus ponens* and is not properly classified as fitting the *modus ponens* inference form. In this respect, the arguments in ArguMed and AI are similar to the kinds of arguments studied in the literature on argumentation schemes. They look like arguments having the *modus ponens* form, and yet in the way they work, they are clearly quite different from deductive arguments.

The question then is whether this common and important form of defeasible inference in AI systems should be regarded as having the *modus ponens* form or not. Judging from the way it is described by Verheij in ArguMed, it looks like it is not being so classified. A step warrant, in Verheij's terms, only plays a role in ArguMed that is analogous to the material implication relation in *modus ponens*. What seems to be suggested is that the inference about Peter cited above does not have the form of *modus ponens*. It has a form that is distinctive as a type of inference but is similar to *modus ponens* in the way it works. It moves forward by detaching the consequent of the conditional as the conclusion, provided the other premise, which is also the antecedent of the conclusion, is accepted as true.

The basic issue at dispute can be formulated simply, using the following example of an inference. This inference has often been discussed in computer science.

THE TWEETY MP INFERENCE
If Tweety is a bird then Tweety flies.
Tweety is a bird.
Therefore Tweety flies.

My contention has two parts. The first is that the Tweety MP inference has the form of *modus ponens*. The second is that this inference is not deductively valid. The first part of my contention, further elaborated, is that the Tweety MP inference has the following form of argument for propositions A and B.

FORM OF *MODUS PONENS*
If A then B
A
Therefore B

The Tweety MP inference appears to have the form of *modus ponens* on the surface, but what is under the surface? Of course, it is quite possible that once we know more about how the Tweety MP inference works, we will see that it will be shown to have a structure that is not that of *modus ponens*. The Tweety MP inference could be represented as having a form with its own special premises. One premise states a general rule in abstraction from applications to a specific case, whereas other premises are based on applications to the specific case. In Walton and Krabbe (1995, p. 180), the following form of inference is put forward as a way of representing a nondeductive inference of the kind associated with default reasoning. Let us call this form★ of inference.

FORM★ OF INFERENCE
(1) (rule n:) $B_x \Rightarrow F_x$
(2) B_t
(3) Rule n applies to the present case

Therefore F_t

Form* of inference has as its first premise a rule (rule *n*) stated at a general level of abstraction. It says that, generally, if something has property *B* it will also have property *F*. The second premise states that individual *t* has property *B*. Normally, by deductive reasoning, the conclusion that individual *t* has property *F* could be detached. But rule *n* has only been stated at (1) in the abstract. It might fail to apply in this case. Once premise (3) is in place, however, we know that rule *n* applies to the case of *t*. Hence the conclusion that *t* has property *F* can be detached. Form* can be taken to represent the form of a default inference such as that in the Tweety case, where *B* stands for the property of being a bird and *F* stands for the property of being something that flies.

CONDITIONALS AND GENERALIZATIONS

Let us begin with a generalization about how logic textbooks treat generalizations. Although these textbooks do write about them very briefly and in an informal manner when treating such fallacies as the fallacy of hasty generalization, they do not write very much about generalizations *per se*. And when they do mention them, they tend to see them as universal generalizations, making a claim about all members of a class, as represented by the universal quantifier, "For all *x*." For example, the most widely used logic textbook (Hurley, 2000)[4] mentions generalization only once (outside the informal fallacies chapter). A general statement (p. 38) is defined as a statement that "makes a claim about *all* the members of a class." The next most popular logic textbook, one by Copi and Cohen (1998), defines "generalization" in its Glossary and Index of Logical Terms (p. 691) thus: "In quantification theory, the process of forming a proposition from a propositional function, by placing a universal quantifier or an existential quantifier before it." But on the same page, the term "generalization, inductive" is defined as follows: "The method of arriving at general or universal propositions from the particular facts of experience." What is suggested by the Hurley account is that there is only one kind of general statement, the kind I would normally call the universal generalization. But is this logical viewpoint consistent with practices of argumentation? What about my generalization about how logic textbooks treat generalizations? Is this a universal generalization, falsified by a single counterexample? I think not. So can there be different kinds of generalizations? The Copi and Cohen approach is more liberal, allowing for three different kinds of generalizations—two in quantification theory and one inductive type.

Perhaps that is too liberal. An existential quantifier in deductive logic is made true by only a single instance being true. It comes out as true even if one thing that has one property also has another property. Is that kind of statement a generalization? It is not the way I would prefer to use the term. Copi and Cohen also define generalization as a process or method. This, too, is less than helpful. I would like to see a generalization defined as a type of statement or proposition.

According to a view I have argued for elsewhere (Walton, 1996a, chapter 5), there are three kinds of generalizations. Distinguishing among these three types of generalizations is vital to getting a grasp of the fallacy of hasty generalization. But why is this view about generalizations relevant to the validity of *modus ponens* inferences? The answer is that the way logic should treat conditionals is closely linked to the way logic should treat generalizations. And corresponding to the three types of generalizations, there are three types of conditionals. This correspondence turns out to be quite important with respect to *modus ponens,* because it reveals that there are also three kinds of *modus ponens* inferences, depending on the type of conditional appearing in the inference. Let us start with the three kinds of generalizations.

The first type is the (absolutely) universal generalization, of the form "All F are G," for classes F and G. The defining characteristic of this type of generalization is that it is falsified by one counterexample. If you can find one thing that has property F but does not have property G, then the universal generalization "All F are G" is false. For example, the generalization "All men are mortal" is falsified by a single instance of a man who is not mortal. We could call this *the single counterexample characteristic.* Both the other two types of generalizations fail to have this single counterexample characteristic. The second type is the probabilistic one of the form "So many F are G," where the quantifier "so many" is represented by a fraction between zero and one, indicating the probability of something that has property F also having property G. An example is the generalization "Seventy-two percent of blue penguins live in New Zealand." The third type of generalization is the plausibilistic generalization, of the form "F are generally G, but subject to exceptions." An example is "Birds fly."

The absolutely universal generalization is familiar from deductive logic, for example in the A-proposition of syllogistic logic, or the universal quantifier. The universal generalization is expressed in modern deductive logic as a conditional of the form $(\forall x)(Fx \supset Gx)$. This way of modeling the universal generalization exhibits the connection with the conditional. The universal generalization is defined in terms of the material conditional (hook). This way of defining it not only ensures that it has the single counterexample characteristic but also indicates why the material conditional would not be suitable for defining either of the other two types of generalizations, for neither of these has the single counterexample characteristic. At present, it is controversial whether the plausibilistic generalization can be reduced to some form of probabilistic generalization or whether it is a distinctive type in its own right.

Alfred Sidgwick noted (1893, p. 23) how logic sometimes assumes that only the universal generalization can "properly serve as ground of inference." But Sidgwick also observed (p. 23): "It is comparatively seldom in actual argument—never, perhaps, where a really difficult or disputed question is raised—that we are able to rest our case in a single faultless generalization, like 'All men are mortal.'" Sidgwick was a precursor both of informal logic and of the recent flowering of artificial intelligence research on defeasible reasoning. He recognized the importance of defeasible generalizations, and the inferences based on them, in practical reasoning in everyday argumentation. But Sidgwick was a voice in the wilderness. The dominant practitioners of logic, both during and after his lifetime, stressed the universal generalization and paid little or no attention to the plausibilistic kind that is open to exceptions. Opinion is now shifting somewhat more toward Sidgwick's view, however. Josephson and Josephson (1994, p. 30) wrote: "The universal quantifier of logic is not the universal quantifier of ordinary life, or even of ordinary scientific thought." In their view, "reasonable generalizations are hedged" (subject to exceptions). Moreover, they added (p. 23): "Predictions from hedged generalizations are not deductions." This view is well supported by the recent computational literature on defeasible reasoning in artificial intelligence.

Anderson and Twining (1991, p. 43) have shown that generalizations, and the reasoning based on them, are centrally important to legal argumentation and evidence. They made a classification of five types of generalizations of the kinds commonly found in law (pp. 368–69). Case-specific generalizations are those that are relevant evidence in a particular case, such as the statement, "In most matters concerning their relationship, Edith dominated Freddie." Scientific generalizations are said to "vary in terms of their certainty" (p. 368) and are based on laws of science, such as the law of gravity. General knowledge generalizations, such as the statement, "Palm trees, rain, and high humidity are common in Miami, Florida" (pp. 368–69), are widely known in a particular community. Experience-based generalizations (p. 369), such as the statement, "Someone who has been unfairly treated by the police may, rightly or wrongly, conclude that police officers are not to be trusted" (p. 369), are based on common knowledge about the way things generally work. Belief generalizations are accepted on a basis of testimony or what others have said, such as the statement, "Members of the certain family (the Hatfields) are untrustworthy." Anderson and Twining pointed out (p. 369) that belief generalizations, based, as they often are, on superficial impressions or prejudices, may be more or less rational. Anderson (1999, p. 459) expressed the variability and limitations of generalizations of the kind used in legal reasoning very well when he commented that generalizations in legal evidence can be classified on a spectrum of reliability ranging from well-tested to largely untested and sometimes untestable intuitions. Basing reasoning on such generalizations is necessary in legal evidence, but it can also be associated with prejudice and rigid thinking in some instances. Twining (1999, p. 357) highlighted the fallibility of such generalizations by showing that although they are necessary in legal argumentation, they are also dangerous because they can "provide invalid, illegitimate, or false reasons for accepting conclusions" in some instances. Thus such generalizations, because of their inherent defeasibility, are best classified as being neither universal nor inductively strong.

To sum up the view that has emerged, I am arguing that there are three types of conditionals, just as there are three types of generalizations.[5] The first type, the absolute conditional, has the characteristic that if the antecedent is true and the consequent is false, the conditional is false. The absolute conditional transfers truth from the antecedent proposition to the consequent proposition. If the antecedent is true, then the consequent is true, and there is no doubt about it. The material conditional (the hook of classic logic) is a subspecies of absolute conditional. The second type of conditional is the probabilistic conditional. Instead of being defined in terms of truth values, it is defined in terms of probability values. It transfers probability from the antecedent to the consequent but leaves open to doubt whether the consequent is true (even if the antecedent is). If the antecedent has a certain degree of probability, then probably the consequent also has a certain degree of probability (depending on the probability of the antecedent and the probability of the conditional link between it and the consequent). The third type of conditional could be called the abductive, defeasible, or plausibilistic conditional. It is defined in terms of plausibility values. It throws a weight of plausibility from the antecedent to the consequent. A weight of plausibility in favor of a proposition's being acceptable only gives a tentative reason for accepting that proposition, subject to doubt and subject to potential retraction. A weight is generally a small amount of evidence that is not very significant in itself but that, taken together with a larger body of evidence, tilts the burden of proof to one side or the other on a balance of considerations. An example is the conditional "If Tweety is a bird then Tweety flies." If the antecedent is accepted in a given case, then a weight of plausibility is shifted to the consequent's being rationally acceptable (other things being equal). But it must be emphasized that this kind of conditional is inherently open to default. If new information comes into the body of evidence in the case indicating strongly that Tweety is a penguin, the conditional no longer gives a reason for accepting the consequent, even if the antecedent is accepted.

For example, the conditional "If Socrates is a good man then Socrates is a man" is an absolute conditional. It can be classified this way because it is not possible for the antecedent to be true and the consequent false. Thus there is no need to add qualifications to this conditional in order to accept it as true. Basing an inference on it as the warrant can yield a *modus ponens* type of inference that is deductively valid. The following argument has the *modus ponens* form and is deductively valid.

> THE SOCRATES MP INFERENCE
> If Socrates is a good man, Socrates is a man.
> Socrates is a good man.
> Therefore, Socrates is a man.

If you examine the Socrates MP inference, you can see that there are no exceptions that might make the conditional premise default. The conditional is acceptable without reservations. Contrast this inference with the Tweety MP inference. It is rightly classified as a default inference. The reason for this classification stems from the conditional that warrants the inference. It is defeasible, and hence the inference itself is defeasible. But the Socrates MP inference is not defeasible. It is deductively valid. It is not possible for both premises to be true and the conclusion false. This is a "tight" or exceptionless kind of inference, one rightly associated with deductive reasoning. How an inference should be classified thus depends on the generalization or conditional that functions as the warrant of the inference.

ABDUCTIVE INFERENCE IN MEDICAL DIAGNOSIS

The issue of differences between types of generalizations and conditionals has now raised a closely related but highly controversial issue. This issue is the logical form of abductive inference. As shown in chapter 1, abductive inference is often taken to be the same as what is called inference to the best explanation, and both are strongly associated with a type of argumentation called argument from sign. An argumentation scheme for argument from sign is presented in Walton (1996a, pp. 47–49).

An excellent example of argument from sign is the following inference of a kind very common in medical diagnostic reasoning.

THE MEASLES INFERENCE
If a patient has red spots (of a certain kind) then the patient has measles.
This patient has red spots (of this certain kind).
Therefore, this patient has measles.

The measles inference appears, on the surface, to have the form of *modus ponens.* Under the surface, it may really have a more complex form such as form★, which may be a special subtype of *modus ponens* inference or may not. It is a kind of inference very commonly used in medical diagnostics (Fox and Das, 2000). It can also be classified as an instance of argument from sign. A sign or indicator is observed, and then, because the sign is linked to a certain condition, that condition or thing is concluded to be present.[6] The thing that is immediately obvious about this inference, and about this kind of inference generally, is that it is not deductively valid. It is possible for the premises to be true and the conclusion false. It may turn out to be the case that when tests are done, the tests will show that the patient does not have measles. So what good is the inference if the conclusion may turn out to be wrong? The function of the inference is to make a guess or hypothesis that can lead to testing. Once the tests have been made, the findings may confirm the guess, or they may show it was false. Either way, knowledge is gained about the patient's diagnosis. If the initial guess can be ruled out, then other diagnoses can be explored and tested. If the guess turns out to be right, then treatment for measles can be undertaken, and the possibility of having to deal with other diseases can be set aside. So even though the inference is not deductively valid, it can perform a very useful function as a kind of reasoning in medical diagnosis.

A study of how physicians reason in arriving at a medical diagnosis (Patel and Groen, 1991) presented physicians with a written description of a case, asked for a diagnosis, and then analyzed how the diagnosis was arrived at from the given evidence. The results of the study showed that expert physicians tend to use forward chaining to reason from given evidence to a hypothesis. In contrast, intermediate and novice physicians were found to use backward chaining. They tended to reason from a hypothesis concerning the unknown and then use backward chaining to reason back to the evidence to test the hypothesis. The key difference between the two patterns of diagnosis seems to reside in the knowledge base of the physician. The expert has a lot of knowledge to work with, whereas the less-expert physician is reasoning, to a much greater extent, under conditions of lack of knowledge. According to Patel and Groen (1991), the efficacious use of purely forward reasoning is the distinguishing mark of an expert, and backward reasoning is used to tie up "loose ends," or aspects of a problem that resist a definitive solution. Generally, then, Patel and Groen found that medical diagnostic reasoning is based on a combination of forward and backward chaining.

Let us take a closer look at the conditional in the first premise of the measles inference. What it means is that if the patient has this kind of red spots then it is a good hypothesis that the patient has measles. The presumptions are that no other contraindicating evidence is available in the case at this point and that these are the kind of red spots that normally indicate measles. What does the "if-then" mean then? It does not mean that if the antecedent is true, the consequent must be true. It just means that if the antecedent is true, then with everything else being equal at this point in the investigation of the case, the consequent is a good working hypothesis to go ahead with, at least as a basis for conducting tests or, if tests are not necessary, as a basis for provisional action or inaction. The conditional has the function that if the antecedent is triggered, a line of actions and further investigations is laid out by moving to the consequent as a working hypothesis. The measles inference is better construed as having the function of narrowing down the search, rather than putting an end to it. Thus conceived, although the *modus ponens* form of inference exemplified in the measles inference seems to be quite reasonable and to have a legitimate and useful function as a kind of reasoning, it is not conclusive. It is not a logically necessary kind of inference of the type associated with deductive logic. Indeed, to understand how it works correctly, you need to appreciate that it is not deductively valid. To see it as deductively valid would be a kind of fallacy—perhaps a fallacy of dogmatic thinking that fails to be sensitive to exceptions to a rule. In traditional terms, it could be classified as a kind of hasty generalization fallacy, or *secundum quid* fallacy of over-looking exceptions to a rule. It is most likely that the measles inference would nowadays be classified in AI as an abductive type of inference. According to Peirce's classification, that inference would therefore not be deductive.

Peirce's analysis, as shown in chapter 1, viewed abduction as a process of forming a hypothesis that can be used as a tentative step in an investigation to explain some observed data. This analysis fits the measles inference very well. The hypothesis that the red spots indicate the presence of a measles virus is just a first step that can be followed up by checking other symptoms and by making diagnostic tests. Peirce (1965II, p. 375) saw abduction as a process of inference to the best explanation, "where we find some very curious circumstance, which would be explained by the supposition that it was a case of a certain general rule, and thereupon adopt that supposition." The conditional part of the kind of inference alluded to by Peirce is the use of a "general rule." What is this general rule? Presumably, it is a medical rule of thumb to the effect that, when on examining a patient you find red spots, one possible explanation would be measles. But of course, all kinds of other explanations are possible, depending on how the spots look and what else is known about the case. Abductive reasoning is not deductively valid. What is clear from the above examples and accounts is that it is some type of inference to the best explanation. What is meant by this phrase is not necessarily inference to the best possible (or maximal) explanation. In a typical case, several explanations of a finding or phenomenon could be possible. The abductive inference narrows down the range of possibilities by weeding out the less plausible ones, restricting the search to more plausible ones or even perhaps to one that stands out as highly plausible. But it does not rule out all the other possibilities. It is not deductively valid, and as indicated above, it would be a kind of fallacy to portray it in this way.

Consider the account of the form of the abductive type of inference given by Josephson and Josephson (1994, p. 14), as presented in chapter 1. What is important to see about this form of inference, so represented, is that it proceeds by excluding other hypotheses. It cuts down the range of competitors. The form given by Josephson and Josephson even indicates that the one selected hypothesis—the so-called best explanation—rules out all the others. But as the Josephsons themselves point out, this terminology is a bit misleading. Characterizing the task as one of "finding the best complete explanation for a set of data" would make the task "computationally intractable" (Josephson and Josephson, 1994, p. 204). What a successful abduction should do is to suggest a hypothesis that is plausible because it stands out as an explanation that fits the case. But there could be other explanations that are equally plausible. In such cases, further tests may need to be devised that distinguish between the two explanations and pick one as preferable to the other. Or in some cases, where two explanations may be equally good, you just need to pick one. In any event, the inference to the best explanation is at its most useful in the exploratory stages of an investigation, where the aim is to narrow down the range of hypotheses for testing and to ascertain (tentatively) which is the most plausible one or ones to pursue.

Abductive inference has two kinds of premises. One is a factual or observational kind, where some observed data or object is classified as fitting a certain pattern. For example, red spots may be observed and then classified as "red spots." This finding then functions as one part of a conditional or generalization that links the finding to a hypothesis. When the two premises are put together in an abductive inference, the finding from the first premise fits into the second premise as antecedent, triggering the detachment of the consequent. The statement in the consequent is then drawn as the conclusion of the inference.

The form of abductive inference is a highly controversial subject, as shown in chapter 1. Some might say that the conditional premise should be turned around. For example, in the measles inference above, the inference should be seen as follows.

If the patient has measles, then the patient will have red spots (of a certain kind).
This patient has red spots (of this kind).
Therefore, this patient has measles.

When the inference is seen this way, it may seem to be stronger, perhaps even deductively valid, because the conditional could be seen as expressing a sufficient condition relation. But the inference has the form of affirming the consequent, a form of inference that is deductively invalid. As indicated in chapter 1, on the basis of an interpretation of Peirce's account of the form of abductive inference, some think that abductive inferences characteristically have the form of affirming the consequent. The controversy over whether abductive inference should be seen as having the form of *modus ponens* or the form of affirming the consequent was extensively discussed in chapter 1. The issue is tied in with a fallacy that Aristotle called the fallacy of consequent, which has to do with turning a conditional around and getting it backward when using argumentation from sign. The complex issues surrounding this alleged fallacy have never been resolved. It will not be until chapter 6 that these issues will be adequately discussed. Suffice it to say here that if abductive inference can be regarded as having a *modus ponens* form, the implications for the fallacy of consequent are interesting.

The real problem here is the antipathy there is, from a viewpoint of traditional formal logic, to seeing inferences that have the form of *modus ponens* as being other than deductively valid. This viewpoint seems to suggest that if abductive inferences to the best explanation can be seen as having some form other than *modus ponens,* some form that is not deductively valid, such as affirming the consequent, then that must be the best way to model them. But an examination of cases suggests otherwise. The considerations adduced above indicate that the conditional in an abductive inference goes from an antecedent finding of fact (observation, indicator, sign) to a consequent that postulates a best explanation of the observed fact. This way of viewing the conditional premise yields an account of abductive inference as displaying the form of defeasible *modus ponens.*

INTRODUCING DEFEASIBLE *MODUS PONENS*

Recent work on argumentation schemes often seems to come very close to assuming the thesis that not all inferences having the form of *modus ponens* are deductively valid and seems to move forward on that assumption. But making the assumption explicit, by stating it as a general principle, is not something easily undertaken. It just seems like too difficult a thesis to argue for, given the contrary view so often expressed or assumed in the field of logic. But sooner or later, as work on argumentation schemes in informal logic starts to converge with work on defeasible argumentation in computer science, the assumption will become more and more explicit. The need to confront the issue was raised most explicitly by a recent review (Blair, 1999c) of some work on argumentation schemes (Walton, 1996a). What was questioned in the review was the apparent assumption that many of the abductive (presumptive) forms of argument (argumentation schemes) presented had the form of *modus ponens,* even though these schemes were not treated as being deductively valid forms of argument. But how could this be so? After all, the conventional wisdom in logic is that if these arguments have the *modus ponens* form, they must be deductively valid. As Blair (1999c, p. 341) commented:

> Several of the formulations of argumentation schemes in Chapter Three represent valid argument forms, whereas Walton is quite explicit throughout the book that presumptive arguments are not deductive entailments. A case in point is the "argument from popularity" or popular opinion which, Walton says, "has the following argumentation schemes" (p. 83):
> If a large majority (everyone, nearly everyone, etc.) accept A as true, then there exists a (defeasible) presumption in favor of A.
> A large majority accept A as true.
> Therefore, there exists a presumption in favor of A.
> Besides the fact that "defeasible presumption" is redundant, this scheme has the form of *modus ponens.* Yet Walton says in the very next line: "This kind of argumentation is deductively invalid"!

These instances of associating argumentation schemes with the *modus ponens* form of inference were questioned by Blair as amounting to an apparent contradiction. That apparent contradiction turned on the assumption that argumentation schemes, such as the one cited above, are not deductively valid, even though they have the form of *modus ponens.* After all, who could deny that all arguments that have the form of *modus ponens* are deductively valid? Blair assumed, with considerable justification, that all readers of the book would also accept this received view without questioning it. This assumption is evidence not only of how widely this view is accepted but also of how it is even held as a dogma, any appearances of contravening it prompting a charge of contradiction.

As long as this dogma is in place, little or no room will be left for the systematic investigation of argumentation schemes as a serious branch of logic. Although many of these schemes do have *modus ponens* forms, it is clear from the way the arguments actually function that they are not deductively valid. Given the current dogma, this apparent impasse leaves no room for further investigation of the inferential structures these arguments really have. One possible solution to the problem comes through the recognition that there are many common forms of inference that look like they have the *modus ponens* form but that, on closer inspection, are found to have a defeasible form of argument like form★. This solution, however, just seems to raise a different problem. How do you determine, in a given case, which form of argument is applicable, *modus ponens* or form★? The problem is that *modus ponens* seems to be the more general form. Form★ would seem to be a special instance. But arguments exhibiting form★ are not deductively valid. The absurd result that seems to follow is that there are instances of *modus ponens* that are not deductively valid. This seems to be the problem that has been plaguing the inquiry all along.

A way of salvaging this solution is to draw another distinction between two kinds of inference. In discussing a related problem, Verheij (2000, p. 5) has drawn a proof-theoretic distinction between two rule-based forms of inference.

MODUS PONENS
Premises:
   As a rule, if P then Q
   P
Conclusion:
   Q

MODUS NON EXCIPIENS
Premises:
   As a rule, if P then Q
   P
   It is not the case that there is an exception to the rule that if P then Q
Conclusion:
   Q

What is most important to notice about these two rules is that they can be applied to two kinds of cases, ones where there are strict rules and ones where there are rules with exceptions. Accordingly, Verheij (2000, p. 5) adopts a policy that suggests the following general principle for applying the two rules to cases. In a case where both strict rules and rules admitting of exceptions might possibly come into play, *modus non excipiens* must always be used. In a case in which only strict rules are involved, *modus ponens* suffices as the appropriate rule of inference.

This policy seems basically right to me from a point of view of applied logic, although I would use slightly different terminology. I would say that there are two forms of argument involved in two different kinds of cases. Both forms of argument can be applied to cases in which the inference is based on a conditional warrant in the form of a general rule or generalization. Where the conditional is purely strict, where no rules that admit of exceptions are involved, *modus ponens* in its deductively valid form can be used. For example, in a theorem-proving case in geometry in which only deductive reasoning is involved (with universal generalizations about all triangles and so forth), the possibility that any of the general statements are open to exceptions may simply not arise. In the other kind of case, the inference is based on a defeasible rule (or generalization) that admits of exceptions. Form★ should be used for modeling defeasible inferences of this kind. Verheij calls this form of argument *modus non excipiens,* but to avoid this expression, which is a little hard to pronounce, I would call it *defeasible modus ponens* (DMP). DMP should be applied only to certain special cases, those where the argument really has the structure of form★. DMP does not need to be used for modeling strict inferences of the kind based on a rule (or generalization) that does not admit of exceptions. Within the confines of a case of this sort, there is no need to use DMP. *Modus ponens* (MP) will do. But considering cases of realistic argumentation in natural language discourse, DMP is clearly the model of choice.

Changing Verheij's notation and method of representation somewhat, we can represent the two kinds of inference as follows. A and B are variables for propositions (statements). The first premise represents what is usually called a "rule" in computing. This can be what Toulmin (1958) called a warrant, meaning that it licenses an inference from one statement (or set of statements) to another statement. The rule in the first inference is prefaced by the operator "absolutely," meaning, in effect, that no exception to the rule is allowed. If there is an "exception," that is, if A is true and B false even in one instance, then the conditional is false. This first form of *modus ponens* corresponds to the familiar kind of inference of this sort in deductive logic. We will call it "deductive *modus ponens.*"

DEDUCTIVE *MODUS PONENS* (MP)
Premises:
    Absolutely (if A then B)
    A
Conclusion:
    B

In deductive *modus ponens*, the conditional premise works like a universal quantifier in deductive logic. One counterexample defeats the rule. This strict form of *modus ponens* can be contrasted with another form of inference that has a comparable structure but is not deductively valid. The warrant is prefaced by the operator "generally but subject to exceptions." This rule, which we can call defeasible, is not falsified by a single case in which *A* is true but *B* is false.

DEFEASIBLE *MODUS PONENS* (DMP)
Premises:
   Generally, but subject to future possible exceptions (if *A* then *B*)
   A
   In this case there is no exception known yet to the general rule
   that if *A* then *B*
Conclusion:
   B

These two rules can be applied to two kinds of cases, depending on which rule is more appropriate to the reasoning used in the case. In some cases it is better to use strict rules, and in other cases it is better to use defeasible rules. Verheij (2000, p. 5) recommended the following policy with regard to applying the two kinds of rules to cases. In a case where both strict rules and defeasible rules might possibly come into play, defeasible *modus ponens* must always be used. In a case where only strict rules are involved, deductive *modus ponens* can be used. For example, in a theorem-proving case in mathematical reasoning, the generalizations may be absolute. Within the confines of a case of this sort, there is no need to use defeasible *modus ponens*. Deductive *modus ponens* can be applied. According to this new way of viewing *modus ponens*, the inference is not always deductively valid. So defeasible *modus ponens* is a highly controversial subject in logic.

Josephson and Josephson, as noted earlier, have also challenged the dogma that inferences based on generalizations of the kind used in everyday reasoning can be analyzed using the absolute (exceptionless) universal quantifier. Their arguments also raise doubts about the capability of deductive formal logic to model such inferences. As noted above, they doubt whether such inferences can be analyzed using the universal quantifier, as we are taught in logic class (Josephson and Josephson, 1994, p. 23). They do not see inferences based on the hedged quantifier of ordinary life as deductively valid. This new view does not restrict the applicability of the *modus ponens* form of reasoning to arguments in which the conditional is of an absolutistic sort only. Deductive logic, in the new view, continues to be applicable to nondefeasible arguments of the *modus ponens* form, such as the Socrates MP inference. But it is no longer applicable to the evaluation of arguments that, like the Tweety MP inference, have a defeasible conditional as the major premise. These arguments exhibit a different kind of reasoning structure (DMP), one that has its own standards for structural correctness of arguments, different from those of deductive logic. Many arguments with the *modus ponens* general form encountered in everyday argumentation and in fields such as law and medicine have the same defeasible structure as the Tweety MP inference. This hypothesis implies that fewer of them than traditionally thought have the deductively valid structure of the Socrates MP inference.[7]

USING DEFEASIBLE *MODUS PONENS* AS AN ARGUMENTATION SCHEME

It is now possible to go ahead and use DMP as an argumentation scheme that can be applied to cases of abductive argumentation of the kind commonly found in law, for example. This way of analyzing the structure of such an argument can be accomplished using *Araucaria*. The first step is to insert DMP into the scheme set in *Araucaria*. Let us reconsider the broken knife case already diagrammed in figure 4.1. DMP can be applied to each subargument. The result is displayed in figure 4.2, a full text diagram that displays each statement from the key list in a text box. The figure displays an argument diagram showing the premises and conclusion of each of the four arguments making up the chain of argumentation in the case. The warrant of each argument is a defeasible conditional, and each subargument is appropriately displayed within a colored border surrounding the premises and the conclusion. Just above the conclusion of each subargument the notation DMP appears, indicating that each conclusion follows from the premises of that argument on the basis of the argumentation scheme for defeasible *modus ponens*.

The method of analyzing an argument by the technique of argument diagramming represented in figure 4.2 is based on the philosophy that there can be different kinds of argumentation schemes. Some of them can be deductively valid schemes, such as deductive *modus ponens*. Some of them can represent inductive forms of argumentation, such as arguing from a sample to a larger population. Still others can be presumptive

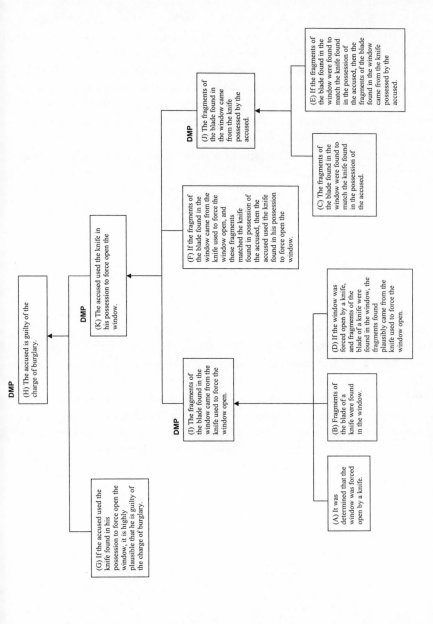

Figure 4.2 Broken knife case with DMP.

argumentation schemes that, like defeasible *modus ponens,* are schemes for plausible reasoning. In logic texts, it is not uncommon to symbolize something in propositional logic that will later be resymbolized in predicate logic. Initially an if-then statement could be symbolized as a material implication even though another symbolization as a modal implication would be better. Thus as a textbook proceeds, students are taught to use the tools they have. The new pragmatic tool of defeasible *modus ponens* has its uses, but it will not displace the material conditional in an introductory logic course that begins with propositional logic and may not go on to advanced topics that require making distinctions between various kinds of conditionals.

Once the hurdle of this chapter has been gotten over, the possibility is open to analyzing all kinds of cases where reasoning is based on presumptive inferences of a defeasible kind. The links in the chain of reasoning in such cases do not need to be deductive or inductive. They are based on argumentation schemes of the DMP form. In some instances, links in the chain of reasoning can be deductive or inductive inferences. But these can be mixed in with links of the DMP form. Another striking implication of the new approach is that the covering law model of explanation, the so-called DN model, needs to be broadened to include explanations based on defeasible generalizations as well as absolute universal ones and inductive ones. Scientific developments, like those in AI, have helped to make it clear that the climate of general acceptance has shifted from the formerly dominant deductive paradigm to new models of rationality. Once we stop trying to bend these arguments into some kind of deductive or inductive format, we can move forward, open to the possibility that they might have a logic of their own. It is only through an open-minded consideration of such arguments that progress can be made in the task of developing a formal structure that is useful for the analysis and evaluation of abductive reasoning.

This chapter began by considering the argumentation scheme called argument from consequences. If the approach taken here is right, arguments of this type do have the DMP form, and they are abductive, reasoning from a hypothesis to a conclusion. But the reader may now ask where this approach is taking us. Suppose we grant that these common arguments are not well represented as being deductively valid even though they have the *modus ponens* form or some variant of it, such as DMP. This is all well and good, but how are such arguments to be evaluated? If they are not adequately evaluated by deductive or inductive standards, then what standard should be applied? It is all very well to say that they are plausibilistic arguments based on defeasible generalizations or abductive inferences based on conjectures, but where does that leave us? Above it was argued that argumentation from consequences is sometimes reasonable. And indeed, this form of argument fits into the model of practical rationality outlined in chapter 3. On the other hand, argument from consequences has been recognized, in at least some instances, as an informal fallacy. So the general problem is posed: how can one judge whether an instance of argument from consequences is reasonable or fallacious?

The way of evaluating argument from consequences suggested by the examples treated above implies that arguments of this form can be stronger in some cases and weaker in others. As illustrated by the cigarette tax example above, in some cases the argument can be quite strong, meaning that it gives good (but not absolutely conclusive) reasons for accepting the conclusion. Some logic textbooks, however, have judged argument from consequences as inherently fallacious. Rescher (1964, p. 82) classified argument from consequences as a fallacy when he wrote, "Logically speaking, it is entirely irrelevant that certain undesirable consequences might derive from the rejection of a thesis, or certain benefits accrue from its acceptance." Examining some examples, we can see why this form of argument has been traditionally classified as a fallacy. The following example is quoted verbatim from Rescher (1964, p. 82).

THE MEXICAN WAR EXAMPLE
The United States had justice on its side in waging the Mexican war of 1848. To question this is unpatriotic, and would give comfort to our enemies by promoting the cause of defeatism.

In this example, it is possible to appreciate why Rescher judged the argument to be "irrelevant" and therefore fallacious. Which side was in the right is a historical, as well as a factual and ethical, question that should be decided by examining the facts—by trying to see how the war came about. What caused it? Who started it? These are the questions that should be asked, and they indicate what sort of evidence is relevant to the issue. Arguing that the United States must be in the right because questioning this claim would be "unpatriotic" in that the consequences might harm U.S. interests is beside the point. The claim that such negative consequences might occur could well be true, but it is not really relevant as an argument for the conclusion that the U.S. had justice on its side. In this particular example, therefore, it does seem justified to say that the argument from negative consequences is fallacious.

But exactly why is the argument fallacious in the Mexican War example when the same form of argument in the cigarette taxes example was not? Trying to explain this is not easy, but one theory was presented in Walton (1996a, chapter 6). According to this theory, there was a shift in the sequence of argumentation in the example from one type of dialogue to another. The example started out to be a critical discussion of the ethical issue of which country had justice on its side. But then, when argumentation from consequences was used, it shifted to a deliberation on the consequences of taking a particular side in this discussion. The shift from a truth-seeking discussion about history to a practical discussion about being patriotic by supporting the interests of one's country underlies the explanation of how the argument from consequences was used in a fallacious way. The practical discussion about patriotism is not relevant to the dialogue about history.

Argument from consequences is not a conclusive type of argument. It is defeasible and best judged on a balance of considerations in a case. Thus it is not really justified to categorize it as a fallacy. Nevertheless, as the Mexican War example shows, it can be fallacious in some cases, and the fallacy involved is a subtle and deceptive argumentation technique that is difficult to recognize and analyze. The difficulty of analyzing some cases can be indicated by citing some controversial examples. For example, arguments for censorship of movies or other literary or artistic works are sometimes based on cited consequences of exhibiting these works to the public. Thus, it might be argued that action movies lead to increased aggressive behavior in children or that the consequences of movies about killing police officers are increases in crimes in which police officers are murdered. Such arguments could be based on good empirical evidence, but are they relevant in judging the artistic merit of crime movies or as arguments for censorship? Such examples of argumentation can be both very controversial and very complex.

The other form of causal argumentation, cited by Hastings (1963, pp. 143–47), is that of reasoning from effect to cause. According to Hastings (p. 143), argument from effect to cause is the same as reasoning from sign, or reasoning from circumstantial evidence—for example, in law. This form of argument appears to coincide with what we would here call abductive causal reasoning or inference to the best explanation. We can sum up, then, by stating that it would appear, on the balance of considerations, that causal arguments should be regarded as important as argumentation schemes. They could even be considered as the primary kind of argumentation under study here. When one expresses such arguments in other forms, such as argument from consequences, the arguments may not appear to be causal because the term "cause" is not explicitly used. And yet, as shown above, they are based on causal generalizations that appear to have a form very much like *modus ponens* or *modus tollens*. The question of the form of these very common causal kinds of argumentation will have to be a subject for further investigation, for even though we may not be able to define "cause" in a way that commands universal agreement, studying causal arguments and causal generalizations cannot be avoided in any comprehensive approach to the study of argumentation schemes closely related to abductive inference.

5

Abductive Causal Reasoning

Causation is an unsolved problem that affects fields as diverse as science, law, medicine, and history. The measles inference in chapter 4 indicated how common causal explanations are in medicine and how important they are to proper medical diagnosis and treatment. But science has not yet come up with any theory of causation that allows precise definition of what causation is. Even in philosophy, a field in which causation is a central concept, the literature is mainly critical and skeptical. Although there are various philosophical theories of causality, none has ever been established as representing an exact, objective analysis of the kind that would be acceptable and useful in science or law. Chapter 4 offers a practically useful approach to the problem. Common forms of causal reasoning are modeled by using argumentation schemes based on defeasible generalizations. Matching each argumentation scheme is a set of critical questions. The argument scheme and the matching critical questions can be used to identify, analyze, and evaluate a given case in which causal argumentation has been used.

The new approach does not portray causal reasoning as either deductive or inductive in its most common uses. Instead, it analyzes the underlying structure of causal reasoning as abductive, meaning that it leads backward from given data as premises to an explanatory hypothesis as conclusion. This structure is based on warrant by defeasible generalizations that are different in nature from either inductive generalizations or absolute generalizations of the kind modeled by the universal quantifier in deductive logic. The structure is based on the familiar concept of cause as belonging to a set of necessary and sufficient conditions in a given case. But the concepts of necessity and sufficiency are analyzed in an abductive way that makes them quite different from the notions of logical necessity and sufficiency used in deductive logic. According to the new approach, a certain skeptical or critical attitude toward causal arguments is generally appropriate. Causal arguments are meant to be questioned, according to this analysis of them, but they can be improved through a process of critical questioning, getting stronger and stronger as each question is answered.

NECESSARY AND SUFFICIENT CONDITIONS

Causation is usually analyzed, in law, science, and medicine, in terms of necessary and sufficient conditions. A condition is said to be necessary for an outcome if the outcome will not occur without the condition. For example, it is a necessary condition, i.e., a requirement, of graduating from a university that tuition fees be paid. At most universities, however, payment of tuition is not sufficient for graduation. Some other conditions, such as passing some courses, have to be fulfilled as well. A condition is said to be sufficient for an outcome if fulfilling that condition is all it takes for the outcome to occur. For example, electrocution is sufficient for a person's death. In statements about causation in ordinary English, sometimes "cause" in the sense of necessary condition is meant, whereas in other cases "cause" in the sense of sufficient condition is meant. As Hurley (2000, p. 505) pointed out, everyday examples show that the term "cause" is ambiguous in this respect. If I say that watering this plant caused it to grow, presumably I mean that watering it was necessary for it to grow. Watering by itself is not sufficient, because proper soil and illumination are also required. But if I say that taking a cold shower caused my body to cool down, presumably I mean that the cold shower was sufficient to achieve the outcome of my body cooling down. Taking the cold shower was not a necessary condition, because the cooling could have been achieved by other means, such as staying in an air-conditioned room.

Philosophers have long struggled with the notion of causation and with the kind of analysis that is based on necessary and sufficient conditions. One of the most common criticisms, associated with the philosophy of David Hume, is that causal connections are not necessary ones.[1] Instead, Hume argued, they are based on regularity or constant conjunction of a kind associated with probability. And yet the latter notions do not seem to be entirely adequate as representations of the kind of necessity and sufficiency characteristic of casual reasoning, for, as will be shown in this chapter, an argument from correlation (based on probability) to causation is sometimes fallacious.

Other problems with defining causation in terms of necessary or sufficient conditions have also been discovered. Scriven (1964) has cited some cases that show that a cause of an outcome is not the same thing as a sufficient condition of the occurrence of that outcome. In one case (p. 408), two men fire at a third. Assuming that each bullet was sufficient for death, the one whose bullet hits the victim first kills him (causes death). In a second case (pp. 410–11), two conditions, unusual excitement and constitutional inadequacies, jointly guarantee that a man will have a stroke at 4:55 p.m. And the stroke guarantees that he dies at 5:00 p.m. But the man also had an unrelated heart attack at 4:50 that is sufficient for his death at 5:00. According to Scriven (p. 411), the heart attack is correctly seen as the cause of death, and the excitement is not. The reason (p. 411) is as follows: the causal chain between the excitement and death was interrupted, whereas the causal chain between the heart attack and death "went to completion." These kinds of cases indicate that a sufficient condition of an outcome is not necessarily the same as a cause of an outcome. The notion of necessary condition seems more closely tied to the causal concept.

Basing the analysis of causation on the concept of a necessary condition is one approach that seems to be widely accepted. For example, Kienpointner's definition of the causal relation (2003, p. 611) is of this type.

Event A is the cause of event B if and only if
1. B regularly follows A
2. A occurs earlier than (or at the same time as) B
3. A is changeable/could be changed
4. If A would not occur, B would not occur (*ceteris paribus*)

The necessary condition requirement is expressed in clause 4. This way of defining the notion of cause has application to law. Let us investigate it further by looking at how causation is treated in legal cases.

The notion of causation is central to the Anglo-American system of law, especially tort law, which is concerned with harm (Hart and Honore, 1962). The causation requirement in tort law relieves the defendant of responsibility for the harm if it can be shown that the defendant's conduct was not the cause of the harm. Causation is also a centrally important concept in any applied subject, such as medicine or engineering. Defining the notion of cause precisely has proved elusive, however. As a result, a skeptical view has been widely held by legal scholars in recent times, based on suspicions that causation has become a tool of manipulation by judges to further socially preferred policies. Despite this skeptical view, it is possible to give a sort of rough but objective definition of causation in law using the notions of necessary condition and sufficient condition.

The test most widely used to determine causation in the necessary condition sense in tort law is the so-called *but-for test*. This test (Wright, 1985, p. 1775) states that "an act (omission, condition, etc.) was a cause of an injury if and only if, but for the act, the injury would not have occurred." The test is thus based on the necessary condition analysis of causation of the kind attributed to Kienpointner above. As one might expect, it does not apply equally well to all cases of causation encountered in legal argumentation. It runs into trouble not only in cases of so-called preemptive causation, such as Scriven's shooting example, but also in cases of duplicative causation, where two sufficient conditions occur together. Consider the following case of the latter sort cited by Wright (1985, p. 1777–78). Arsenault and Flamand start separate fires. Each fire by itself would be sufficient to burn down Tutela's house. The fires converge and burn down Tutela's house. In Scriven's shooting case, the but-for test would rule that the first shot that hit was not a cause of death because it is not true that but for the shot, the death would not have occurred. In the house-burning case, the but-for test would rule that neither Arsenault's nor Flamand's fire was a cause of the burning down of the house because it is not true that but for the fire, no matter which fire you pick, the house would not have burned down. In short, these cases provide counterexamples to the but-for test. As shown in the survey of Wright (1985, pp. 1777–88), there have been numerous attempts in the literature on legal causation to modify the but-for test in order to deal with these counterexamples. But Wright argued convincingly that none of them have been successful. Using similar examples from science and everyday causal reasoning, Scriven (1964, p. 408) argued they cannot be analyzed as just being necessary conditions or as just being sufficient conditions.

This impasse has led many writing on causation to opt for an analysis that combines necessary and sufficient conditions. For example, according to Scriven (1964, p. 408), a cause is an outcome of a set of necessary conditions such that the whole set, taken together, is sufficient for the occurrence of the outcome. But two qualifications must be added. One is that causes are not themselves necessary. The set of conditions is therefore described by Scriven (p. 408) as "contingently sufficient." The other qualification is that each of the causal conditions has to be nonredundant, meaning the rest of the set cannot alone be sufficient for the outcome (p. 408). Putting all these requirements together, Mackie (1965, p. 245) formulated the INUS condition model of causation: "If C is a cause of E (on a certain occasion) then C is an INUS condition of E, i.e. C is an insufficient but necessary part of a condition which is itself unnecessary but inclusively sufficient for E (on that occasion)." The INUS condition model appears to provide a test for causation that is essentially similar to what is called the NESS (necessary element of a sufficient set) test in law. A succinct statement of the NESS test was presented thus by Wright (1985, p. 1790): "A particular condition was a cause of (condition contributing to) a specific consequence if and only if it was a necessary element of a set of antecedent actual conditions that was sufficient for the occurrence of the consequence." Note that in this statement of the NESS test, "a set" allows for the possibility of a plurality of sets, each of which is sufficient. The NESS test adds to the but-for test by taking account of how a set of necessary conditions can be combined to form a sufficient condition for an outcome. Hart and Honore (1962) were led to a recognition of the NESS test by studying the problems arising from the shortcomings of the but-for test arising from counterexamples such as the ones cited above. They observed (p. 116) that nearly all modern writers who use the but-for test to deal with the legal notion of causation tacitly acknowledge the central importance of the assumption that the necessary condition be part of a set of conditions that is sufficient for the outcome. Hart and Honore (1962, p. 119) incorporated the but-for test by adding a sufficient condition requirement. Thus they are credited with showing the importance of the NESS test in cases of legal causation.

The NESS (INUS) test can be modeled schematically by the diagram in figure 5.1. Figure 5.1 shows a set of conditions, each of which is individually necessary for the outcome to occur. But the outcome will occur in a given case only if each and every one of the necessary conditions is present in that case. Thus the combined set of necessary conditions is said to be sufficient for the occurrence of the outcome. Hart and Honore observed that in typical cases of causation in law, one of the given set of necessary conditions is picked out from the others as being the cause. It is picked out by pragmatic criteria. The two chief pragmatic criteria Hart and Honore identified are voluntariness and abnormality.

Because the underlying structure of causation is that of necessary and sufficient conditions, causal reasoning is based on *modus ponens* and *modus tollens* forms. But these forms, as shown below, are not the same as

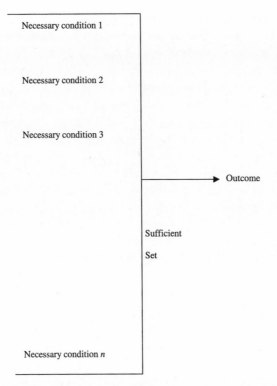

Figure 5.1 Schematic model of the NESS test.

the familiar ones used in deductive logic. Below it will be argued that the notions of necessary and sufficient conditions, as applicable to casual reasoning, need to be seen as provisional and defeasible in nature. They need to be analyzed as based on conditional warrants (causal rules) that contain a *ceteris paribus* clause stating that the connection only holds if all other factors in a case are assumed to be constant or "held equal."

FORMS OF CAUSAL ARGUMENTATION

Whether causal forms of argument are necessary for the systematic development of argumentation schemes appears questionable at first. There is no universal agreement on how to define the causal relation, as noted above, and hence the best approach might seem to be to avoid using the causal idiom altogether. That is, it seems misdirected to try to develop causal argumentation schemes based on a primitive but undefined causal concept. On the other hand, from a practical point of view, it does seem that causal forms of reasoning are not only very common but also very important. From this viewpoint, it is hard to avoid using the language of causation altogether.

As noted in chapter 4, Hastings (1963, pp. 65–77) devised an argumentation scheme to represent a kind of reasoning he called "argument from cause to effect." He described this type of argument as based on a prediction of the future from existing conditions. This type of argumentation applies causal reasoning of the most common sort. For example, if I strike the white billiard ball, and it moves toward the black one in the usual way, then it is reasonable to expect that (everything else being equal) the black ball will move forward. A version of the argumentation scheme for argument from cause to effect similar to the one given by Hastings was presented in Walton (1995, p. 140) as follows. In this account, the variables A, B, C, . . . , stand for "states of affairs," or statements describing events.

> Generally, if A occurs, then B will (might) occur.
> In this case, A occurs (might occur).
> Therefore in this case, B will (might) occur.

This form of argument looks similar to *modus ponens,* but it is different from it because the generalization in the first premise is not absolute. The latter claims that A is a sufficient condition for B in a sense that does not require epistemic closure. All the premise warrants is that, in normal circumstances of the kind that we are familiar with, if A occurs in a known context, then you can reasonably expect B to occur as well, all things being held constant, but subject to exceptions.

Schauer (1988) has shown how legal argumentation is typically based on rules that are subject to arguable exceptions. Defeasible reasoning is extremely common in legal argumentation. As shown in chapter 4, Verheij (1999) implemented this insight in a computational model. In this model, typical instances of legal reasoning are based on generalizations (often called rules) that warrant *modus ponens*–type inferences that are subject to defeat when a case is shown to be an exception. For example, consider the rule that if Peter has violated a property right, then he has committed a tort. Suppose Peter has in fact violated a property right. Then it follows that he has committed a tort. But this inference is defeasible, for if Peter had a good reason for violating the property right, it may be that he did not commit a tort. To accommodate such reasoning, it was shown in chapter 4 how Verheij (2000, p. 5) drew a proof-theoretic distinction between the usual kind of *modus ponens* inference used in deductive logic and a defeasible form of *modus ponens*.

Now the question is how these new ways of regarding *modus ponens* apply to causal reasoning. In the case of an argument based on a causal prediction, the generalization warranting the argument would presumably be defeasible, unless epistemic closure can be assumed. Why? The reason is that causal reasoning is typically based on a conditional that makes a prediction about the future in a complex situation where not all the relevant factors can be known with much confidence. Such inferences need to have a *ceteris paribus* clause built in. Thus they are defeasible. In such cases then, to model the logical form of the reasoning, we would find it better to use defeasible *modus ponens*. Causal rules, the kind that typically support causal inferences, are defeasible warrants.

Thus far it has been shown how causal reasoning can take two forms. It can take the form of argument from cause to effect, based on the defeasible *modus ponens* structure, or it can take the form of argument from effect as given datum to inferred cause, based on the abductive structure. But a third form of causal reasoning is also centrally important in both legal and scientific argumentation. In this kind of argumentation, the premise is a set of empirical data in the form of observations or experiments reporting correlations between two events or conditions. The conclusion is the claim that one event or condition is a cause of the other. This form of causal reasoning is partly based on probability, because the premise reports a claimed statistical correlation. But because the conclusion is a causal claim, the reasoning may also be partly abductive, or based on abduction or defeasible *modus ponens*.

ARGUMENT FROM CORRELATION TO CAUSE

One of the central problems of causal reasoning concerns the traditional *post hoc* fallacy (*post hoc ergo propter hoc*). Arguing from correlation to cause is not always fallacious. In fact, statistical evidence in the form of correlations between perceived events is the normal kind of evidence used, and properly used, to support causal predictions and generalizations. Thus the problem is to provide a means of judging when such an inference is fallacious and when it is not.

There is an existing method (Walton, 1995) of analyzing and evaluating cases of causal reasoning associated with problems of the *post hoc* fallacy based on an argument form and a set of critical questions addressed to the form as instantiated in a given case. This method assumes that the argument from correlation to cause will be defeasible and will be strong or weak, depending on the particulars of the case. It is especially important to recognize that this analysis sees arguing from correlation to cause as a reasonable kind of inference in many cases. It is not, on this account, an inherently fallacious form of argument. But it often tends to be a weak kind of argument that can easily go wrong or be overestimated. The fact is that we often leap to causal conclusions too quickly or uncritically, without taking account of proper reservations and qualifications. The existing method takes this fallibility, as well as the variable strength of reasoning from correlation to cause, into account. The method sees the basic argument from correlation to cause as generally quite weak, but open to strengthening as the appropriate critical questions are answered.

One account of the argument form (or so-called argumentation scheme) for the argument from correlation to cause has been given in Walton (1995, pp. 140–43). This argument form is displayed in the following scheme (p. 142).

There is a positive correlation between A and B.
Therefore A causes B.

Matching this argument form is a set of seven critical questions.

1. Is there a positive correlation between A and B?
2. Are there a significant number of instances of the positive correlation between A and B?
3. Is there good evidence that the causal relationship goes from A to B and not just from B to A?
4. Can it be ruled out that the correlation between A and B is accounted for by some third factor (a common cause) that causes both A and B?
5. If there are intervening variables, can it be shown that the causal relationship between A and B is indirect (mediated through other causes)?
6. If the correlation fails to hold outside a certain range of cases, then can the limits of the range be clearly indicated?
7. Can it be shown that the increase or change in B is not solely due to the way B is defined, the way entities are classified as

belonging to the class of *B*s, or changing standards, over time,
in the way *B*s are defined or classified?

The seventh critical question is relevant because changing definitions, or standards for classification, can affect causal reasoning. The classic case was that of cancer statistics. Increases in incidence of cancer, which for a while seemed to show more people getting cancer, turned out to be a function of better technology for diagnosing cancer in patients tested. In effect, the increase was due to the population of patients initially classified as "cancer patients." Even though the earlier diagnosed cases were better able to be treated, the cancer statistics seemed to show an alarming increase in cancer over the years. Once it was realized that the increase was only due to earlier diagnosis, the apparent conclusion that cancer was on the increase was shown to be illusory.

The danger of unknowingly committing the *post hoc* fallacy may be less in fields such as medicine and law, where the terms that are used tend to be defined in a precise way. If a mistake is made in medical research, for example, it can be corrected when the fault is detected in subsequent research. In such medical diagnosis, a disease tends to be defined in a careful, official definition, and physicians are expected to adhere to that definition in making a diagnosis in a given case. But as in legal argumentation, they can also correct and update the definition as the diagnosis proceeds. In the case of the *post hoc* fallacy with regard to cancer statistics, for example, the problem was corrected once it was realized through further investigations that the statistical data were biased by a faulty definition. In law, terms such as "contract" and "murder" are defined by statute and then even more precisely by rulings of courts.

Causal findings in the social sciences are often used to set social policies on matters of public concern such as crime and poverty. But here scientific and legal definitions are not used. One problem is that statistics can be inflated by opting for a broad or highly inclusive definition. For example (Best, 2001, p. 68), feminists have argued that rapes should automatically be classified as hate crimes because rape is motivated by gender prejudice. The problem is that identifying a "hate crime" requires identifying the criminal's motive. This loose definition leaves plenty of room for political activists to inflate crime statistics and then use the statistics in the media to "create" a social problem. In other cases persuasive definitions are used that are the outcome of political decisions. These definitions are often disputed. Advocacy groups often use inflated definitions to give rise to what Best (2001, p. 93) calls "mutant statistics" to support their cause. There are official definitions given by government statistical agencies, but these definitions can be decided on in a manner that is not free from politics and is often disputed. They might even be classified as persuasive definitions in the sense of Stevenson (1944). These statistics are often then used to make predictions based on causal generalizations. The predictions are then used to set social policies. The use of statistics is necessary and important for setting social policies. Nevertheless, because the general public tends to be receptive to claims about new social problems, we tend not to think critically about how social statistics are calculated (Best, 2001, p. 19). There is always a grave danger of the *post hoc* fallacy being committed, especially when the statistics are gathered or deployed by groups who have an interest at stake. For example, we should recall that, for decades, the tobacco industry denied any causal link between smoking and lung cancer.

Some of the difficulties in using causal reasoning to set policy have been outlined by Rein and Winship (1999). For the reasons stated above, the social sciences tend to provide only "weak" explanations and causal analyses of social problems. But it is tempting for social activists to interpret such causal findings as what Rein and Winship call "strong" causal reasoning. They cited the example of social science findings about the causes of poverty being used to set social policies on how poverty can be eliminated. The most famous initiative of this sort was President Lyndon Johnson's War on Poverty. As noted above, there are problems about defining "poverty" in a way that is scientifically precise enough and is not open to critical questioning and social controversy. The tendency to assume that strong causal reasoning can be used to infer a conclusion on how to act in setting social policy is the source of so many instances of the *post hoc* fallacy. The reality is that causal analysis in social science is based on weak causal reasoning of a kind that should be open to critical questioning. Causal analysis has little predictive power in most instances. But, deferring to the scientists, the public tends not to think critically about conclusions drawn from social statistics. This situation represents a danger in a deliberative democracy, where social policy is supposed to be set by the citizens on the basis of intelligent deliberations about how best to solve problems. By creating mutant statistics to define the problem and then using the media to promote their own solution, interest groups preempt the possibility of the citizens coming to their own conclusions based on intelligent and informed deliberation.

The argument form and matching critical questions can be used to analyze and evaluate any given case of argument from correlation to cause relative to the evidence known. The argumentation can be seen as a dialogue. The proponent has put forward an argument that moves from correlation to cause. The respondent can ask critical questions about the case. As each appropriate critical question is adequately answered by the proponent, the argument from correlation to cause becomes stronger and stronger. Thus the evaluation of this form of argument can range from stronger to weaker, depending on the particulars of the given case. In medical and legal argumentation the dialogue is guided by careful definitions of key terms, and the process of dialogue can then test out a causal hypothesis by refining and correcting it. In some cases, the hypothesis can be refuted. Where social policies are set through public deliberation based on statistical findings of the social sciences, the dialogue tends less to take the form of a cumulative amassing and testing of evidence. Instead, there is a much greater danger of the *post hoc* fallacy being committed in a way that is hard to detect and correct. There tends to be argumentation about definitions of key terms such as "poverty" and "crime" between competing interest groups who have a political agenda. The causal statistics claimed by the right tend to be highly different from those claimed by the left. The conclusions drawn by each side from their own statistics also tend to be opposed. Their arguments are based on scientific data, or purport to be. But because they are based on soft causal reasoning, they should be seen as open to critical questions.

ABDUCTIVE CAUSAL REASONING IN LAW

In chapter 1, I showed that the kind of reasoning typically used in citing legal evidence is defeasible and that a very good case can be made for classifying this kind of reasoning as abductive in many instances. But how does abductive reasoning work in cases of evidential reasoning in law where causation is at issue? It would seem that it would work somewhat differently from how abductive inference works in science. The framework of inquiry and the standards of what counts as evidence seem to be stricter in science. Scientists are also much more diffident about making causal claims or holding them as confirmed hypotheses. To get a better idea of how causal reasoning is used in cases of legal evidence, we might find it helpful to examine a legal case that has been analyzed using techniques of AI.

A system for the reconstruction of causal evidence in such a case has been devised by Prakken and Renooij (2001). The system is typical of those used in AI in that it is based on reasoning that applies to a set of facts and a set of rules that apply to the case. The so-called facts represent items of legal evidence collected in the case. For example, a proposition might be accepted as a fact if a witness has testified that it is true. A "fact" in this sense is not necessarily true. It is merely a tentative finding based on evidence and is accepted by the court on that basis. Legal reasoning works by drawing inferences from a given set of facts in a case. An example presented by Prakken and Renooij (2001, pp. 132–33) illustrates how causal rules can apply to a given sets of facts in a case to warrant conclusions explaining what happened by abductive inference. A summary of their presentation of the case is given below.

THE ACCIDENT CASE

A driver and passenger were returning home from a birthday party late one night when the driver lost control of the car on the highway. In the ensuing crash, the passenger was injured. The passenger sued the driver claiming he had lost control when there was no car or other obstacle in sight. In reply, the driver claimed that the passenger had suddenly pulled the handbrake, and that this act had caused the accident. This was a Dutch Supreme Court case (HR 23 October 1992, NJ 1992, 813), a civil case in which the judge is supposed to decide on the basis of the facts adduced by both parties. These facts were as follows. The police found that the accident took place just beyond an S-curve. Tire marks caused by locked tires (skidmarks) were detected past the curve, and just beyond that point, tire marks caused by a sliding vehicle (yawmarks). When the car was found, the handbrake was in the pulled position. The driver said three times after the accident that the passenger had pulled the handbrake. The passenger was found to have consumed some alcohol. An expert witness said that pulling the handbrake can cause the wheels to lock.

In this case, then, there were two opposed arguments. The passenger argued that it was the careless driving of the driver that caused the accident. The driver argued that the pulling of the handbrake by the passenger caused it. The court found (p. 133), on the basis of the nature and location of the skidmarks, that there was insufficient evidence to support the passenger's claim that the driver was speeding just before the S-curve. As support for the hypothesis that the accident was caused by the passenger's pulling of the handbrake, the court cited four main items of evidence: (1) the testimony of the driver that the passenger pulled the handbrake, (2) the position of the handbrake after the accident, (3) the expert testimony that pulling the handbrake can cause the wheels to lock, and (4) the location and nature of the tire marks. Two other items of evidence also taken into account by the court were (1) the fact that the driver and passenger were returning from a birthday party late at night, and (2) the fact that the passenger had consumed alcohol. On the basis of this evidence, the court ruled against the passenger's claim that the driver's careless actions had caused the accident.

What is especially interesting about Prakken and Renooij's analysis of the evidence and argumentation in this case is that they use an abductive model based on causal rules. This model (p. 134) is based on a set of observed facts F and a set of causal rules T. The rules are applied to the facts by producing one or more explanations of the facts. An explanation H (for hypothesis) is a set of possible causes for the facts using the causal rules. Prakken and Renooij (2001, p. 134) gave the precise definition of an explanation of this sort as set H, such that

$H \cup T \mapsto f$ for every $f \in F$; and
$H \cup T$ is consistent.

To represent the causal rules that apply to the facts, Prakken and Renooij (p. 134) began with a set of so-called literals $c_1 \ldots c_n$, standing for causes that in conjunction produce the effect. The causal rules T are then expressed in the following general form.

$c_1 \wedge \ldots \wedge c_n \rightarrow e$

These causal rules can then be chained so that an outcome of a cause can itself be a cause of a new outcome. Using these components, Prakken and Renooij (2001, p. 136) set up an abductive causal structure representing the facts in the case and the various alternative explanations that can be offered for each fact (see figure 5.2).

The outcome of the case depends on what caused the accident. The ultimate fact to be explained is the *accident*. The problem is to find the best explanation. The evidence contains the following facts.

Fact 1: ~*obstacles*
Fact 2: *tire marks present*

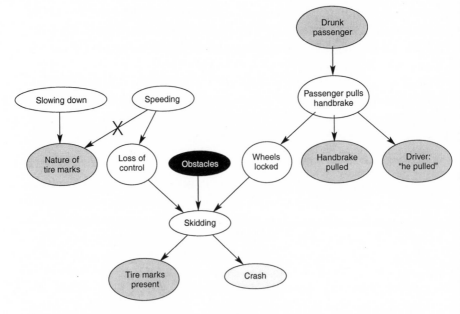

Figure 5.2 Causal structure for the accident case (Prakken and Renooij, 2001, p.136).

Fact 3: *observed nature of tire marks*
Fact 4: *handbrake in pulled position after accident*
Fact 5: *driver said "passenger pulled handbrake"*
Fact 6: *passenger was drunk*

The causal theory used to explain the facts is based on twelve rules (p. 137).

Rule 1: *skidding ⇒ accident*
Rule 2: *skidding ⇒ tire marks present*
Rule 3: *obstacles ⇒ skidding*
Rule 4: *loss of control ⇒ skidding*
Rule 5: *wheels locked ⇒ skidding*
Rule 6: *speeding in curve ⇒ loss of control*
Rule 7: *speeding in curve ⇒ ~observed nature of tire marks*
Rule 8: *slowing down in curve ⇒ observed nature of tire marks*
Rule 9: *passenger drunk ⇒ passenger pulls handbrake*
Rule 10: *passenger pulls handbrake ⇒ wheels locked*

Rule 11: *passenger pulls handbrake ⇒ handbrake in pulled position after accident*
Rule 12: *passenger pulls handbrake ⇒ driver said "passenger pulled handbrake"*

To pick the best explanation, we have to look at the arguments on both sides of the case. The passenger's argument is based on the hypotheses of speeding in a curve and loss of control as the cause of the accident. Let us call this hypothesis the passenger's hypothesis, or PH. The driver's argument is based on the passenger's pulling the handbrake as the cause of the accident. Let us call this hypothesis the driver's hypothesis, or DH. According to the analysis of the judge's decision proposed by Prakken and Renooij (2001, p. 137), DH is better because it explains more of the given set of facts taken as evidence and contradicts fewer of them. The passenger's main argument is composed of the following proposed explanations.

(P1) PH explains the absence of observed tire marks before the curve by the hypothesis of the driver's speeding in the curve.
(P2) PH explains the observed tire marks after the curve by the hypothesis of skidding.
(P3) PH additionally explains the skidding by loss of control by the driver.
(P4) PH contradicts the observed nature of the tire marks, not indicating speeding before the curve.

The driver's main argument is composed of the following proposed explanations.

(D1) DH explains the passenger's pulling the handbrake by rule 9, citing the hypothesis that the passenger was drunk.
(D2) DH additionally explains facts 2, 4, and 5.
(D3) DH contradicts none of the facts in the case.

The passenger was the plaintiff and had the burden of proof. Thus the issue is resolved by the court's finding that the passenger's solution is not more likely than that of the driver. The rationale (Prakken and Renooij, 2001, p. 137) is that the driver's solution explains more of the evidence and contradicts less of it. This solution follows the general approach of the Josephsons to abductive inference. The better explanation is the one that covers more of the given facts and contradicts fewer of them.

What is most interesting about this case and the analysis of it presented by Prakken and Renooij is that it shows how an abductive model of reasoning can be applied to a typical legal case involving causation. This case is very typical of how an abductive type of defeasible reasoning is used in law to set up arguments on both sides of a disputed issue, based on a set of facts brought into the court through the rules of evidence. Causality is not seen in this example as based on a set of necessary and sufficient conditions that give a causal reason for an outcome as necessarily flowing from these conditions. Instead, there are two competing causal hypotheses aimed at explaining the observed facts, and each of them is claimed to be stronger by its proponent than the competing hypothesis. The problem is to judge which argument is stronger on a balance of considerations. The judge has to make the decision based on the rules of evidence. In particular, the final decision in the case is based on the rule, set in advance of the trial, governing burden of proof. In Dutch civil law, the burden of proof is set by the requirement that the side wins who presents an argument in the form of a hypothesis that explains more of the facts better than the opposed hypothesis. Thus the dialogue model applies extremely well to a legal case such as this one. Causation is no longer a matter of a necessary outcome of a set of conditions. Instead, it has become a matter of which side in a dispute has the better reasons to support its claim of causation. Expressed in this framework, causation makes a lot more practical sense than when viewed in its old metaphysical guise of necessary and sufficient conditions for an outcome, where necessity and sufficiency are seen as deductive. If this reasoning is reexpressed in terms of provisional, context-sensitive necessity and sufficiency based on an inference with a defeasible warrant, causation begins to make sense. Within the dialogue framework, it becomes possible to show how to draw a causal conclusion abductively from the given set of facts and causal rules of a case. Causal reasoning, when analyzed abductively, provides a model that is useful for evaluating argumentation of the most common and important kind in legal evidence gathering.

The process of crime investigation can be seen as a diagnostic task much like that of medical diagnosis by a physician on the basis of observed symptoms of a patient. The symptoms are the pieces of evidence collected by the investigators. The argumentation in both kinds of cases can be seen as abductive. There is a given body of findings in the case, and competing explanations that plausibly explain the data are compared and evaluated. As Keppens and Zeleznikow (2002, p. 2) have shown, a pattern of this kind of reasoning is evident whenever police officials find a body. The evidence can vary widely, but the hypotheses always fall into four options: homicide, suicide, accident, or natural causes. A common problem in such investigations is that the police focus on a single hypothesis and neglect to collect further evidence on any other hypothesis. This single-hypothesis approach leads them to ignore other lines of investigation that might turn up new evidence while the trail is still fresh.

Interestingly, once such a case gets to trial, the argumentation tends to continue to follow an abductive pattern of argumentation. Josephson (2001, p. 1623) showed how the prosecution argument in a murder case can be seen as a best explanation argument of the following form: "Suppose a prosecutor argues that a man is a murderer because: (1) there was a death; (2) the death cannot be satisfactorily explained by natural causes; (3) the death cannot be satisfactorily explained as an accident; and (4) the death cannot be plausibly or satisfactorily explained as a suicide; (5) thus, it was a homicide." Suppose, in addition, that the prosecutor continues with the following arguments (p. 1623). The hypothesis that the defendant could have committed the murder is not ruled out, because he has no alibi. And there is plausible evidence that he had the means, motive, and opportunity. Suppose there is no other nearly so plausible hypothesis that has been investigated and that suggests some other individual was the perpetrator. In such a case the conclusion will seem to follow that the defendant is guilty as the best explanation of all the facts that have been collected. What the defendant needs to do to undercut this argument is question whether other avenues should have been explored and other evidence collected that might lead to some other plausible explanation of the death. Once the facts are supposedly in, however, and the case has gone to trial, it can be extremely hard to backtrack and propose reopening the investigation. These factors indicate that the order of the sequence of asking and answering questions in an investigation is fundamentally important in abductive argumentation. These factors will turn out to be vital to the theory of abduction as a dialogue process in chapters 6 and 7.

CAUSAL ABDUCTION IN MEDICAL EXAMINATION AND DIAGNOSIS

One of the most important and convincing applications of abduction is to the kind of reasoning so common in medical diagnosis. As indicated in the measles example in chapter 4, this kind of reasoning is typically based on argument from sign. Recent initiatives in using computer systems to aid in this kind of reasoning have been highly successful. Expert systems technology has proved to be very useful for diagnostic problem solving in medicine. An expert system is a database made up of a set of facts and rules in a particular domain. A rule is composed of a left-hand side, called the antecedent in traditional logic, which contains multiple requirements that have to be satisfied in order to infer the right-hand side. The right-hand side corresponds to the consequent of a conditional in traditional logic. In other words, the rule has an if-then form, where the hypothesis or iffy part is the left-hand side, and the consequent, or what follows from the hypothesis, is the right. If the requirements in the left-hand part are satisfied in a given case, then the right-hand part can be inferred. Thus a rule in AI, along with the set of facts required to satisfy the right-hand part of the rule, sets up a *modus ponens* type of inference to the conclusion in a case. The rules apply to the facts, enabling a conclusion to be drawn. The conclusion can be seen as a hypothesis that is justified by the rules and facts. Thus the rules and facts can be said to give reasons to support the hypothesis, or conversely, the hypothesis can be said to offer an explanation of the facts.

An example of an expert system used for causal problem solving is the Electrodiagnostic Assistant (Jamieson, 1990), used by neurologists to diagnose nerve and muscle disorders. The rules take findings of nerve conduction studies and needle examinations as facts for input. These findings reference the "location, severity and pathology of a nerve or muscle disorder" (Jamieson, 1990, p. 374). Certain combinations of findings are packaged under definitions of a type of disorder. For example (p. 378), carpal tunnel syndrome is defined and is associated by means of rules with certain symptoms or factual findings, such as axon loss, motor amplitude reduction, and sensory slowing. The more of these factual findings that are found in a given case, the more plausible is the hypothesis that the cause is carpal tunnel syndrome.

Measles is a common name for two distinct diseases caused by different viruses. Rubeola, or seven-day measles, can affect persons of all ages, but if you had it as a child, you will be immune. Babies of mothers who have had rubeola are also immune for about a year after birth. Many children have been vaccinated against rubeola, and anyone who has been vaccinated should be immune. The first symptoms are those similar to a cold, such as sneezing, cough, and nasal discharge. There is also a high body temperature. The characteristic rash appears from three to five days after the onset of the other symptoms. The fever subsides when the rash appears. Complete recovery occurs in a few weeks, but the patient should be isolated to avoid spreading the disease. Rubella, called three-day measles or German measles, is, like rubeola, a contagious viral disease characterized by spots or a pink rash that appears on the face, neck, and body. The symptoms of rubella are mild. There may be fever and tenderness in the lymph nodes. The rash disappears after one to three days. Recovery requires no specific treatment, and one attack gives immunity for life. Rubella can cause birth defects in the first three weeks of pregnancy. There is a vaccine against rubella.

To consider a simple example, let us go back to the measles example in chapter 4. How will diagnosis work when a patient appears with a complaint that looks initially like it might fit the disease recognized as rubeola, or seven-day measles? Let us say that the patient exhibits some evidence of the characteristic rash and complains of feeling sick. The process will go through several stages. First, the physician will ask the patient questions to get more information. This process of question and answer takes the form of an examination dialogue. The purpose is to expand the database by asking relevant questions and by physically examining the patient. During this examination stage, the physician will formulate a hypothesis or diagnosis, and the questions asked will be guided by that diagnosis. At the same time, the physician will consider alternative diagnoses or hypotheses that are not yet ruled out. For example, initially the physician might think the problem could be either rubella or rubeola, and so the questions will be designed to rule out one of these competing hypotheses and possibly thereby help to confirm the other. This part of the dialogue is basically information seeking. The aim is to collect and expand a database of relevant information. But already the argumentation in the dialogue may be described as abductive, or as based on a pattern of abductive argumentation. The reason is that the physician's questioning is partly determined by an attempt at best explanation. Which questions are relevant to the examination dialogue is partly determined by the hypothesis that is plausible at that point in the dialogue and by which competing hypotheses are still plausible as well or have been eliminated as implausible.

For example, the physician may begin by examining the patient's lymph nodes and asking whether the nodes feel tender. The physician may ask whether the patient recalls being inoculated against measles when a child and, if so, which kind of measles the inoculation was for. The physician may ask when the patient first began to feel ill and what the symptoms were. Each of these questions not only collects data but also guides further questioning by making one hypothesis more plausible or another hypothesis less plausible. While running through this examination dialogue, the physician will eventually arrive at a diagnosis. The diagnosis could involve more than one hypothesis, or it could be a "don't know yet" diagnosis, where several hypotheses could be possible but no one or two are much more plausible than others. It could also come down to one hypothesis that is much more plausible than the other explanations that are in the running. Especially if the outcome is one of the latter two kinds of cases, the diagnosis might proceed to a testing stage. A blood sample might be taken, and tests for the most likely diagnoses might be conducted at a lab. The tests can be used to eliminate hypotheses as well as to provide evidence confirming a hypothesis.

What is important to realize is that the abductive reasoning used in the process of diagnosis is not only a form of reasoning in which premises are accepted and a conclusion proved or supported at the end of the sequence. It is also a dialogue process. What is vitally important to the process is that questions are asked and answered and that the abductive reasoning moves forward in a dialogue format as the answers come in, providing data. As the database expands through the information-seeking dialogue, each step in the sequence of abductive reasoning only makes sense as relevant and useful insofar as it is based on the previous question-answer moves in the dialogue and insofar as it guides the dialogue forward to its ultimate objective of determining a cause of the illness. In the argumentation stage, various alternative hypotheses are considered by the physician, and the process moves by question and answer to evaluate the plausibility of various hypotheses. The process has to be understood not just as reasoning but as reasoning guided by a dialogue or investigation framework that has a goal. This goal shapes the investigation and determines the relevance of a sequence of questions and replies.

A sample sequence of dialogue can be represented in the dialogue sequence below.

Physician	Patient
When did you first notice the rash?	Just yesterday.
How did you feel before that?	I had a bad cold and still have it.
Have you had measles before?	Yes, when I was in grade school.

Can you recall what type it was?	Not for sure, no.
Have you been inoculated for measles?	Maybe, but not that I can recall for sure.
Is it tender here (lymph nodes)?	No.
Did you have fever during the cold?	Yes.
How many days did you have the cold?	This is the fifth day I would say.

It can be seen by looking over the sequence that the physician's line of questioning is methodical and is guided by an aim. That aim is to make a diagnosis. The aim is pursued by collecting a database of information and then trying to explain the data collected at any given point by forming a hypothesis or set of hypotheses. This hypothesis formation then moves the dialogue forward by determining which questions will be asked next. The function of questioning is to collect more relevant data that will enable evaluation of the various hypotheses, showing some to be less plausible and some more plausible.

Thus it would seem that what is really needed to grasp the logical form of abduction as a process of reasoning is to go beyond seeing it as a single inference, called abductive inference, with characteristic premises and conclusion. What is needed is even to go beyond seeing abduction as a chaining of reasoning with several inferences connected in a sequence. One need is to grasp the ultimate aim of such a sequence by seeing the reasoning as used within a larger framework. The need to take pragmatic factors into account, such as the purpose an argument is being used for, was already evident in the J&J model of the form of abductive inference cited in chapter 1. In the J&J model, the last so-called pragmatic factors used to evaluate any instance of abductive inference concerned such matters as the need to arrive at a decision versus the need to collect more facts. These factors already indicate that abduction cannot be evaluated merely as an isolated inference in abstraction from the context of a dialogue or investigation. Instead, it needs to be evaluated as a process of hypothesis formation that is guided and judged in relation to which facts have been collected up to a given point and to what kind of decision is to be made, once all or enough facts have been collected and examined.

It is natural to think of an expert system for medical diagnosis along the lines of a dialogue model. The system offers advice in the form of a hypothesis, or possible diagnosis, to the physician who uses it. But all expert systems have a question-answering capability. A user can ask the system questions. For example, a user can initially ask a system to explain given symptoms by producing a diagnosis matching those symptoms in the form of a hypothesis. The user can then ask further questions or input more information if the diagnosis seems questionable. The expert system does not replace the physician's judgment, but it does allow quick access to knowledge in a domain with which the physician may not be familiar. Such a system is especially helpful in dealing with uncommon cases that a physician has not encountered. Thus an expert system can make a physician's diagnosis more comprehensive by taking more relevant data into account.

When producing a hypothesis from a knowledge base composed of a set of facts and rules, a medical expert system can be seen as carrying out a form of causal reasoning. This is because the hypothesis links physiological mechanisms to disease manifestations. A causal chain may be set up, for example, that explains a visible symptom by linking it to other conditions. For example, leg edema, observed as swelling of the leg, may be explained by the hypothesis of hepatic congestion. But then this condition, in turn, may be explained as congestive heart failure. Once this diagnosis has been hypothesized, further tests can be run for hepatic congestion. If these tests are positive, the hypothesis will be strengthened. If they are negative, it will be weakened. In expert systems, rules and facts are assigned numerical confidence factors (CFs). There is no universally accepted single system of determining how the CFs are combined to judge the confidence value that should be assigned to a hypothesis. Many different systems are in use. They all tend to be rough estimates. The Bayesian system of attaching numerical probability values to all facts and rules, and then using a numerical formula to calculate the outcome, is not all that helpful in measuring how a decision should be arrived at in many cases. Even so, it does seem reasonable to say that citing facts and rules is a good method of giving reasons to support a hypothesis. It could well be that, as an alternative to the Bayesian model, the dialogue model explains better how causal reasoning in medical diagnosis should be evaluated as weak or strong. According to the dialogue model, one should critically examine all the arguments on both sides and then reach a decision based on a balance of considerations. In other words, one should sum up the total body of evidence on each side of a case and then reach a holistic dialogue-based assessment of which argument is the stronger. This type of assessment is not wholly determined by numerical calculations, although it can help to assign numerical values or CFs to the facts and rules. The CF attached to a statement represents a judgment of how plausible the statement is. Then the CFs can be raised or lowered as one statement is connected to others by arguments based on causal rules. The causal rules are themselves regarded as defeasible. That is, they are typically plausible to some degree, realizing that as new information enters a case, that degree may decrease. In some cases, a hypothesis that was plausible at an earlier stage of dialogue may be refuted altogether at some later stage.

Such considerations suggest that there are two levels at which abduction can be identified, analyzed, and evaluated. The preponderance of the literature dwells on the reasoning level. Abductive inference is seen as a logical inference, comparable in kind to deductive or inductive inference, but having additional characteristics that set it off as distinct from either of these other types. Beyond this level, there is the hint in some of the literature that abduction needs to be defined within some larger framework in which data are being collected and processed with some overarching frame of reference in mind. As noted above, strong hints of this pragmatic aspect of abduction are evident in the analysis of its logical form presented by the Josephsons.

This aspect is also clearly visible in Peirce's writings on abduction. Peirce saw abduction as the central form of reasoning in the process of scientific discovery. He saw it as representing the creative stage of scientific discovery in which guesses are made by formulating new hypotheses that have not yet been verified or perhaps even tested. It is thus a creative part of science. This view of abduction actually fits quite nicely with the dialogue model of medical diagnosis outlined above using the measles example. Of course, medical diagnosis and scientific investigation are in certain respects quite different, although related, processes. In medical diagnosis, the physician examines a single patient, with all the imponderables that are involved in trying to apply science to the single case. Scientific investigation is often held to have the properties of the inquiry type of dialogue, especially by the neopositivists. But Peirce made room for a discovery stage that precedes the testing and verification or falsification stages of scientific reasoning. This discovery stage is creative, and thus it can be likened to a dialogue process in which questions are asked and a dialogue moves back and forth as different hypotheses are formed and judged as more plausible or less plausible. If this approach is right, the dialogue model can be used to provide a framework to show how abductive argumentation moves forward by formulating a sequence of questions, these guided by the answers and by the incoming data they provide.

CAUSAL REASONING AS DYNAMIC IMPROVEMENT OF A HYPOTHESIS

Causal reasoning, in the theory proposed above, is not only abductive but also dynamic. The causal conclusion takes the form of a hypothesis that is derived by inference to the best explanation of the data. But as new evidence comes into the case, the hypothesis can be better and better confirmed, making it more and more plausible as critical questions are answered. For example, a correlation between two events A and B may suggest that the one event is a cause of the other. The correlation may be asserted only on the basis of a few observed instances. But as more data come in, and more and more instances are observed of B occurring after A, the evidence indicating a causal connection may build up. The hypothesis that A causes B becomes more plausible. Then new evidence, in various forms, may enter the case. There may be no negative instances found where A occurs but B does not. Or it may be ruled out that the correlation can be explained by the existence of a third event C that is causing both A and B. As new evidence builds up in a case and the case evolves, the hypothesis that A causes B may be better and better confirmed. This dynamic sequence of reasoning is one of retesting and improving the causal hypothesis as each new bit of evidence comes in. Seeing such a sequential buildup of evidence for a causal hypothesis in a case is just the sort of evidential framework that can and should be used to evaluate argumentation from correlation to cause. So it is just this sort of dialogue framework that allows rational argumentation to deal with cases where the *post hoc* fallacy is an issue. Of course, such reasoning is not deductive in the most common and controversial kinds of cases. It does not seem to be entirely inductive, either. It seems to be an abductive kind of reasoning that is based on defeasible causal generalizations and is plausibilistic in nature. It has been shown above how this kind of causal reasoning is highly typical of legal evidence. A good case can be made that it is also typical of much reasoning of the kind used to gather scientific evidence. Simmons (1992) has represented the generate-test-and-debug (GTD) paradigm as a model for argumentation in a scientific inquiry. The sequence starts

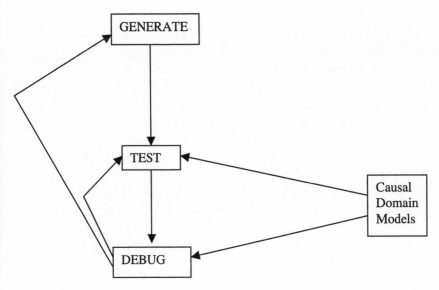

Figure 5.3 The generate-test-and-debug (GTD) paradigm (Simmons, 1992 p. 159).

with the formulation of a problem and a hypothesis representing a possible solution. The next step is the testing of the hypothesis. The debugger then modifies the hypothesis and resubmits it for testing. Alternatively, of course, the test could falsify the hypothesis, thereby refuting it. Given that kind of outcome, an alternative hypothesis needs to be considered. The argumentation in the GTD paradigm can be represented by the flowchart in figure 5.3 (based on the more complex diagram in Simmons, 1992, p. 161). The argumentation diagrammed in figure 5.3 is goal-directed, and the sequence takes the form of a feedback cycle. As the hypothesis is continually retested, experimental support for it builds up. The hypothesis becomes more and more plausible. It is never regarded as beyond testing, however, even though it may become highly confirmed at an advanced stage of testing, especially once it has been highly refined and expressed very precisely within the language of a scientific theory.

This pattern of improving dynamic causal reasoning by continued retesting of a causal hypothesis is highly characteristic of scientific reasoning from data to a hypothesis. For example, this kind of argumentation is evident in typical diagnostic reasoning in medicine, where the cause of a disorder is sought. Peng and Reggia (1990, pp. 6–7) have described the characteristic sequence of inferences as hypothesize-and-test reasoning. The first stage, which consists of the asking of a question or posing of a problem, is called "disorder evocation." A perceived "disorder" in a given case is cited (Peng and Reggia, 1990, p. 6). In the second stage, a hypothesis is formed to explain the given manifestation. This stage is called "hypothesis generation" (p. 6). The third stage, called "hypothesis testing," consists of updating an existing hypothesis by evaluating it in relation to new information. The sequence of reasoning in medical diagnosis is portrayed by Peng and Reggia as circular. It is one of continued refinement of a hypothesis through steps of observing, explaining, and testing. Each time new observations come in, the hypothesis is retested, and the existing explanation is either confirmed or refuted. At each step, as the existing explanation is confirmed again and again, it becomes more and plausible that it is the "best" explanation of the given data at that point.

Thagard (1999, pp. 118–19) has identified four stages in the development of medical understanding of the cause of a disease. The first stage (p. 118) is the identification of the disease with its own symptoms. The second stage (p. 119) is the specification of possible causes by correlation, by setting up a hypothesis that some unobserved factor is the cause, and by biochemical analysis. The third stage (p. 119) is the use of experimentation to support the conviction that the cause of the disease has been found. The fourth stage (p. 119) is the elaboration of the mechanism by which the cause is connected to the effect. Thagard presented many case studies of the causation of diseases such as scurvy and peptic ulcers to support his analysis of how scientific argumentation goes through a sequence of reasoning that builds a better case for a conclusion about the cause of disease. His analysis of the argumentation used in such cases makes it clear that the reasoning is abductive and dynamic. The causal conclusion drawn from the data becomes more and more plausible as more refined and improved explanations arise from asking and answering the right questions at each stage.

THE THESIS THAT CAUSAL REASONING IS ABDUCTIVE

Pearl (2000, p. 1) has constructed an interesting paradox about causal arguments. The paradox begins by asking the reader to accept two plausible premises.

(1) My neighbor's roof gets wet whenever mine does.

(2) If I hose my roof it will get wet.

It would appear that these two premises logically imply the following conclusion.

(3) My neighbor's roof gets wet whenever I hose mine.

But statement (3) is implausible. How is it, then, that two plausible premises can lead by what appears to be a deductive inference to an implausible conclusion? This is a paradox. But as Pearl observed (p. 2), the paradox disappears if (1) is restated in a defeasible form.

(1*) My neighbor's roof gets wet whenever mine does, except when it is covered with plastic, or when my roof is hosed, etc.

Recast in this defeasible form, (1) is seen as a generalization that is subject to exceptions. Pearl (2000, p. 1) drew the general conclusion that "most assertive causal expressions in natural language are subject to exceptions, and those exceptions may cause major difficulties if processed by standard rules of deterministic logic." If we treat causal generalizations such as (1) and causal conditionals such as (2) as defeasible rather than as universal generalizations, Pearl's paradox disappears. Treating causal arguments as abductive and moving from deductive *modus ponens* to defeasible *modus ponens* solves the problem.

But there is another option to be considered. Could causal reasoning be based on probability? When Hume overturned the older view of causation as a necessary connection, he moved to seeing the causal relation as probabilistic. Now it is time to take a third step and view causation as abductive in some instances. In science, these instances occur at the discovery stage of an investigation, where there is more than one hypothesis on what is the cause of a set of data. In law, there are competing explanations of the given facts, even if both sides agree on the facts. In both science and law, there is a network of facts and causal rules leading to a conclusion or to several possible conclusions. There is uncertainty about what is the cause, and there are various hypotheses. In some such cases, Bayesian methods can be extremely useful to compute the strength of the argumentation (Pearl, 2000). But in other cases, putting numbers onto a causal graph and then using Bayesian methods to calculate an outcome is not as useful as looking over the hypotheses and deciding which is most plausible. According to Pearl (2002, p. 1), in many instances causal relations are built up from causal generalizations that represent "everyday knowledge" such as the statement, "Symptoms do not cause disease." It is arbitrary, and not all that helpful, to assign precise statistical numbers to these kinds of generalizations. How, then, can causal argumentation be evaluated in such cases?

One way is to classify the arguments as abductive rather than inductive and to evaluate them dialectically. In so evaluating a causal argument in a given case, the first step is to judge whether the argument is at midstage in a dialogue or whether the closing stage has been reached. If it is judged that the closing stage has been reached, what needs to be done is to assess the whole network of argumentation and ascertain the weight of evidence on both sides. If the dialogue has not reached the closing stage, then the step is to identify the argumentation scheme. The method of evaluation in such a case is pragmatic and contextual. It is not well served by specifying a probability and then carrying out a Bayesian calculation. One reason is that it is not possible to prove that each single item of evidence is independent of the others. Another is that the assessment of plausibility is based on defeasible generalizations rather than statistical ones. The exceptions that may make the generalization default may not be predictable inductively. They may simply appear as the dialogue goes on and new evidence comes in.

On the other hand, probability judgments are involved in causal reasoning. In the argument from correlation to cause, for example, the premise is based on a statistical correlation. It is this correlation that is in fact the basis of the fallacy, making it seem natural, when the correlation is statistically strong, to jump to a causal conclusion. But when viewing the causal argument in the abductive and dialectical model, asking more questions before jumping to a causal conclusion is the stance to take. Before unconditionally accepting the causal conclusion, the dialectical move would be to ask one of the critical questions matching the argumentation scheme. In the dialectical analysis, the premise of the causal argument, if acceptable, shifts a weight of plausibility onto the conclusion as a hypothesis that explains the data, but is only one among competing hypotheses. This abductive analysis, of course, is most useful during the argumentation stage of a causal investigation, where the investigation is still open to new evidence. Once the dialogue ends, epistemic closure may apply, and the causal argument may even be seen as deductive. But in many intermediate cases, the causal argument may best be seen as inductive, and the Bayesian methods of Pearl (2000) will thus be very useful. On the other hand, Pearl (2002, p. 1) claims to be only "half-Bayesian." He has left room for the utility of causal argumentation based on defeasible generalizations that are everyday pragmatic assumptions rather than statistical generalizations.

The hypothesis supported by the examination in this chapter of how legal and scientific argumentation has been modeled in AI systems is that the causal reasoning is abductive in both instances. It is a plausibilistic kind of reasoning that typically takes the form of a chain of defeasible *modus ponens* inferences. It is not deductive or inductive for the most part, although deduction and induction are involved in the process through which evidence moves forward and is tested and confirmed. It has been shown that causal reasoning becomes much clearer and amenable to useful modeling when taken to be a species of inference to the best explanation. For example, suppose it is said that, in what is often thought to be the simplest sort of case, the cause of the black billiard ball's moving forward is the movement of the white billiard ball striking it. What is meant, in the analysis of this chapter, is that the best explanation of the movement of the black ball is to be found in its being struck by the white ball. The black ball's moving forward is the given datum. And the best explanation of the given datum is its being struck by the white ball. In this abductive analysis of causation, there is a close connection between causation and explanation. Hypotheses about causes drawn as conclusions by inference from observed data are formulated as explanations. In a given case, there will be many possible explanations of the given data, some of which are more plausible and better fit the data than others. The particular explanation selected as cause, or "best" explanation, is the one that best fits the data. In this analysis, causal conclusions are reached by a form of inference that is defeasible and nonmonotonic. A causal hypothesis is tentative, and said to be relatively plausible or not, comparable with other explanations. It is generally open to defeat, and therefore best regarded as defeasible, in legal argumentation and at the discovery stage of scientific argumentation. As new information comes into a case, the hypothesis that seemed the most plausible one may be replaced by another hypothesis that now becomes the most plausible one, given the expanded database. Hence causal reasoning, in this analysis, is nonmonotonic, meaning that it can support a different conclusion as the premises of the argument change.

The hypothesis that causal argumentation in law and science takes this defeasible form recalls the characteristics of abductive reasoning encountered in previous chapters. It especially takes us back to the analysis of the form of abductive inference given by Josephson and Josephson (1994, p. 14). In this form, called *abductive inference* in chapter 1, *H* is a variable that stands for a hypothesis, and *D* is a variable that stands for a given collection of data that can change over time. How should any given instance of abductive reasoning be evaluated as strong or weak? The conclusion to be inferred by abductive reasoning in a given case is the best explanation of the given data, relative to the given data in the case. Of course, what is or is not given data in a case can change. Therefore, an abductive inference results in a conclusion that is a plausible assumption, except in a case where the database may be regarded as closed (epistemic closure). It is typical of real cases of causal reasoning, however, that they occur in a situation of incomplete knowledge. Epistemic closure cannot realistically be assumed. On the contrary, it is often emphasized in writings on causation that causal reasoning should be epistemically open. Schauer (1988, p. 536) has shown how epistemic openness is characteristic of legal reasoning: "Legal systems often reject closedness because they must deal with a large array of problems presented by a complex and fluid world." But the same observation can also be applied to scientific reasoning in applied sciences such as medical diagnosis or engineering. Generally, one thing is said to cause another relative to a set of circumstances that can be assumed to represent all the relevant factors in the case, as far as is known. This *ceteris paribus* condition, often emphasized in connection with causal hypotheses, suggests that epistemic closure is generally not a realistic assumption. Causal reasoning is typically based on defeasible generalizations of the kind described in chapter 4.

CAUSAL EXPLANATIONS

In order to define causation, we need to have some account of the concept of a causal explanation. Causal explanation, following the general analysis of explanation in chapter 3, can be seen as dialectical in the sense of having a distinctive kind of purpose or function, as a special type of speech act in a goal-directed process of communication. The dialogue-based theory of chapter 2 postulated a framework in which two participants take part in a goal-directed communicative exchange. In this framework, the purpose of an explanation should be that one participant verbally transfers understanding to the other, thereby fulfilling a clarifying function of the communication. So conceived, a causal explanation begins with a question, typically a why question asking about the cause of an event.

Explanations are often based on an account of some matter that is in turn based on our capability to fill in links in a chain of causal or practical reasoning. This capability is based on scripts of the kind described in chapter 1 that allow us to fill in gaps in the chain. For example, consider the explanation offered in the following dialogue.

THE RADIATOR DIALOGUE
Questioner: Why are radiators usually located under windows, when windows are the greatest source of heat loss?
Respondent: The windows are the coldest part of the room, and that is why the radiators are placed underneath the windows. The air that comes in contact with the windows is cooled and falls to the floor. This creates a movement of air in which the cold air from the window is heated when it passes the radiator. But if the radiator were placed at an inside wall, then the warmest part, toward the inside, would stay warmer, and the coldest part of the room, where the windows are, would stay colder. This placement would not be a comfortable arrangement for habitation of the room. Therefore, the radiators are normally placed beneath the windows in a room.

Here the question is based on two factual assumptions. One is that the radiators are usually located under the windows in a room. The other is that the windows are the greatest source of heat loss. The question poses a puzzle, a sort of oddity that calls for an explanation. Why? The answer is that if the windows are the greatest source of heat loss, presumably the heat gained from the radiators would be lost by its proximity to the windows, a location that is cool, without heating the interior of the room. The puzzle is that the usual placement of the radiators under windows does not appear to be practical because it is presumed that, normally, our purpose in constructing a house is to minimize unnecessary heat loss. Locating the radiator under the window would appear to defeat this purpose.

The explanation offered by the respondent solves the puzzle. The radiators are normally placed under the windows, the respondent explains, because the movement of air in this arrangement is comfortable for the inhabitants of the room. The movement of air, as the cold air falls from the window and hits the warm radiator, mixes the air, keeping it at a uniform temperature. If the radiator were on an inner wall, the difference between the warm part of the room, where the radiator is, and the cold part, where the window is, would be uncomfortable. A goal is comfort. Normally, a design for heating a room would try to avoid a situation where the person living in that room would be uncomfortable because of a persistent difference in temperature between two parts of the room.

The problem of abduction is to see how one gets from the given facts in a case to a best explanation. Of course, part of the process is one of choosing between explanations to pick the best one. But how are the explanations generated from the facts in the first place? The radiator dialogue offers some insight into how this process works. A set of given facts is placed into a sequence of causal reasoning with some implicit assumptions and some generalizations or conditionals of a defeasible kind. The network of causal reasoning in such a case can be formalized in a diagram that looks somewhat like an argument diagram. For example, figure 5.4 represents the sequence of causal reasoning in the radiators explanation. The radiators explanation is all about how things are normally done, subject to exceptions. It is about generalizations on how things normally happen in a room, such as warm air rising and cool air falling, subject to exceptions. It is about what is generally comfortable or uncomfortable in heating arrangements. Thus all the statements that appear in the boxes above the bottom one can be classified as plausible assumptions. Connected together in the sequence indicated by the arrows, they exhibit a chain of plausible causal reasoning. When all are put together, the whole package does a nice job of offering a plausible explanation of why the radiators are normally placed under the windows in a room.

What we see in this case is a forward-backward pattern that is also characteristic of abductive reasoning as a process of inference to the best explanation. For example, we see what look like bear tracks in the soil. The best explanation is that a bear was there, and that is the conclusion drawn from the data by abductive reasoning. But looking at the reasoning in reverse, we see that the bear's being there presumably caused the prints. It is this causal inference that underlies the argument from sign. Similarly, in the radiators case, the explanation, as expressed in the statement in the bottom box of figure 5.4, is successful because of the chain of causal reasoning (with its incorporated segment of practical reasoning) indicated in the diagram.

The problem posed is how to grasp the relationship between the forward and backward chains of reasoning in such a case. Somehow all the parts of the causal sequence above the bottom box fit together in a coherent account. When you put the whole account together and fill in the missing bits, you understand why the radiators are normally placed under the windows in a room. The account yields understanding because

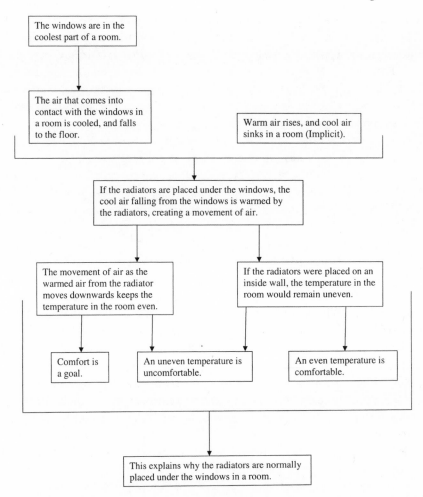

Figure 5.4 Reconstructed sequence of reasoning in the radiators explanation.

all of the parts make sense, the causal steps of inference between make sense, and thus the whole account makes sense as an explanation.

THE CHAIN OF REASONING IN THE ACCIDENT CASE

One thing that was especially interesting about the analysis of the accident case of Prakken and Renooij (2001) is how the abductive system for resolving the dispute is based on a set of rules that have an if-then or conditional form. The twelve rules each postulate a possible cause as the antecedent and the possible effect or outcome as the consequent. Thus it seems like the reasoning goes from the cause to the effect in a *modus ponens* type of inference. Or does it? Some would say that the reasoning in such a case goes backward, from the effect to the likely cause. For example, rule 2 is applied by inferring from the given fact of the tire marks being present to the hypothesis of skidding. So here is a theoretical problem brought out graphically by this type of case. What form does the abductive-causal reasoning in it take? Is it a *modus ponens* type of reasoning that goes from antecedent to consequent of a conditional? Or is it a reverse type of *modus ponens* reasoning that goes from the consequent to the antecedent? This question appears to be highly controversial, yet it is basic to understanding the nature of abductive inference.

The two theories or general approaches to reconstructing the logical form of the argumentation used in abductive reasoning can be stated more precisely as follows. One is the *modus ponens* approach, which sees any case of abductive inference as having the form, "If *A* then *B*; *A*; therefore *B*." The opposed approach sees an abductive inference that goes in a backward *modus ponens* pattern. According to this theory, the *B* is the given fact used to explain the *A*. In this theory, the form of an abductive inference should be represented as "If *A* then *B*; *B*; therefore *A*." Prakken and Renooij (2001, p. 137) claim that their reconstruction of the accident case follows the *modus ponens* approach, which, they write, is "very usual in nonmonotonic logic." Thus a good place to begin to resolve, or at least cast some light on, this issue is with Prakken and Renooij's reconstruction of this case. Does it really fit the *modus ponens* theory, or does it better fit the backward *modus ponens* theory? As we will see, this question poses a somewhat thorny issue.

The issue is raised by Prakken and Renooij (p. 138) by the following question. Should causal knowledge be represented by forward (causal) rules of the form "cause ⇒ effect" or by backward (evidential) rules of the form "effect ⇒ cause"? The analysis of the argumentation in the accident case showed that both types of rules are needed. Evidential rules are needed because it is necessary to use explanations to derive causes from effects. For example, we needed to look at the given fact of the pulled handbrake as an effect and to apply a backward rule to explain it by the hypothesized cause that the passenger pulled the handbrake. But we also needed causal rules to make predictions by deriving effects from causes. For example, we must be able to predict by means of a forward rule that the wheels will be locked from the assumption that the passenger pulled the handbrake. Hastings (1963, pp. 65–77) made this point very simply when he distinguished between two causal argumentation schemes. One he called reasoning from cause to effect. The other he called reasoning from effect to cause. The first of these was associated with prediction by Hastings, as noted in chapter 4. It represents the kind of argument in which a prediction of some outcome is attempted, based on the causes that are supposedly present in a case and will likely produce that outcome. The second argumentation scheme corresponds to what is now called abductive reasoning. It represents the kind of reasoning that proceeds backward from some given data to a hypothesis concerning the factors that are held to be the causal antecedents explaining how these data came to be.

Prakken and Renooij (2001) pointed out that there are two ways of reconstructing the causal reasoning in the accident case. The first, called the abductive-logical analysis (p. 140), is represented by the reconstruction outlined above. This way based the outcome of the reasoning in the case on the twelve causal rules used to derive conclusions by a series of explanations from the given six facts of the case. The abductive-logical reconstruction was based on the causal structure of the accident case represented in the sequence of connected explanations in figure 5.1. In this model, we reason backward from the known facts through a series of explanations to a set of hypotheses. The second way is called the argument-based analysis. In this reconstruction, we move forward from the various facts, from one conclusion to the next, in a series of argument-steps. With the use of this model, the arguments on both sides can be summed as follows (Prakken and Renooij, 2001, p. 139).

THE PASSENGER'S ARGUMENT
accident + ~obstacles

---

speeding in curve

---

loss of control + speeding in curve

---

driver caused accident

THE DRIVER'S ARGUMENT
handbrake is in pulled position + driver said "passenger pulled handbrake"

---

passenger pulled handbrake

---

wheels locked

---

skidding

---

accident + passenger pulled handbrake

---

passenger caused accident

Prakken and Renooij (2001, p. 140) commented that it is difficult to choose between these two ways of formalizing the argumentation in the accident case and that a decision should not rest on any single case. They added, however, that the argument-based model "seems closer to the text of the decision" made by the judge in the case and is therefore more natural. The abductive-logical model, they believed, is "deeper" as opposed to the more "shallow" argument-based model. Perhaps both models can be useful, depending on the interests of the analyst of the case. It would also seem that the one model is structurally equivalent to the other in several senses. Both models use the same set of facts and rules. Both are dialogue models based on explanation, hypothesis, and abductive inference. Both will come to the same outcome in any given case, provided they start with the same set of facts and rules.

If we examine the passenger's argument and the driver's argument once again, we can see that they have the basic structures exhibited by Prakken and Renooij's analyses of them. But further examination will show that they also have a deeper structure. This deeper structure is revealed once some missing implicit premises are stated. In particular, inserting implicit defeasible conditionals can help us to understand the structure of the argumentation.

The passenger's argument, as analyzed by Prakken and Renooij, contains two subarguments. The first has two explicit premises. The first premise is that in the accident, the car ran off the road (A). The second premise is that there were no obstacles that the driver had to steer around ($\sim O$). An implicit premise also plays a role in the argument: there was a curve in the road just before the place where the car went off the road (C). An implicit conditional can also be formulated as follows: if the car ran off the road, and there were no obstacles the driver had to steer around, and there was a curve in the road just before the place where the car went off the road, then it is plausible to assume that the car was speeding in the curve. When all four of these premises are grouped they lead to the conclusion that the car was speeding in the curve (*S*). Thus the first subargument of the passenger's argument has the following structure.

First Premise: A
Second Premise: ~O
Third Premise: C
Conditional Premise: If *A* & ~*O* & *C* then *S*
Conclusion: S

The form of the argument is that of defeasible *modus ponens*. On the assumption that all four premises are true, it is plausible that the conclusion is true.

The first subargument then links to the second subargument stated by Prakken and Renooij. Let us assume that the conclusion of the first subargument is right and that the car was speeding in the curve (*S*). If that is right and if, as supposed in the first subargument, the car ran off the road in the accident (*R*), then it is reasonable to assume that the driver lost control of the car (*L*). Given this whole package of assumptions, it follows that the driver caused the accident (*D*). Thus the second subargument has the following form.

First Premise: S
Second Premise: R
Third Premise: If *S* & *R* then *L*
Fourth Premise: If *L* then *D*
Conclusion: D

The reasoning in this argument is based on two defeasible *modus ponens* arguments. The first has the following form.

First Premise: S
Second Premise: R
Third Premise: If *S* & *R* then *L*
Conclusion: L

The second defeasible *modus ponens* inference is the one below.

First Premise: L
Second Premise: If L then D
Conclusion: D

These last two *modus ponens* arguments can be connected together in a chain linked by the common element L, which functioned as the conclusion of the first argument and then as a premise in the second. This chain of reasoning forms the second argument, which is then linked to the first subargument. The whole chain of reasoning culminating in the ultimate conclusion D makes up the passenger's argument.

The driver's argument also has two subarguments. The first subargument is based on two premises. One is that the handbrake was in the pulled position (P). The other is that the driver said the passenger pulled the handbrake (H). The following statement is an implicit conditional: if the handbrake was in the pulled position and the driver said it was, then it is plausible that (T) the passenger pulled the handbrake. Because the statements in the antecedent of the conditional are supposedly true, based on the facts of the case, the consequent may be drawn as a plausible conclusion, based on defeasible *modus ponens.*

First Premise: P
Second Premise: H
Third Premise: If P & H then T
Conclusion: T

But once this conclusion has been drawn, it sets up a chain of causal reasoning. If it is true that the passenger pulled the handbrake, then that would cause the wheels to lock. But if the wheels were locked, that would cause the car to skid. The car's skidding was the cause of the accident. Putting the two subarguments together, we get to the conclusion that the passenger's pulling of the handbrake caused the accident. Thus the argumentation has chained forward, from the causes supposed to have been at work to a conclusion about the cause of the accident as a whole. The ultimate conclusion of this chain of reasoning is that the passenger caused the accident.

The passenger's argument takes the form of a chain of reasoning that can be represented by an argument diagram as shown in figure 5.5. The driver's argument takes the form of a different chain of reasoning, which can be represented by an argument diagram (see figure 5.6) in which letters are assigned to statements as follows.

W = The wheels lock.
K = The car skids.
B = The passenger caused the accident.

Each diagram represents a chain of reasoning that moves forward to an ultimate conclusion that makes a claim about what caused the accident. Viewed in this way, they are typical argument diagrams that depict a set of premises leading to a conclusion by way of a chain of reasoning. But you can also view each diagram in a different way. You can see each diagram as a chain of backward reasoning proceeding from a posterior event or alleged fact to some prior set of events or alleged facts that best explain the posterior one. The same observation is true of the diagram representing the causal structure of the accident case (figure 5.1). It represents a forward chaining of reasoning that goes at each link of the chain from cause to effect. But from an abductive point of view, you can also look at it as a chain of reasoning that goes backward from a given event or alleged fact to some prior set of events or alleged facts that supposedly explains how the given event or alleged fact came about.

The forward chain of reasoning in such an argument diagram can be represented as a chaining of several defeasible *modus ponens* arguments that leads to some ultimate conclusion. The same diagram can also be used in another way. It can be taken to represent a series of steps backward from a given event or alleged fact to a prior set of events or alleged facts that explain it. Or at any rate, the claim made is that the event cited is explained by the other events that supposedly preceded it.

INSIGHTS INTO CAUSAL ARGUMENTATION YIELDED BY THE ABDUCTIVE THEORY

One of the major problems with the analysis of the accident case is how to understand the causal rules Prakken and Renooij cited in their analysis. Let us consider some of these rules once again.

Rule 1: *skidding* ⇒ *accident*
Rule 2: *skidding* ⇒ *tire marks present*
Rule 3: *obstacles* ⇒ *skidding*
Rule 4: *loss of control* ⇒ *skidding*

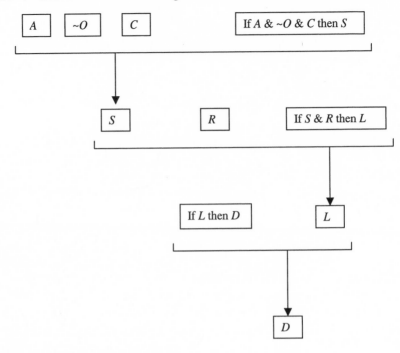

Figure 5.5 The passenger's argument.

Rule 5: *wheels locked* ⇒ *skidding*
Rule 6: *speeding in curve* ⇒ *loss of control*

According to Prakken and Renooij (2001, p. 134), these rules are made up of so-called literals such as *skidding* and *accident*. The causal rules made up of the literals and the causal arrow can be chained so that an outcome of a cause can itself be a cause of a new outcome. But what else do we know about the relation symbolized by the causal arrow? For example, what properties do arguments made up from this relation have? To examine this question, let us associate each literal with a proposition that describes the occurrence of the event cited by the literal in a case. For example, the literal *skidding* is associated with the proposition, "There is skidding in this case." And the literal *accident* is associated with the proposition, "There is (or was) an accident (meaning a car accident) in this case." What then does rule 1, for example, say? It says that skidding causes accidents generally, we may assume. But it does not say that every case where there is skidding is a case where there is an acci-

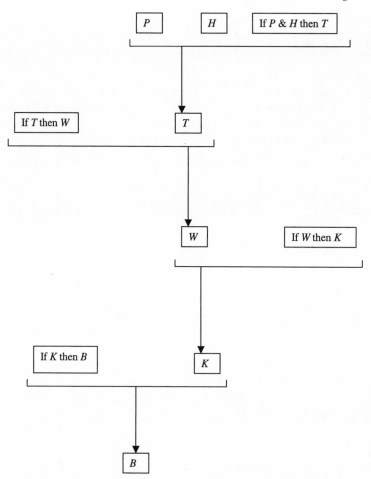

Figure 5.6 The driver's argument.

dent. It seems to say that skidding is a causal factor in accidents. In such an interpretation, it seems to say that if you have skidding in a case, along with a number of other factors, such as enough speed, then the skidding, along with these other factors, is sufficient for the occurrence of an accident. But what does "sufficient" mean here? It does not mean logically sufficient. It seems to refer to some defeasible notion of sufficiency.

Consider this form of argument as an example. In this form of argument, we have transposed the ⇒ relation so that it applies to propositions of the kind that contain literals.

THE CAUSAL MP ARGUMENT
$A \Rightarrow B$
A
Therefore B

The following argument is an instance of the causal MP argument.

THE SKIDDING ARGUMENT
If there is skidding in a given case, then there is an accident in that case.
There is (was) skidding in this case.
Therefore there is (was) an accident in this case.

The skidding argument shows that the causal MP form of argument is not deductively valid. It is logically possible for the premises to be true and the conclusion false, assuming we take the conditional premise not to imply that every case of skidding is a case where there is (or was) an accident. A better way to interpret the skidding argument, a species of argument from cause to effect in Hastings's terminology, is as a DMP type of argument. The first premise says that, generally, if there is skidding in a case of a car accident of the kind being considered, the skidding, along with such associated factors as traveling at a good rate of speed or traveling on a curved road, is a defeasibly sufficient condition for there being an accident in the case. This means that skidding is one factor that, combined with other factors in a case, could plausibly cause an accident.

The thesis that argument from cause to effect has a *modus ponens* form that is different from deductive *modus ponens* was stated quite explicitly in Walton (1995, p. 141): "Argument from cause to effect has the form of *modus ponens* except that the conditional in the major premise is presumptive, instead of being strict: the presumptive conditional is open to qualifications and exceptions as applied to a particular case." This statement is quite radical. It suggests that argument from cause to effect has a *modus ponens* form but is not a deductively valid type of argument. Nobody noticed this radical suggestion, it appears, because it was not challenged or questioned in any reviews or commentaries on the book as far as I am aware.

The theory that causal reasoning can be analyzed as abductive throws new light on various important species of causal argumentation. It is especially useful in relation to the study of such causal fallacies as the *post hoc* fallacy. One form of argumentation where *post hoc* is a special danger is argument from sign. As shown in chapter 4, argument from sign is especially common in medical diagnosis. A familiar and common nonmedical example is the kind of case where someone sees a certain kind of track on a trail and identifies it as a grizzly bear track. Using argumentation from sign, the tracker can conclude that a grizzly bear passed along the trail. Argument from sign can easily be seen as a species of inference to the best explanation. The best explanation of the given datum (the track mark) is the hypothesis that a bear passed along the trail. Of course, there could be other explanations. Someone could have made the mark by impressing an imprint on it to deceive anyone who came later on the trail. But in the absence of such a plausible explanation, it would be reasonable to infer, by default, that the best explanation is that a grizzly bear passed along the trail. Thus argumentation from sign, in this kind of case, is a defeasible and nonmonotonic kind of reasoning.

It is also not difficult to see how argument from sign is based on causal reasoning. Presumably what licenses the inference to the conclusion that a bear passed along the trail is the following explanation. Because the imprint matches the familiar track of the grizzly bear, it can be reasonably (but defeasibly) inferred that this imprint was caused by a grizzly bear walking along the trail. Normally (barring evidence indicating other plausible explanations), one would infer, in a context where the imprints were found on a trail that grizzly bears are known to use, that these tracks were caused by a grizzly bear. The sequence is not difficult to work out. Grizzly bears are heavy, and if the ground is soft enough, they will normally leave a certain characteristic type of track, with big pads and long claw marks, that can be identified by someone familiar with bear signs. In other words, the whole process of argumentation from sign in such a case works because it is based on a pattern of reasoning backward from effect to cause. This pattern of reasoning is a common argumentation scheme. We often reason backward from a given sign as datum to the cause that supposedly produced that effect in the given case. What is shown is that there are two distinctive types of causal reasoning that are used differently in different cases. In forward causal reasoning and in making predictions we reason from the cause to the effect. This form of causal reasoning underlies the familiar form of argument known as argumentation from consequences. But as shown above, another kind of causal reasoning is also commonly used— backward causal reasoning from effect to postulated cause. This type of causal reasoning is closely associated with argumentation from sign and is very nicely analyzed as a species of abductive inference, or inference to the best explanation.

Yet another important implication of the abductive theory of causal reasoning concerns the traditional *post hoc* fallacy. As noted above, the form of argument on which this fallacy is based is called argument from correlation to cause.

There is a positive correlation between A and B.
Therefore A causes B.

The general problem for analyzing the *post hoc* fallacy, as noted above, is that this form of inference is, in many cases, not unreasonable. In fact, causal hypotheses are typically based on positive correlations, and there seems to be nothing wrong (in principle) with that. A question then arises: how do such inferences go wrong, or become fallacious? In working out an answer to this question, the abductive theory of causal reasoning is extremely useful. The abductive theory can show that causal reasoning is dynamic, defeasible, and nonmonotonic and can become stronger (or become weaker, or even be refuted) as new evidence enters into a case. Thus the abductive theory can support the view that reasoning from correlation to causation can be evaluated in a range of ways, depending on the evidence in the case. In some cases it can be a very weak form of argumentation—simply a conjecture or guess. Even so, it could be not altogether worthless or fallacious as an inference. In other cases, the argument from correlation to cause could be stronger. In still other cases, it could be very strong and even backed up by a theoretical link of explanation between cause and effect. The argument could also be fallacious because available evidence leading to a different conclusion is overlooked or ignored. According to the abductive theory, all these possibilities can be accommodated without falling into the simplistic approach that would require argument from correlation to cause to be always fallacious or always reasonable.

In *post hoc* reasoning a causal generalization is the conclusion of the inference. The abductive theory works well in such cases provided it is made clear that causal generalizations are (generally) defeasible and have a *ceteris paribus* clause built in. Causation has been such a problem for philosophers because they see generalizations as "all" statements of the absolute kind modeled by the universal quantifier of deductive logic. But typically, causal generalizations of the kind featured as conclusions of *post hoc* inferences are not absolute generalizations. They are generalizations supported or argued against by statistical findings, for example in drug trials or experiments. Even so, it is best to see such generalizations, in many instances, as abductive rather than inductive. They are abductive when they are rough guesses or hypotheses at the discovery stage of a scientific investigation. As the investigation goes on, and more evidence is collected and assessed, the *post hoc* argument can become inductive. If the investigation ever reaches the stage where a theoretical connection between the two events is established at a level of generality appropriate for a science, the *post hoc* argument could even assume a deductive form. Such a form, however, would be based on an assumption of epistemic closure. This assumption can be made at the level of abstraction appropriate for a scientific theory. But in any real case, it would be one that is inherently questionable.

The abductive theory works best when applied to particular cases where the outcome has actually occurred because, when it comes to predictions, we never really know whether a set of conditions is sufficient. For example, if I strike the white billiard ball and it moves toward the black one, we can never be sure in advance that the white ball will actually hit the black one and move it. But once the event of the white ball hitting the black ball has happened, we can then confidently say, with hindsight, that the movement of the white ball caused the movement of the black one. We can say that the one occurrence was a sufficient condition for the other. We do not mean "sufficient" here in a sense of expressing logical necessity. We just mean that, because the second event actually happened, the set of conditions that were there, such as the table being flat, the white ball moving, and so forth, were evidently sufficient for the occurrence of the second event. Before Hume, the conventional wisdom in philosophy was that causation is a logically necessary relation. Hume argued convincingly that this view of causality does not accord with everyday experience. His being right is often taken to be strong evidence for the hypothesis that causal reasoning is inductive. The analysis of cases in chapter 5, however, better supports the hypothesis that it is abductive. At any rate, the abductive model of causation presented in chapter 5 has been shown to apply exceptionally well to singular instances of causal inference in cases of real or allegedly real events, such as those so commonly found in law and history.

The argumentation schemes for abductive inference are based on a defeasible conditional of the form $A \Rightarrow B$ that is different from the material conditional of the form $A \supset B$ in deductive logic. Evaluating a statement or argument containing only simple statements or statements containing material conditionals is possible using a context-free procedure. The truth or falsity of the whole conditional, or the validity of the argument, is merely a function of the truth-values of the component statements. The truth-value of the whole conditional can be calculated from the truth-values of the components by an algorithm that is independent of the context of use of the conditional. Evaluating a statement or argument containing one or more defeasible conditionals is not possible using a context-free procedure. The truth or falsity of the whole conditional, or the structural strength of the argument, is not merely a function of the truth-values of the component statements. The simple statements and the conditionals in an argument of this sort can be assigned a weight of plausibility, often called a confidence value in AI. There are various ways of calculating the plausibility of an argument, say one of the defeasible *modus ponens* form, from the confidence values of its component statements. One of these is the least plausible premise rule: the plausibility value assigned to the conclusion must be at least as high as that of the argument's least plausible premise. But none of these rules for calculating confidence values is all that useful for the general run of defeasible arguments. A better method has been called the argumentation approach, as opposed to a Bayesian approach, which bases evaluation on numerical calculations such as the probability calculus (Fox and Das, 2000). The argumentation method is to collect all the arguments on both sides of a case, to get a holistic evaluation that the mass of arguments provides as the strongest evidence, and then to make a decision for one side or the other based on the burden of proof appropriate for the type of dialogue.

The notion of argument chaining is fundamental to both the forward and the backward argumentation schemes for abductive inference. In the cases of abductive reasoning that have been studied, such as the accident case, the abductive argumentation on each side can only be evaluated once it has been displayed as a connected chain of reasoning representing the mass of evidence on that side of the case.

Whether you choose to use the argument diagram or the search graph of the kind used in heuristics, the structure nicely represents the chaining forward and chaining backward of a sequence of reasoning. Thus both techniques are useful for representing a chain of abductive reasoning such as that in the accident case. But notice that in the accident case, and comparable cases where abductive argumentation has been used, there is an argument diagram on both sides of the case. This phenomenon suggests that the argument diagram method, or any comparable method of representing the chaining of the reasoning, is inherently limited. It is very clear from the analysis of the logical form of abductive inference given by the Josephsons (the J&J model of chapter 1) that pragmatic considerations are involved.

6

Query–Driven Abductive Reasoning

Chapter 6 analyzes abduction as a query-driven form of inference to the best explanation in which the conversational context of an abductive chain of reasoning must be considered. According to this theory, the structural correctness of an abductive inference depends on the transfer of understanding from one party to another in a dialogue. The best explanation is one that increases the understanding of a questioner as that individual moves forward through a search process. Of course, what increases understanding depends on the nature of the investigation. An explanation that produces better understanding in a court of law may not produce it in a scientific investigation and vice versa. A pair of argumentation schemes for abductive argumentation is presented in a dialogue format. An abductive argument that is put forward by a proponent and meets the requirements for the scheme is to be evaluated in a given case with respect to how a respondent's critical questions are answered in a dialogue. The aspects that need to be judged at this level are how the argumentation is contributing to the dialogue and whether the chain of reasoning is aiming at the ultimate conclusion to be proved.

ARGUMENT EXTRAPOLATION BY CHAINING FORWARD

The analysis of cases so far has shown that evaluating abductive reasoning is a matter of judging where an argument plausibly seems to be going in relation to a given set of facts to be explained in a case. The presumed framework is one of an argument going forward aiming at proving or discovering something in a given case. The method of argument diagramming, as Schum (2001, p. 181) recognized, can be used as a model of this forward chaining of argumentation. As Schum noted

(p. 181), Wigmore was at least sixty years ahead of his time as an exponent of argument diagramming by virtue of his use of the chart method as applied to legal evidence: "As Wigmore realized, the construction of an inference network is an exercise in imaginative reasoning." Schum recognized that abductive reasoning is a matter of "how one might construct different plausible chains of reasoning" from evidence given in a case. The argument diagram begins with a particular case in which the argumentation is given as a product, so to speak. There is a given text of discourse in which some argument, or perhaps an explanation, has been put forward. The task is to state the premises and conclusions in the chain of argumentation, filling in the inferential steps joining them, along with missing statements needed to make sense of the argumentation, and build up an argument diagram. The problem, however, is that abduction is an imaginative process related to discovery. Thus to analyze cases of abductive reasoning, we need to go beyond the notion of argument as a product and view the argument as a process.

The analysis of relevance in argumentation put forward in Walton (2004) is based on argument diagramming but assumes that the diagram of the argument as a product may be incomplete in a certain way. It might show us very well how the argument has reached a particular conclusion, but it may not show where that same argument seems to be going, as aimed toward some ultimate conclusion in a case. In some cases, however, it may be known that such an ultimate conclusion (thesis to be proved) exists in a given case. This thesis to be proved can provide an aiming point that indicates a direction for the chaining forward of the argumentation past the point of the evidence modeled by the argument diagram. Thus it might be possible to adopt a broader perspective by judging argumentation as a process moving in a direction toward proving some ultimate thesis or moving away from that direction. This perspective is the one needed to make judgments of relevance of argumentation and thereby to evaluate cases in which it is suspected that a fallacy of irrelevance may have been committed. Argumentation is relevant, in this sense, if it is on track in leading toward the ultimate conclusion that is to be proved. It can be judged to be irrelevant if it is going off track and perhaps leading toward some conclusion different from the one to be proved. The notion of relevance described here is dialectical in that it presumes that argumentation in a given case is part of some dialogue between a proponent and a respondent. The proponent has a designated proposition called the thesis, and the goal is to prove it by putting forward a chain of argumentation leading to it. The respondent either has an opposed thesis or has the job of casting doubt on the proponent's attempts to prove his or her thesis.

The method used to determine dialectical relevance of the kind described above is called *argument extrapolation* in Walton (2004). The method works by examining the argumentation in a given case and judging whether it aims toward the thesis to be proved or, if not, whether it might aim somewhere other than the thesis to be proved. To arrive at such a determination on the basis of evidence, the evaluator must attempt to extrapolate the given chain of argumentation even further forward to get an indication of where it is leading. The place to begin is to construct an argument diagram of the argument as product, based on the text of discourse actually given in the case. The diagram can be used as a basis for forward extrapolation. To carry out such an extrapolation, one needs to examine the chaining of argumentation shown in the diagram and attempt to extrapolate forward to see if its plausible chains of reasoning can be moved even further forward. In the case of a relevance determination, one looks to see whether the chain aims at the ultimate conclusion to be proved by the argumentation in the case. In some cases of analyzing abductive reasoning, such as those of scientific discovery, one does not know where the chain of argumentation is aiming. In other cases, such as those of legal evidence, one may know this, as illustrated by the broken knife case discussed in chapter 4. Here the problem is getting from the given facts of the case along a chain of argumentation that leads to the ultimate *probandum* of the argumentation in the case.

Some recent work in computing has tried to answer the question of how to provide an infrastructure for Web explanations by mapping an explanation onto an inference structure that traces how a conclusion was proved from data. This research takes proofs or proof fragments and rewrites them into abstract structures that can be used to provide the foundations for what is presented to a user who asks for an explanation. McGuinness and da Silva (2003) have taken on the technical task of reconstructing an explanation in a given case by viewing it as a transformation of a proof trace. In other words, they have taken an inference engine, which can represent a chain of inferences as a set of inference steps chained together by inference rules, and applied this to the explanation. This yielded what they called an inference web proof, in effect a forward chaining of a sequence of steps of inference. They then used this inference structure to generate follow-up questions in a dialogue sequence representing an explanation. This line of research is very promising in representing a technical development compatible with the dialogue theory of explanation. The main reason is that it reconstructs an explanation as a query-driven sequence of reasoning that is mapped onto a forward chaining of argumentation representing a proof or attempted proof of some conclusion. This technology relies on the notion of an explanation having the structure of a set of statements connected by inference steps and rules that link the steps into an account. This approach sees explanation as based on a prior justification attempt represented by a chain of reasoning. Thus it represents a technology that connects the structure of an argument, of the kind that could be represented in an argument diagram for example, with the structure of an explanation.

COLLIGATION IN CHAINING BACKWARD

The process whereby a conclusion is derived by argumentation schemes chaining forward from the given facts of the case to an ultimate conclusion is fairly clear. Unstated premises and conclusions, often generalizations or conditionals of a defeasible sort, need to be filled in, and then the whole sequence of argumentation can be modeled using an argument diagram. The full text figure of the broken knife case (figure 4.2) presents a simple example of how such a process works. The diagram exhibits the structure of the argument that chains forward from the given facts and other premises to the ultimate conclusion that is proved (or plausibly supported by the evidence). It would appear from many remarks in the literature on abduction considered so far that abduction is a process of inference to the best explanation that is the reverse of this argumentation process. Instead of reasoning by chaining inferences forward in a series of DMP steps, as figure 4.2 displays, abduction reasons backward from the given facts to the best explanation of those facts. The one process, it is supposed, is the reverse of the other. But is this reversal hypothesis really a good account of how abduction works? To test it, let us look back at the broken knife case and review figure 4.2.

Three facts were given in the broken knife case.

(A) It was determined that the window was forced open by a knife.

(B) Fragments of the blade of a knife were found in the window.

(C) The fragments of the blade found in the window were found to match the knife found in the possession of the accused.

To grasp how abduction works in such a case, you have to consider the context as well. First, we know that the case is one where a burglary was committed. We know that the aim of investigating the case (by the police and possibly later by a court) is that of trying to determine who committed the burglary. Third, it is assumed that no other relevant facts of the case are known at the time the broken knife is being considered. Given this context of the case, how then is the best explanation generated from the facts?

The process has been called marshaling of evidence by Schum (2001). As Schum (2001a, p. 1678) pointed out, Peirce used the term "colligation," with reference to abduction, to refer to the "binding together of ideas that, in combination give rise to new ideas" in scientific discovery. In light of the dialogue theory of explanation presented in chapter 2, an analysis of the process can be offered as follows. First, a question is being asked in the case. The question is, "Who committed the burglary?" Along the way toward answering this question, another question is prompted: "How was the burglary committed?" We know quite a bit about the answer to this question and can give an account of how the burglary was committed. The burglar gained entry through a window by forcing it open with a knife. This tells us quite a bit, because we are familiar with actions of this sort. We understand how the knife would be forced into the crack between the window and its frame. Thus fact *A*, along with the script representing our commonsense knowledge about actions, represents an account of how the burglary was carried out or that part of it that concerns entry into the house. But what happens when fact *B* is added to the set of things to be explained? The account is expanded through a process of colligation. Because we are familiar with how a knife would be used to force open a locked window, we understand very well how fragments of the blade might be left in the window. We now have an account of how the actions in the burglary fit together based on routines of the kind with which we are generally familiar. We may never have actually used a knife to force open a window, but we have a pretty good idea of how it would work. We understand this sort of action because we are familiar with it in our daily activities; we often use knives when we have to pry something open. The colligation of *A* and *B* has given rise to a new, expanded account of what happened. Inferences can be drawn from this expanded account. The next step in the process of colligation is to add the third fact C and move on to asking the question, "Who committed the burglary?" The fact of the accused person having been found in possession of a knife matching the fragment of the blade found in the window presents a plausible answer. The fragments must have come from this knife. But how could that have happened? The best explanation that immediately offers itself is that this was the knife used to force the window open. The accused person is thus linked to the means used to carry out the burglary. Practical reasoning is used to draw inferences from the account that has been bound together at this point in the process of colligation. The explanation of all these facts is colligated in an account comprising all of them in which the accused person used this knife to open the window, gain entry to the house, and thereby commit the burglary. The explanation as a whole of what presumably took place offers understanding to an investigator by colligating a series of more and more complex accounts. The inference engine is a sequence of practical reasoning made up of actions with which the investigator, or any human agent for that matter, is familiar.

At each step in this process, a successful explanation can be given only if the person who asked the question understands the new account that has been given once the new account is marshaled together. The new information has to fit together not only with all the information given in the account at that point but also with whatever else the questioner already understands. How do we know what the questioner already understands? We have to look at the previous dialogue between the questioner and the respondent, and we have to consider what the respondent can reasonably be expected to understand, given the context of the dialogue. In a scientific investigation, for example, it could be presumed that participants accept and understand the basic facts and principles of the scientific field in which the discussion is taking place. In a legal case of a criminal investigation, such as the broken knife case, it can be presumed that the investigators, and those who use its results to carry the case forward to trial, understand the normal routines of prying open some closed object, such as a window, with a sharp object, such as a knife. What sort of explanation is successful, and how the marshaling of evidence proceeds at each stage of the process of colligation, depends on the context of dialogue and on what the questioner and the respondent both accept and understand as basic facts and principles.

Once we look at this process carefully, in light of the analysis of explanation offered in chapter 2, we see that it is based on a sequence of reasoning going from a set of facts to the best explanation. But the sequence of reasoning is not exactly the reverse of the sequence of argumentation displayed in the *Araucaria* diagram of the broken knife case. It is not a chain of backward *modus ponens* inferences leading from the facts *A, B,* and *C* to the ultimate *probandum* of the case. As Prakken and Renooij (2001, p.140) observed, abductive reasoning is a deeper process that seems closer to the text of discourse of a case. From a legal and logical viewpoint, it may appear to be a less natural process than forming a chain of argumentation from premises to a conclusion. The process of abduction is one in which facts are given and some question is posed in relation to these facts and in relation to a context of dialogue. The context, for example, may take the form of an investigation in which there is a questioner and in which answers to questions are derived from the facts found so far. There are normally a series of such questions asked in an orderly dialogue. A typical question in such a dialogue asks for an explanation. In the dialogue theory of explanation, it asks for the respondent to help the questioner to understand something in light of the given facts of a case with which both are, at least to some extent, already familiar.

Notice, however, that this dialogue generally takes the form of a process that is roughly the reverse of the forward chaining of argumentation in a case. In the broken knife case, it is taken as factual that (A) the window was forced open by a knife and that (B) fragments of the blade were found in the window. These two facts, taken together, can be explained by offering an account of the connection between them, namely (I): the fragments of the blade found in the window came from the knife used to force the window open. It would not be right, however, to say that *I* comes from *A* and *B* through a reverse *modus ponens* inference in which the defeasible conditional *D* is added as a missing premise. That is not how the process works. Instead, it works because an account of *A* and *B* can be colligated by virtue of our understanding of the familiar action of forcing a window open with an implement such as a knife. Parts of the blade are fragile, and we know very well from common experience that they could fragment when pressure is applied on the blade in an action such as forcing a window open. We understand all this very well, and the account forms a script of the kind described in the theory of explanation in chapter 2. It hangs together nicely and generates an explanation that is highly plausible. This is not a reverse *modus ponens* inference. But it is a process of colligation in which facts are explained by offering a series of accounts, each of which can be well understood by anyone familiar with such common actions as using knives and prying objects open. One idea, in Peirce's terms, gives rise to new ideas through the binding together of the ideas in a sequence.

The process of colligation is made possible because an agent who is familiar with everyday actions such as using a knife or other tool to pry open some object such as a window has knowledge of how such an action can normally be expected to work. In chapter 2, a theory explaining how this ability is possible was based on the notion of a script in AI and the concept of an anchored narrative as a device of reasoning in legal evidence. Colligation is possible because an account is composed not only of explicit statements but also of commonsense background knowledge about such matters as how common actions are performed. These implicit statements need to be expressed and added to the account at each stage before it can be seen how inferences are drawn from the statements in the account at that stage. Thus one can see a point of comparison with the reverse process of how a chain of argumentation chains forward from a set of premises in a given case to an ultimate conclusion. As we have seen, this process is based on missing premises or conclusions, often in the form of defeasible conditionals or presumptive generalizations. In such cases, each argument in the chain is often an enthymeme, and the chain cannot move forward until the unstated parts have been filled in. The process of colligation is similar because an account produced at each stage of an abductive sequence has to be filled out by adding implicit statements to it that are understood and would be accepted by both parties in the dialogue.

Despite these similarities, however, it needs to be made clear that the two processes, that of backward chaining abduction and forward chaining argumentation, are inherently different in structure. Abduction is a process of asking a series of questions, each of which requests an explanation. As each question is answered, an account is given of what needs to be explained in order to answer the question. At each step new statements are added to the account, and through a process of colligation a new account is produced at each step. This process is creative in that in each step the respondent, guided by the questions of the other party in the dialogue, has to try to produce a new account that will explain all the facts colligated together at that point. There may be more than one account that can be given. Then the question of which account is the better explanation arises. The best one is not necessarily perfect in explaining all the statements in the account. It is only the best in the sense that it is better than the others that can be given at that point.

THE FORM OF ABDUCTIVE
INFERENCE REVISITED

A main problem of abduction is how to model it as a distinctive form of inference. Four models have been developed. In chapter 4, two models of causal reasoning were identified: the abductive-logical model and the argument-based model. In chapter 1, two formal structures were postulated as possibly representing the logical form of abductive reasoning. One is the defeasible *modus ponens* form. The other is backward inference from the given data to the best explanation, which, as noted in chapter 1, could be seen as taking the form of the deductively invalid type of inference called affirming the consequent. As noted in chapter 1, Magnani (2001) has adopted this theory of abductive inference. He presented the following example (p. 21) of what he took to be a deductive inference to illustrate his point.

THE PNEUMONIA EXAMPLE
Premise 1: If a patient is affected by pneumonia, his/her level of white blood cells is increased.
Premise 2: John is affected by pneumonia.
Conclusion: John's level of white blood cells is increased.

To say that this argument is deductively valid means that if both premises are true, then necessarily the conclusion must be true. Magnani stated (p. 22) that in this example, we can infer the conclusion from the premises by deduction. As he showed (p. 22), the argument has the form traditionally called *modus ponens* in deductive logic.

If A then B
A
Therefore B

Assuming that the conditional in the first premise is represented by the material conditional, which comes out false if A is true and B is false, any argument of this form is deductively valid. All this said, however, there is another way to look at the reasoning in the pneumonia example.

It could go the other way around. In a medical diagnosis, a physician could reason backward from the given sign, the increased white blood cell count found in a test, to the hypothesis that John is affected by pneumonia. This kind of reasoning is abductive. The physician reasons from the given finding of the white blood cell count to the best explanation. What form of reasoning would be used in such an abductive inference? Magnani (2001, p. 22) tells us that it "corresponds to the well-known fallacy called affirming the consequent," which he represented as follows.

If A then B
B
Therefore A

As noted in chapter 1, this hypothesis that abductive reasoning has the form of a reversed type of *modus ponens* argumentation of the kind called affirming the consequent had already been suggested by Peirce's remarks on the subject[1] and even more strongly by the analysis of abductive reasoning in mathematics offered by Polya (1954). Magnani took a next step by arguing that abductive inferences generally, of the kind commonly found in medial diagnoses for example, can be expressed as taking this form. In general outline, Magnani (2001, p. 23) adopted the view that all three types of reasoning—deduction, induction, and abduction—are involved in the kind of reasoning typically used both in scientific discovery and in medical diagnosis. Abduction is the process of making a guess that results in a plausible hypothesis. Deduction is then used to explore the consequences of the hypothesis. Finally, induction is used to test the hypothesis against the given data. In Magnani's view, deduction and abduction are quite distinct, and yet there is a close structural relationship between them. An abductive inference is taken to have the form of a *modus ponens* argument with the conditional premise reversed.

The Peirce-Polya-Magnani model represents abductive inference as a backward form of reasoning. It is a reverse MP inference. The analysis I will present contrasts with this approach in that it postulates two basic forms of abductive inference, neither of which has the form of $MP.$ I will argue that the abductive-logical model fits in with the backward form of reasoning and that the argument-based model fits in with the forward *modus ponens* form of reasoning. Once the models are integrated in this way, two more general models are articulated, each having a claim to represent abductive reasoning. Following up this approach, I will present below a new analysis of the form of abductive inference as a kind of argumentation scheme. The argumentation scheme represents abductive reasoning as moving from antecedent to consequent of a conditional. The new view of abduction based on the argumentation scheme draws its philosophical justification from the lengthy argument presented in chapter 4. According to this argument, there can be arguments that have the form of *MP* but that are not deductively valid. Of course, such a view has not been popular, or even expressed, in the past, because the general assumption in logic has always been that all arguments having the MP form are deductively valid. Thus it appears to be a theory that contrasts sharply with the Peirce-Polya-Magnani view of abduction as a reverse *MP* inference.

The argumentation scheme for abductive argument is based on two variables. The variable *D* stands for data or a set of given facts in a case. The data can be viewed as a set of statements that describe the so-called facts, or what are presumed to be the facts, in a given case. They are called "facts" because they are presumed to be true statements, or at least their truth is not in question for the present purposes. The participants in the dialogue agree on them or at least agree not to dispute them. The variable *E* stands for an explanation. But what is an explanation? According to the account in chapter 2, on which the argumentation scheme below is based, the concept of explanation is dialectical in the following sense. A set of statements *E* is judged to be a satisfactory explanation of a set of data *D* if and only if *E* is a set of statements put forward by an explainer in a dialogue that enables the respondent to make sense of *D*. An explanation, so defined, is an appropriate response offered to a particular type of question in a dialogue. The success of an explanation, so considered, depends on the type of dialogue the two parties are engaged in, on the respondent's commitments, on how far the dialogue has progressed, on what has been said in the dialogue before the explanation was attempted, and on the collective goal the dialogue is supposed to fulfill. So conceived, abduction is a form of argument that has the structure of an inference to the best explanation, as postulated by the accounts of Peirce and the Josephsons.

As indicated in chapter 1, Peirce postulated, according to Fann's interpretation, that abductive inference has the form of argument called affirming the consequent in logic: if *A* then *B; B;* therefore *A*. This form of inference, called Peirce's form of abductive inference in chapter 1 and called the Peirce-Polya-Magnani model above, is deductively invalid.

But it was also shown in chapter 1, and highlighted in Polya's account, that there is an *MP* counterpart of Peirce's form of abductive inference. This form of inference, as explained in chapter 4, is deductively valid, but it was argued in chapter 4 that as well as this deductive form, it also has a defeasible form. So which form fits abductive reasoning, the forward *modus ponens* or the reversed version with the conditional premise turned around? To explore this question, we might find it useful to re-examine the form of abductive inference postulated by Josephson and Josephson (1994, p. 14) and discussed in chapter 1. The J&J form corresponds roughly to Peirce's form of abductive inference in the way it represents the direction and nature of abductive reasoning. In Peirce's form, the inference goes from the data or "surprising fact" to the hypothesis. Similarly, in the J&J form, the reasoning goes from the data to the hypothesis. There are also some significant differences, however. Peirce represented the inference as being based on one premise that is a conditional. He did not use the term "explain" in presenting the form of the inference, although he often used it to describe abduction. The J&J form used the term "explain" twice and did not represent any premise as a conditional.

Which is the better representation of the form of the abductive type of inference? Both give a useful account of abductive inference and emphasize features that each of the theorists took to be important. From the viewpoint of the theory argued for in this book, two features are of special interest. One is the defeasible *modus ponens* form of abductive reasoning. The other is the dialogue model of explanation put forward to provide the underlying basis of the notion of inference to the best explanation. These two features are emphasized in the two new proposed argumentation schemes I now set out as models of the two forms of abductive inference. One scheme represents a typical abductive inference of the backward type, going from data to a best explanation. A_i is a particular account selected from among a given set of accounts, A_1, $A_2, \ldots , A_n$. Each is successful in explaining D, but some are more successful (better) than others. Each account is a set of particular and general statements that can be colligated together, but some fit the data better than others.

BACKWARD ARGUMENTATION SCHEME FOR ABDUCTIVE INFERENCE
D is a set of data or supposed facts in a case.
Each one of a set of accounts $A_1, A_2, \ldots , A_n$ is successful in explaining D.

A_i is the account that explains D most successfully.

Therefore A_i is the most plausible hypothesis in the case.

Always corresponding to this backward abductive inference in a given case is a matching forward abductive inference of the following form. Such an inference can be represented by an argument diagram made up of defeasible *modus ponens* inferences.

FORWARD ARGUMENTATION SCHEME FOR ABDUCTIVE INFERENCE

D is a set of data or supposed facts in a case.

There is a set of argument diagrams G_1, G_2, . . . , G_n, and in each argument diagram D represents premises of an argument that, supplemented with plausible conditionals and other statements that function as missing parts of enthymemes, lead to a respective conclusion C_1, C_2, . . . , C_n.

The most plausible (strongest) argument is represented by G_i.

Therefore C_i is the most plausible conclusion in the case.

The forward scheme for abductive inference corresponds roughly to the *MP* counterpart of Peirce's form of abductive inference. The backward scheme is comparable to the J&J form of abductive inference. Both schemes represent abductive reasoning, but they represent two different uses of it. The backward scheme represents the inference from given data, or supposed facts in a case, to a hypothesis claimed to be the best explanation of those facts. In the causal variant, the various hypotheses represent causal explanations of how the data came about. The forward scheme represents abductive inference as having a *modus ponens* form, based on a set of conditionals. In the examples presented in the previous chapters, these conditionals were illustrated as being defeasible generalizations of the kind often called "rules" in AI. In the causal variant, they are causal rules of the kind one might find in legal argumentation in a trial, as illustrated by the accident case of Prakken and Renooij (2001, pp. 132–33).

BELIEF-DESIRE-INTENTION AND COMMITMENT MODELS

The dominant approach to providing a structure in which to analyze the form of abductive reasoning has been to apply the belief-desire-intention (BDI) model. This model has been the paradigm in analytical philosophy and cognitive science for many years, and it appears to have influenced recent work in AI very strongly. For example, the conversational policies in agent communication languages (ACLs) have been expressed in terms of the beliefs and intentions of the agent. An example (Singh, 1998) is a communication policy requiring that one agent can "inform" another agent of something only if the sending agent believes it and can establish that the receiving agent does not believe it. The purpose of setting such a conversational policy in an ACL is to minimize the sending of useless messages by confining the communication to information the sender thinks is correct. Conversational policies of this general sort are useful in computing in order to allow software agents to gather and transmit data in an efficient manner. Recently, however, questions have been raised about whether the BDI approach is the best way to build conversational policies. Singh (1998, p. 435) has questioned whether the BDI model should be emphasized so heavily, because it requires, perhaps unrealistically, that one agent can judge what the beliefs or intentions of another agent really are. The big problem in ACLs resulting from this approach is that conversational policies are hung up on devising complex formulae about what one agent believes another agent believes and so forth. These formulae quickly become abstruse. The BDI makes them so by expressing them in a mentalistic jargon that is less than helpful. It is not that the BDI approach is wrong. It is just that it is not all that helpful as a place to begin a formal analysis of speech acts in dialogues.

Fortunately, another model has come out of argumentation theory, and Singh (1999) has advocated applying it to help untangle conversational policies of the kind needed for ACLs. The commitment model has arisen out of the various formulations of dialogue theory in argumentation originally developed by Hamblin (1970) and Barth and Krabbe (1982). Da Costa and French (1993) have argued that scientific discovery can be better understood in a pragmatic model of acceptance than in a belief model. They cited the case of classic (Newtonian) mechanics, which is known to be false, strictly speaking, but is still used in the construction of bridges and buildings (p. 145). They described this situation by saying that Newtonian mechanics may be accepted in the sense that it is believed to be only partially true or pragmatically true in the domain it models (p. 145). Da Costa and French (1993, pp. 148–55) cited inconsistency in a scientific theory as a factor that can be explained within an acceptance model of scientific discovery. They cited Bohr's theory as a case in point (p. 148). It was an accepted theory, even though it was inconsistent. It was accepted and played a role in scientific discovery, but then later it gave way to better theories. Da Costa and French argued, citing cases of this sort, that seeing scientific theories as beliefs, or as true statements, may not be the best vantage point from which to view scientific discovery. Viewing the process as one of commitment or acceptance, even including temporary acceptance of statements that later turn out to be false or inconsistent, may be a better vantage point.

Hamblin (1970, p. 257) explained the issue by insisting that commitment, in the sense of the term appropriate for dialogue theory, is not the same as belief. Commitment is more like acceptance, which of course need not coincide with belief, even if it often does. Belief is often taken to mean rational belief, but even so it has a psychological component that requires the existence of some sort of internal mental state. Commitment, as indicated above, is determined purely by the moves made in a dialogue, where some record has been kept of those moves and where there are rules about whether some move is appropriate or not. So defined, commitment is a normative concept that binds a participant in a dialogue. Once a certain type of move in a dialogue has been made, such as asserting a particular statement to be true, the participant is then bound to certain other statements that flow from that assertion. Belief is a richer notion than commitment, meaning that belief in the truth of a statement implies commitment to that statement, but commitment does not necessarily imply belief. Thus, in a research program to study abductive reasoning, it is better to begin by modeling this kind of reasoning in a commitment-based system and then later on use this simpler framework to study richer notions of abductive reasoning based on knowledge and belief.

In the commitment framework, when a participant in a dialogue puts forward an argument designed, let us say, to rationally persuade the respondent to accept some designated proposition, that argument will have a form. It might be deductive or inductive, or the argument might be of a plausibilistic type that falls under one or other of the presumptive argumentation schemes. How will putting forward such an argument affect the commitment sets of the participants in the dialogue? Let us say, for example, that the dialogue is a persuasion dialogue of the permissive persuasion dialogue (*PPD*) type studied in Walton and Krabbe (1995). The answer, then, is that if the respondent is committed to all of the premises, that commitment will automatically transfer forward to the conclusion. Thus the respondent becomes committed to the conclusion unless, at the next move, that individual can raise doubts about the acceptability of the argument by asking one or more of the appropriate critical questions. But suppose the respondent, just at the point in the dialogue where this argument was brought forward, was already committed to the negation of the conclusion. Then we have the typical sort of problem that has to be solved within the framework of *PPD* set out in Walton and Krabbe (1995). Depending on the exact type of *PPD* dialogue the participants are engaged in, the rules will generally require that the respondent make a retraction in one of two ways. The respondent either must retract the commitment or commitments that give rise to the inconsistency or must make other moves that enable retraction of commitment to the conclusion of the argument.

As the dialogue continues, an argument diagram can be constructed to represent the longer sequence of argumentation if the argument is chained forward or backward. Suppose a participant retracts any statement that has some place as a premise or conclusion in such a chain. The retraction of that single proposition (according to the rules for the *PPD* type of dialogue) will very likely affect the respondent's commitment to other propositions that have places in the chain. If so, a readjustment of the participant's commitment set will have to take place. How this readjustment should be carried out in a *PPD* dialogue, as noted above, is through an internal or an external stability adjustment. The exact mechanisms or rules for such adjustments are not so important here. What is important is that they can be computed in a dialogue according to the rules for that type of dialogue. These will include rules for making certain types of moves, such as putting forward an argument, and rules for the incurring and retracting of commitments. They will also include rules for the asking of questions, such as the kind of why question that requests an explanation. It is within this general framework, according to the dialogue theory of abductive reasoning, that an abductive argument should be identified, analyzed, and evaluated. Instead of a belief-revision solution to the problem, which leads to metaphysical and psychological mysteries about iterated beliefs, desires, and intentions, the recommended approach redefines the problem as one of commitment management in a dialogue structure. This approach is different for several reasons. One of the most important is that there are different solutions for different types of dialogue. Thus evaluating any abductive argument used in a given case will be taken to depend on what type of conversational exchange the participants are supposed to be engaging in.

THE ABDUCTIVE PROFILE OF DIALOGUE

The concept of the profile of dialogue was originally devised in Walton (1989, pp. 65–71) as a tool to evaluate problematic examples of argumentation involving the asking and answering of questions. One of the problems treated with the use of this tool was the fallacy of many questions associated with tricky questions such as "Did you stop abusing your pet?" The problem is that if the respondent gives a direct answer to the question, such as "yes" or "no," the person is admitting to pet abuse, but if pet abuse has not occurred, the person needs to find some method of deconstructing the question. The profile of dialogue technique is such a method. It can be used to break down the overall question into a set of further connected questions put into a certain order. For example, the first question to be asked is whether the respondent has a pet. The next is whether the respondent has abused that pet in the past. Only if the answer to the first two questions is "yes" should the proponent be allowed to proceed to asking the original question. The profile of dialogue technique is applicable not just to question- asking problems and fallacies but also to many kinds of argumentation. It can be applied to any problem where a technique is needed to represent a connected sequence of moves in a local segment of a larger dialogue. Conversational analysts in linguistics such as Schlegloff (1988, p. 56) have used schematized dialogue sequences that are in effect profiles of dialogue to analyze natural language dialogues. Krabbe (1991) has analyzed fallacies of irrelevance using profiles of dialogue to evaluate sequences of argumentation in which problems concerning irrelevance typically arise. The profiles technique was employed in many examples in Walton (1996b) to analyze and evaluate problematic sequences of argumentation associated with the traditional fallacy of argument from ignorance or *argumentum ad ignorantiam*. The profiles technique has turned out to be especially applicable to problematic cases where the problem centers on a relatively short sequence of questions and replies or other speech acts that fit a pattern and have a place within a larger framework of dialogue (Krabbe, 1999). This tool is useful to focus on a relatively short sequence at a local level instead of having to deploy the elaborate and often cumbersome dialogue apparatus as a whole.

The profiles technique is nicely suited to the analysis of abductive reasoning as it occurs in particular cases. If we take any given case of abductive reasoning, it can be seen as an argument having the form of the backward or the forward argumentation scheme for abductive inference set out below in this chapter. The recommended method to evaluate the argument is to use the set of four matching critical questions cited below. Hence, the task of analyzing and evaluating any case of abductive reasoning is dialogical. But that is only part of the story. We need to see how these components fit into some wider pattern or format that itself fits into a dialogue framework. The profiles technique is the best method to accomplish this task.

There can be many profiles of dialogue representing abductive arguments, but they all fit into one basic structure, which could be called the basic profile of dialogue for abductive reasoning. To see how this basic profile works, we begin by considering a typical kind of dialogue situation where abductive reasoning is being used to put forward an argument. Two parties are engaged in a persuasion dialogue. The proponent is committed to a particular proposition E, and the respondent doubts E. In this typical type of situation, the proponent offers an argument designed to persuade the respondent to accept E. Let us say the proponent uses an abductive argument and that the dialogue takes the following form.

Respondent: Can you give me a reason to accept E as true?
Proponent: Because E is the best explanation of some data D.

Now at this point, the respondent has several options. This individual can simply accept the argument and thus become committed to E or can make any one of four other moves. The respondent can ask any one of the following critical questions.

CQ1: Is E successful as an explanation of D, and if so, how successful is it?
CQ2: Are there other explanations that might be better?
CQ3: How thorough has the search for these other explanations been?
CQ4: Instead of accepting E, would it be better to collect more data and continue the dialogue before making a commitment for or against accepting E?

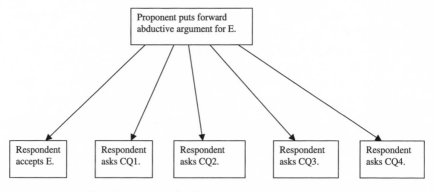

Figure 6.1 Profile of dialogue for abductive argument.

These four critical questions are complete at this level of abstraction, meaning that there are no other options for the respondent to make as the next move in the dialogue. The dialogue structure can be represented by the basic profile of dialogue in figure 6.1. Of course, many instances of abductive argumentation are much more complex than the dialogue sequence represented by the basic profile of dialogue. The respondent can ask critical subquestions of any of the four basic critical questions. The dialogue can then take the form of a sequence of questions and replies under this critical question.

For example, the respondent might ask a question having the form of CQ1, and the proponent might reply by giving some reason for the respondent to accept the explanation. But the respondent might not be satisfied with this answer. The respondent might go on to argue that the explanation offered by the proponent is unsuccessful for some reason. An explanation can fail to be successful for several reasons. It can be inconsistent. It can be circular and thus fail to increase the respondent's understanding of what was at issue. It can be inconsistent with other known facts accepted as data. It can have logical holes in it, that is, inferences can be drawn from it that lead to implausible consequences. Indeed, some explanations can be empirically tested against known facts and fail the test. But basically, explanations fail because they do not meet the requirements of the dialogue model of a successful explanation. The main reason is that the explanation attempt fails to give a coherent account that fills the gap signaled by the respondent's why question in the dialogue. Another way the dialogue might continue is that many alternative explanations might be proposed and evaluated in a lengthy discussion that comes under CQ2. The proponent and the respondent may go through a lengthy process of framing different explanations and then considering each in turn.

Schaffner (1980, p. 179) has argued that Hanson and his critics in their writings on abduction never distinguished clearly between two kinds of logic. One is what Schaffner calls a logic of generation, meaning a method for articulating a new hypothesis. The other he calls a logic of preliminary evaluation, meaning a way in which a "hypothesis is assessed for its plausibility." Schaffner's distinction corresponds at least roughly to a distinction long made in logic between two uses or functions of logical reasoning. One is the use of standards of inference to test arguments to see whether they meet standards of structural correctness. This use is highly familiar in logic as conventionally taught. But there is also a longstanding tradition of using logical reasoning to invent arguments called the *ars inveniedi,* or art of finding. This process looks not for all possible arguments but only for the plausible ones (Kienpointner, 1997, p. 225). The first art of this type was developed by Aristotle and was based on so-called topics (*topoi*), representing common forms of argumentation. The theory of the topics was continued in the Middle Ages and is still useful in the modern theory of debating. But many of the traditional topics correspond quite well to defeasible argumentation schemes. As research on argumentation schemes moves ahead, new uses of the topics are being found. They certainly have a potential role in an abductive discovery device that extrapolates a line of argumentation from a database in order to judge whether the argumentation moves toward some ultimate thesis to be proved or disproved in a dialogue. The problem is to embed this chaining forward of argumentation in a context of dialogue.

One can appreciate why some cases of abductive argumentation can only be modeled, in all relevant details, by a complex sequence of dialogue moves. For example, a proponent may put forward an explanation in order to meet a respondent's request for an abductive argument in support of a queried proposition. But this explanation may have some statement in it that is inconsistent with a statement to which the proponent is already committed. How should the inconsistency be resolved? Perhaps the proponent may decide to retract the earlier commitment or try to resolve the apparent inconsistency by some other means. Whatever response the proponent attempts, the rules of persuasion dialogue, or of whatever type of dialogue is in progress, will require that such an inconsistency be dealt with. No attempt is made here to deal with a number of such cases, for they can be highly variable, depending on the type of dialogue and on the critical subquestions. The most important point is to see how such cases all come under the basic profile of dialogue for abductive argumentation.

ABDUCTION AS A QUERY-DRIVEN PROCESS

As shown in previous chapters, abductive argumentation is fundamental in areas as diverse as medical diagnostics, legal evidence, and explanation-based reasoning in history and the natural and social sciences. What is suggested by the varied examples presented is that abductive inference should be evaluated in the context of a dynamic investigation of the facts. The database is not fixed. New facts are always coming into the circumstances of the case. This dynamic aspect suggests that abductive inference is best evaluated as an evolving dialogue between two parties. Several other aspects of the account of abductive inference given above also suggest the contextual variability of this kind of reasoning. One is that abductive inference is query driven, meaning it is triggered by the asking of a question and then moves on as other relevant questions are asked in a dialogue. How did something happen, or why did it happen? Another aspect is that abduction is based on the notion of explanation. And it has been argued in chapter 2 that explanation is itself a dialectical notion that can only be analyzed by seeing it in a context of dialogue between two parties. It was argued above that a process of explanation can move forward as the respondent puts forward an account, and then that account, once colligated, enables the drawing of inferences that lead to more questions that request further explanations offering increased understanding. Another aspect is the Tidmarsh example that was presented by the Josephsons (see chapter 1); it is in the form of a dialogue. In fact, presenting the abductive inference in this form best shows the process of reasoning that is characteristic of abduction. All these aspects combined suggest that query-driven abductive inference could very nicely be modeled as a presumptive form of reasoning, fitting the many other argumentation schemes (forms of inference) for presumptive reasoning presented in Walton (1996a).

The term "hypothesis," used so often by Peirce in his account of abduction,[2] suggests that abductive inference is a form of presumptive reasoning. The conclusion is only a tentative assumption, relative to the progress of an investigation to a given point. It is not proved beyond doubt by the premises but only set in place as an assumption that both parties to the dialogue should accept for the time being so that the dialogue can progress further. As the dialogue proceeds, the abductive conclusion may stay in place, or further evidence may dislodge it. Things could go either way. The abductive conclusion can be seen as having a certain "weight" behind it. But that weight can be lightened or even removed through the asking of appropriate critical questions by the other party in the dialogue. What are these critical questions? The evaluation factors of Josephson and Josephson cited in chapter 1 offer guidance. The following critical questions provide a basis for evaluation that centers on many of these same factors or comparable ones.

CQ1: How successful is E itself as an explanation of D, apart from the alternative explanations available so far in the dialogue?
CQ2: How much more successful is E than the alternative explanations available so far in the dialogue?
CQ3: How far has the dialogue progressed? If the dialogue is an inquiry, how thorough has the search been in the investigation of the case?
CQ4: Would it be better to continue the dialogue further, instead of drawing a conclusion at this point?

In line with this pragmatic analysis, the six factors cited by the Josephsons can be viewed as critical questions matching an abductive argument used in a given case. The abductive argument can be plausible to begin with, if the premises are well supported by the case. But its plausibility can be strengthened each time a critical question is answered adequately. Thus even though epistemic closure may not be achieved, the abductive argument can get stronger and stronger, relative to the pragmatic criterion of how well it answers to the appropriate critical questions. This form of pragmatic analysis can also be applied to causal argumentation. Almost needless to say, such a dialogue-based analysis of causal explanation will be quite different from the purely inferential models so long advocated in traditional analytical philosophy, such as the deductive-nomological model of Hempel (1965). Explanation, in this pragmatic analysis, should be seen as a dialogue exchange in which the respondent has asked a specific question. The form of the question is important. It could be a why question or a how question of a certain sort. Then the proponent gives an answer.

The forward and backward argumentation schemes for abductive inference can be used to analyze and evaluate abductive arguments at three levels. First, at the local level, the given discourse can be examined to see (a) whether the given argument as put forward by the proponent meets the requirements of the argumentation scheme and (b) how the critical questions have been asked and answered. At the second level, the given discourse can be examined at greater length, with more of the context and adjoining discourse being taken into account. At this level, the larger mass of evidence represented by an argument diagram showing the chaining of the argumentation in the case is the basis for evaluation. At the third level, the wider context of dialogue can be taken into account. As Peirce showed, the value of abduction is that it enables a selection of a hypothesis from among a set of alternative possible explanations. The hypothesis can then be tested. This hypothesis-formation argumentation at the discovery stage moves the process of scientific investigation forward through an empirical testing stage to a stage of theory formation. Once the theory has been precisely expressed using mathematical methods, its deductive and inductive implications can be drawn out. A comparable process is observable in Wigmore's analysis of how legal evidence is judged during the trial process or through other procedures of legal investigation. What makes abduction useful is that it can lead to the use of more exact forms of reasoning once a plausible hypothesis begins to take shape. It is not the hypothesis itself that is so valuable, but how the hypothesis turns out to be useful in the wider process of investigation as the dialogue moves forward to a conclusion.

The evaluation procedure outlined above explicitly analyzes abductive arguments as dialectical. Each abductive argument put forward in a given case has some weight in a dialogue, making its conclusion an assumption that should be reasonably accepted for the present. But each single abductive argument needs to be evaluated in a dialogue containing other abductive arguments as well. Some abductive arguments can conflict with others because none of them, by themselves, tends to be conclusive or have very much weight. The small weight of plausibility of each argument needs to be evaluated, and then possibly reevaluated, within the larger body of evidence compiled as the dialogue proceeds. Only after the dialogue is completed will the mass of evidence on both sides be weighed and compared. The prior distribution of the burden of proof, presumably set at the beginning of the dialogue, will determine the final conclusion to be drawn. Typically, however, single abductive arguments as used in a given case need to be evaluated provisionally at a midpoint of the dialogue. Hence, such arguments are typically defeasible in nature. Even so, they can be useful as rational arguments because they can play a small but potentially important part in the final outcome.

DISCOVERY AS AN OPEN PROCESS

The view that some single dialectical model could be used to evaluate all cases of scientific argumentation is absurd. Many different kinds of cases seem to involve different kinds of argumentation. Abductive reasoning is, of course, most closely associated with scientific discovery, especially at the early stages of an investigation. But much of the controversy in recent years between rationalist philosophy of science and relativist sociology of science stems from Kuhn's famous book titled *The Structure of Scientific Revolutions* (1970). The kind of argumentation on which Kuhn based his theory occurs where a new theory is advanced that involves a so-called paradigm shift, and the exponents of the new theory then engage in argumentation with the exponents of the old theory. Kuhn saw this kind of argumentation as having a rational basis. But he had difficulty saying what makes it rational, and he fell back on allusions to persuasion as being a way of advancing good reasons. The question of what makes such reasons persuasive, however, is one that Kuhn could not really answer. Nowadays, the resources of argumentation theory could be deployed to model this kind of argumentation as a species of persuasion dialogue. But of course, for those who are not open to dialectical models of rational argumentation such as persuasion dialogue, there is a tendency to see persuasion as purely rhetorical and subjective or as something that can only be explained sociologically by referring to groups and institutions.

Hintikka (1998, pp. 508–11) argued against the assumption that abduction can be equated to inference to the best explanation by citing several cases from the history of science. One is Einstein's discovery of his theory of relativity (p. 508). Another is Newton's discovery of his theory of gravitation (p. 510). Hintikka argued that these discoveries were not based on abduction, as attempts to explain specific scientific facts. Indeed, the discovery of these very general theories falls very easily under the kind of paradigm shift model offered by Kuhn. But Hintikka is not on strong ground in arguing that these cases of scientific discovery do not fit the model of abductive reasoning. They may be accommodated by a theory about conflicting high-level scientific theories, and the dialectical model that seems to best fit is persuasion dialogue. The abductive model may more obviously apply to historical cases of scientific discovery at a much earlier stage, where the data have not been tested yet, at least not very fully, and hypotheses have not yet been formulated at a high level of abstraction and with mathematical precision.

In these cases, abduction can very plausibly be equated with inference to the best explanation, providing a highly appropriate model of the process of reasoning used in discovery. But even at a later stage, where there is a clashing of scientific theories, abduction could still have an important role, even if other kinds of argumentation are more at the forefront. For example, in theoretical discussions, the more abstract arguments used may be deductive or inductive. For example, one scientist may use an abstract argument to attack the consistency of the theory advocated by the other. Even here abduction could be involved, even if more distantly, because empirical findings such as experimental results and how to best explain them are still relevant. Still, it seems a reasonable conjecture that abduction is most visible at the discovery stage.

It seems that the discovery stage could take various forms, but what characterizes it especially is an openness to the possibility of new findings. The argumentation schemes used at this stage tend to be of the defeasible sort. To model the kind of argumentation involved, we need to think of it as situated in a framework of dialogue that is open to future moves and developments. It is not yet at the stage of epistemic closure, and it does not take the form of an inquiry. It is this openness to new findings in a dialogue that makes abduction ampliative, meaning that it yields new information. According to Hintikka's analysis (1998, p. 505), abduction is ampliative, and that is what makes it different from deduction. Deductive inference is tautological, meaning that it does not yield any new information. It follows that abduction is not truth preserving, nor is it the same as induction (Hintikka, 1998, p. 505). In Peirce's account, it is making a good conjecture or guessing well. It is directed to an open future that could go one way or another depending on responses to questions that have not even been asked yet. Its success or failure is to be judged on this future dialogue sequence.

An excellent example is the case of the fossil hunter (Leakey and Lewin, 1992) cited in chapter 1. Judging from the flattish shape of the skull fragment and the faint brain impression on the inner surface, the fossil hunter drew an inference to the best explanation that what he found was part of a *hominid* skull. Of course, this conclusion was only a plausible hypothesis. Later investigations could confirm or refute it. But at the point the fragment was found, it was a reason for carrying the investigation forward with further excavations of the site. As it turned out, the discovery led to a nearly complete *homo erectus* skeleton, an amazing scientific discovery. But it could have gone the other way. Nobody knew until more evidence was collected and assessed. The fragment that was found only led to a plausible hypothesis that led to further questions, pointing the investigation in a certain direction.

The basic problem with the Peirce-Hanson account of abduction is that it fails to provide a systematic model to accommodate and explain this feature of openness. The form of inference that Peirce, and later Hanson, put forward looks more like a semantic structure. It displays the central structure of the abductive form of inference as having a characteristic set of premises and a conclusion. But the bare inference, to be a useful analysis of abductive reasoning, has to be embedded in some enveloping notion of scientific discovery as a guided, rational process that moves forward in time toward some goal. The case studies and remarks of Peirce and Hanson that place the central inference in some sort of context of scientific discovery are highly motivating and exciting. But as the reaction of critics to them over the years has indicated (Nickles, 1980), they have not provided a clear and sufficiently developed normative framework in which the central inference can be situated. What is needed is to see abductive inference as a local form of inference that is used, over and over again, in some wider framework of investigation or discovery that moves forward toward the future. As new evidence comes in, a hypothesis is drawn as an abductive inference and then either supported or defeated as the argumentation process moves forward. New data keep coming in, and the argumentation has to be open to revision or correction along the way. Once the argumentation reaches a closing stage, however, the data are closed off. Epistemic closure is reached. At that point the way the argumentation is to be evaluated changes abruptly. All these dynamic and temporal notions of data collection and refinement of successive hypotheses to explain the data at given points in a forward-moving sequence of argumentation are implicit in the Peirce-Hanson account and in the case studies of scientific discovery they presented. The problem is that none of this dynamic structure was modeled by some clear and exact structure that would satisfy the many critics and positivistic doubters. How, then, can one accommodate this open-ended feature of abductive reasoning, seeing it as based on defeasible inferences used within some sort of overarching structure representing discovery?

Defeasible arguments are open ended, meaning that they are subject to defeat in the future by a sequence of argumentation that is not known yet. They are not conclusive and closed in the way deductive arguments are, and they are even more open than inductive arguments are. To illustrate this characteristic of openness, let us begin with the canonical example of a defeasible argument.[3] Suppose that the proponent claims that Tweety flies because Tweety is a bird and birds fly. The respondent should accept this conclusion unless evidence can be brought in about Tweety that might defeat the inference. But this acceptance is tentative. The Tweety issue still remains open, and it needs to be seen that way by both parties. Suppose the dialogue continues for a while, and then the respondent brings in evidence showing that Tweety is a penguin. If the proponent agrees that this is good evidence, the proponent must then give up the earlier claim that Tweety flies. If the proponent accepts that Tweety really is a penguin according to the facts of the case and that penguins are birds that do not fly, then the proponent must concede the defeat of the earlier argument. Thus at the point where the proponent first put forward the Tweety argument, and during the subsequent interval where it remained undefeated, the argument was open to defeat. This characteristic of defeasible arguments can be formulated as follows.

> *Openness to Defeat (OTD) Condition:* When a proponent has put forward a defeasible argument at some move in a dialogue, the proponent must be open to giving it up and admitting its defeat at any future move should the respondent bring in new evidence that defeats the argument.

Defeasible arguments such as the Tweety argument are based on defeasible generalizations that are subject to exceptions. The OTD condition requires that if the respondent comes up with an exception to the rule, at that point in the dialogue the proponent has to give up the argument. Thus it is presumed that prior to that point, the argument has to be seen by both parties as open and incomplete. The proponent must be willing to retract the argument if the respondent makes moves that defeat it. But in typical cases, the proponent will be unable to predict when a respondent may come up with such a defeater or even whether the respondent will. Thus openness is a very important feature.

A dialogue always has four stages: a confrontation stage, an opening stage, an argumentation stage, and a closing stage (van Eemeren and Grootendorst, 1992). During the argumentation stage, a defeasible argument might be put forward. As defeasible, it must remain open until either it is defeated or the argumentation is closed. There is a characteristic of reasoning in a database called the closed world assumption in AI. The closed world assumption is said to be met if all the positive information available contained in the database is listed, and it is assumed that no information is missing. Reiter (1980, p. 83) has presented the airport example to illustrate how the closed world assumption works.

THE AIRPORT EXAMPLE

Consider a data base representing an airline flight schedule and the query "Does Air Canada flight 113 connect Vancouver with New York?" A deductive question-answering system will typically treat the data base together with some general knowledge about the flight domains as a set of premises from which it will attempt to prove CONNECT (AC113, VAN, NY). If this proof succeeds, then the system responds "yes."

Suppose the system has searched for a flight of the designated type and has failed to find one in the database. It will reply that no such flight is listed. Under the closed world assumption, a user would be entitled to conclude that there is no such flight. Reiter (1980, p. 83) described this sequence of knowledge-based reasoning as follows: "Failure to find a proof has sanctioned an inference." This form of inference is known in logic as the *argumentum ad ignorantiam*. Once the database is closed off, the argument from ignorance is conclusive. Essentially, it becomes deductively valid. Closure of the dialogue, once assumed, also closes off the formerly defeasible argument. Closure of a dialogue is, of course, perfectly appropriate under the right circumstances. But in other cases, defeasible arguments need to be viewed as just having been put forward and as still open to defeat. In such cases, it needs to be assumed that the dialogue is still open and is still proceeding through the argumentation stage. At this stage, commitment to the conclusion of the argument is subject to possible retraction as the dialogue proceeds.

Now there may be a question about what type of dialogue is involved. The answer is that it depends on the context. In scientific argumentation, abductive arguments are most useful at the discovery stage. But a scientific investigation typically passes from a discovery stage to a testing of hypotheses stage and then to a theory formation stage. At the testing stage, inductive reasoning is dominant. At the theory formation stage, deductive reasoning is dominant. Legal argumentation goes through different stages, sometimes leading up to a trial. And even within scientific argumentation, there can be different types of dialogue in different cases. Many cases of discovery concern the testing of new drugs or medical treatments for curing diseases. Many such cases studied in the philosophy of science concern the development of scientific theories. For example, Finocchiaro (1980) studied the case of Newton's theory of gravitation. But there are also interesting practical cases of problem solving that led to new inventions, such as that of the jet engine. The dialogue in this kind of case is a form of problem-solving deliberation. The problem was one of how to take the existing ramjet engine, a device that was not very useful practically, and transform it into a useful propulsion device. The ramjet could only propel an aircraft once it had attained enough speed to get air flowing rapidly through the burner. This practical problem was solved by building a turbine into the engine that could force enough air through to the burner to enable the aircraft to get off the runway under the power of the jet engine. The result was the creation of the jet engine as a practical means of propelling an aircraft. Although the sequence of argumentation in this process of discovery involved theory and much testing of devices, the dialogue is best classified as one of deliberation on how to solve a practical problem.

Thus it can be seen that no one type of dialogue or framework of investigation is always involved, even in scientific cases of discovery. What is common to them all is that when abductive reasoning is used, the dialogue must be regarded as open to new evidence and future developments as the dialogue proceeds. What is characteristic of abductive reasoning is that it is used at the early stages of a dialogue, before epistemic closure has been achieved and very often even before much empirical testing has been carried out. That does not mean that abductive reasoning is chaotic or pure intuitive guesswork. It has certain characteristics as a form of argumentation. And one of these is its defeasibility. It is a type of inference that needs to be seen as used in a context of dialogue that is still open.

RETRACTION OF COMMITMENT

Magnani (2001, pp. 145–69) posed the problem of hypothesis withdrawal in science by studying cases from scientific reasoning where a hypothesis had to be withdrawn. The need for withdrawal of a hypothesis that was previously accepted on a basis of abductive reasoning can occur for many reasons. A contradiction can be found and can only be resolved by moving to a different hypothesis or by modifying the old one. New data can come in. Or even in the absence of new data or a contradiction, a better explanation of the given data may be found. Such a need for retraction of a previously accepted hypothesis is character-istic of abductive reasoning in science. But it raises many questions about scientific methodology. It suggests that scientific argumentation, at least at the discovery stage, is not an inquiry of the kind that is cu-mulative, meaning that retractions are not allowed. It suggests that sci-entific argumentation at this stage allows for retraction in an orderly way and for moving to a different explanation from the one previously accepted. The problem of retraction is not exclusive to scientific argu-mentation. It has been studied in relation to other contexts of argument use as well.

The problem of retraction in formal dialogue systems was stated in Walton (1984, p. 135) in relation to persuasion dialogue. In a persuasion dialogue, the proponent has a thesis to be proved. To fulfill this goal, the proponent needs to present a structurally correct argument to the re-spondent with premises that are all previous commitments of the re-spondent. But in devising a realistic model of persuasion dialogue that has this aim as its central goal, one encounters a practical problem. If the proponent overtly asks the respondent to commit to an argument prov-ing a conclusion that is the proponent's own thesis, the respondent is hardly likely to accept it. Indeed, the respondent's aim in the dialogue will be to resist any argumentation of this kind. Once the respondent sees what the conclusion is and that the argument proves it by the re-quired standards of the dialogue, the respondent will automatically look to see which premise can be retracted as a commitment. This is the no-commitment problem.[4] The early systems of formal dialogue con-structed by Hamblin (1970; 1971) did not have any method of solving this problem. Later extensions of Hamblin's systems did have rules to deal with it (Mackenzie, 1981, 1990; Walton, 1984), but these rules were of a simple sort and did not seem very realistic. Of course, the first so-lution that comes to mind is simply to ban retraction or to impose some penalty on it that would make it a very difficult or onerous move to make. But this solution will not work for persuasion dialogue.

There is a definite need for considerable freedom to retract commit-ments in a persuasion dialogue. First, one needs to see that capability for retraction of commitments is necessary for the goal of a persuasion dia-logue to be fulfilled (Krabbe, 2001, p. 143). In the critical discussion, a widely recognized type of persuasion dialogue, it is necessary to allow for retraction of a thesis in order for the goal of the dialogue to be fulfilled. A critical discussion can be successful in its aim of resolving a conflict of opinions only if the respondent is persuaded by the rational argumentation of the proponent to give up the commitment to a thesis (van Eemeren and Grootendorst, 1992, p. 34). This clearly requires capability for retraction. Another factor is that retraction is quite common in everyday argumentation of the persuasion dialogue type. Formal models of persuasion dialogue will model such everyday arguments better if the participants have the capability to retract commitments with a reasonable degree of freedom (Krabbe, 2001, p. 144). On the other hand, this freedom could easily lead to the no-commitment problem if it is not restrained to some degree. As noted above, the respondent to an argument should not be so free that the individual can retract as soon as there seems to be any danger of being defeated by the argument.

To solve the no-commitment problem in persuasion dialogue, Walton and Krabbe (1995, p. 147) introduced a device called a stability adjustment. Two types of stability adjustment are possible, an internal type and an external type (Walton and Krabbe, 1995, section 4.3.3). The internal stability adjustment involves a change of commitments in one's own arguments (Krabbe, 2001, p. 149). Suppose the proponent of an argument has retracted commitment to a statement A but had an argument that offered premises giving reasons to support A. In such a case the respondent will also have to retract commitment to at least one of these premises. The need to make such an adjustment before retracting delays the proponent from retracting a conclusion too quickly, i.e., once the proponent sees it might cause trouble. It prevents the possibility of a quick retraction with no penalty. Hence, requiring an internal stability adjustment is helpful as a device for helping with the no-commitment problem. The external adjustment can also be helpful in this regard. The term "external" refers to the following kind of case (Krabbe, 2001, p. 155). A proponent puts forward a valid argument, and the respondent is committed to all of its premises. Can the respondent retract commitment to one or more of the proponent's premises once the respondent realizes they lead to the conclusion? The device of the external stability adjustment requires that the respondent can do this only if that individual first retracts commitment to one or more of the premises.

Imposing the need for making a stability adjustment makes argumentation in a formal system of dialogue "sticky." An arguer has the freedom to retract a commitment at any point, but the retraction may take more than one move. Indeed, the process is recursive. Premises that are retracted may be based on other premises in a previous argument. But now the stability adjustment will require that these commitments need to be retracted as well. This stickiness makes it not so easy for an arguer to retract a commitment and so helps to fix commitment. An arguer cannot simply retract a commitment when it is seen that it might be used to persuade that individual rationally to accept a conclusion that is not liked or might be used against the person. This means that the proponent of an argument can build up a line of argumentation, adopting a strategy of securing some commitments first and then using them as premises to try to get other commitments in place. Argumentation, in other words, involves strategic maneuvering of the kind described by van Eemeren and Houtlosser (2002).

A scientific investigation, once it moves along to the stage where a hypothesis is being tested, has a structure quite different from a persuasion dialogue. Once a hypothesis has been accepted, there is a commitment to going through a generate-test-and-debug cycle with it, and then commitment is determined by the outcome of the test. As noted in chapter 5, the GTD cycle has a pattern. Suppose at the discovery stage, a hypothesis has been selected as the best explanation of what has been found at that point in the investigation. Suppose the hypothesis has been tested empirically against some data, and it passes. Then, according to the GTD procedure, commitment to the hypothesis is retained. If it fails the test, then the hypothesis will be rejected, and the search for one that might pass the test will begin. Thus the process for maintaining or retracting commitment has a pattern. Commitment is determined by empirical data and by whether a hypothesis passes or fails tests that indicate its empirical implications.

In some respects, however, conditions for retraction of commitment are similar in a persuasion dialogue and in a scientific investigation. Inconsistency is a serious charge in both types of dialogue. In a persuasion dialogue, if a proponent has a set of commitments that are inconsistent with each other, and a respondent points out the inconsistency, then the proponent is obliged to remove it, or at least to deal with it somehow. Otherwise, the respondent can attack the proponent's position, using argument from inconsistent commitment. The argumentation scheme for argument from inconsistent commitment is said to have the following form in Walton (1998a, p. 252). The small a is an agent, and the capital A is a proposition.

ARGUMENTATION SCHEME FOR ARGUMENT FROM INCONSISTENT COMMITMENT

a is committed to proposition *A* (generally, or in virtue of what has been said in the past).

a is committed to proposition not-*A,* the conclusion of an argument presently advocated.

Therefore *a*'s argument should not be accepted.

In this argumentation scheme, the contradiction in an arguer's commitment set is taken to be a reason for rejecting that argument. Argument from inconsistent commitment is a special subtype of the more general scheme called argument from commitment. It is also closely related to the circumstantial type of *ad hominem* argument, but it is not the same thing. A circumstantial *ad hominem* argument uses argument from inconsistency as the basis of a personal attack on an arguer's ethical character and credibility. Thus, although based on argument from inconsistent commitment, it also contains an essential element of personal attack on character. It is important to stress these distinctions because argument from commitment and *ad hominem* argument have often been taken to be the same.

In a scientific investigation, inconsistency of commitments is also taken as a serious indicator of error and of the need to retract commitment. But a finding of inconsistency can occur in different ways. A hypothesis may be found to be inconsistent with data that are very clear or have been highly confirmed as accurate and true. It may be found to be inconsistent with some well-founded and generally accepted body of scientific knowledge. It may be found to be internally inconsistent. Or it may be found to be, or appear to be, inconsistent with a scientific theory that is widely accepted. None of these findings absolutely requires that the hypothesis be rejected, but any of them will be taken as evidence that the hypothesis is highly questionable and may in many instances be taken as a good reason for retracting commitment to it.

Describing Galileo's methods of scientific investigation, Finocchiaro (1975, p. 123) portrayed him as typically beginning by posing a problem that involves difficulties. The problem is often one of drawing out the logical consequences of a received view. Hamblin (1970, p. 132) cited the famous dialogue from Galileo's *Dialogues Concerning Two New Sciences* as "perhaps the greatest thought-experiment in the history of science," noting (p. 131) that the form is that of a dialogue.

Salviati: If we then take two bodies whose natural speeds are different, it is clear that on uniting the two, the more rapid one will be partly retarded by the slower, and the slower will be somewhat hastened by the swifter. Do you agree with me on this opinion?
Simplicio: You are unquestionably right.
Salviati: But if this is true, and if a large stone moves with a speed of, say, eight while a smaller moves with a speed of four, then when they are united, the system will move with a speed less than eight; but the two stones when tied together make a stone larger than that which before moved with a speed of eight. Hence the heavier body moves with less speed than the lighter; an effect which is contrary to your supposition.

Here the argument begins with a received view and shows that it leads to an absurdity in the form of a contradiction with the original view. The form of the argument is that of *reductio ad absurdum,* a familiar form of reasoning in logic. But its being put explicitly in a dialogue format also brings out that, as an argumentation scheme, it is an argument from inconsistent commitment. In solving such a problem, Galileo is explaining not just by deducing from general laws but by explaining a difficulty. The explanation is successful because it takes something incomprehensible and shows that it can be understood.

Inconsistency in a hypothesis is a fairly common phenomenon in scientific discovery (Da Costa and French, 1993), and apparent inconsistency between opposed theories has become a commonly discussed problem in logic and the foundations of mathematics (Woods, 2003). Instead of seeing scientific discovery as an accumulation of truth or a process of increasing knowledge or true belief, it may be better to view it as a process of acceptance and rejection of statements. This process can be seen as a dialogue, or process of investigation, in which commitments are incurred and may later be retracted.

THE FOUR PHASES OF ABDUCTIVE REASONING

Any case of abductive reasoning proceeds through four phases: dialogue setting, formation of explanation attempts in dialogue, evaluation of explanations, and dialogue closure. Each phase has its requirements that must be met in order for the conditions for an abductive argument to be there. These phases do not necessarily correspond to the temporal order in which abductive argumentation proceeds in any given case.

Instead, they represent normative requirements that a dialogue should logically proceed through in order for an abductive argument to be reasonable. Specific requirements of the argumentation during each phase are set out below.

The Dialogue Setting

THE TYPE OF DIALOGUE

The type of dialogue could be any of the kind described in chapter 2. For example, it could be an inquiry in which facts are being collected and verified. In a scientific investigation, the ultimate aim is to prove or disprove some hypothesis. But at the early stage of trying to find a hypothesis, the argumentation can take the form of a persuasion dialogue in which there is a conflict of opinions.

THE COMMON STARTING POINTS

Both parties agree not to dispute some commonly accepted statements, or "common starting points," as they are called by van Eemeren and Grootendorst (1984). In abductive argumentation, there is a given set of facts, or data *D*, known to both the proponent and the respondent in a dialogue.

THE COMMON UNDERSTANDING

Third, the participants share some common understanding of the subject being discussed, but the proponent is presumed to have understanding of some things that the respondent lacks. The notion of understanding is defined relative to the type of dialogue. Thus scientific understanding of a subject could be quite different from legal understanding of the same subject.

THE USE OF EXPLANATION TO FILL GAPS

The respondent's role is to ask questions and in particular to ask the proponent to explain some things (statements or propositions) that the respondent does not understand. The proponent's role is to fill in gaps in the understanding of the respondent to help the latter make sense of something that is professed not to be understood.

SPEECH ACTS AND COMMITMENTS

Both proponent and respondent can perform other functions as well. They can collect new facts as evidence, enlarging the data set. They both have commitment sets. They can also retract statements from these commitment sets.

Formation of Explanation Attempts in Dialogue

THE INITIAL QUESTION STARTING THE SEQUENCE

First, the respondent asks the proponent a why question of the kind requesting an explanation of some specific item in the data set.

THE OFFERING OF AN ANSWER TO THE QUESTION

Second, the proponent offers an explanation that answers the question. More precisely, what the proponent offers is an explanation attempt in the form of a hypothesis. In the forward argumentation scheme for abductive inference, the hypothesis functions as the antecedent of a rule (conditional generalization) that has the statement in the why question as its consequent.

THE REPEATED SEQUENCE OF QUESTIONS AND REPLIES

Third, this process goes on and on in a finite repeating sequence that can be modeled by a profile of dialogue. In the repeating sequence, the respondent keeps asking the same why question, and the proponent, each time, offers a different hypothesis.

THE TERMINATION OF THE QUESTIONING SEQUENCE

Fourth, the sequence is repeated until all the plausible hypotheses are collected into a set. Then the sequence of asking and answering questions is terminated. The decision to terminate questioning is often a practical one. It does not necessarily mean that all possible, or even all plausible, explanations have been exhausted. It may be affected by such factors as the costs of continuing an investigation and collecting more facts.

Evaluation of Explanations

THE EVALUATION OF PLAUSIBILITY

Each explanation attempt is evaluated in answer to two questions. How plausible is it in itself as an explanation? How plausible is it relative to the other explanation attempts?

THE SELECTION OF THE BEST HYPOTHESIS

The most plausible explanation is selected, or if there are several, one is selected as the best hypothesis with which to move forward.

Dialogue Closure

THE JUDGMENT OF COMPLETENESS

The abductive inference to the best explanation needs to be judged as relative to the progress of the dialogue to that point. Several questions need to be asked to make this judgment. How complete has the collection of data been? How deep has the examining all the possible or plausible explanations been? These questions correspond to CQ3 in the list of critical questions earlier in this chapter.

THE RECONSIDERATION OF CLOSURE

After answers are given to these last two questions, two choices are possible. One is to cycle back to the terminating of questioning point and reopen the sequence of seeking further explanations. This option is represented by CQ4 in the list of critical questions earlier in this chapter. The other choice is to close the dialogue and tentatively accept the best explanation found to the point reached in the dialogue so far.

THE KNOWLEDGE BASE ASSESSMENT

If the closure option is taken, and the decision is made to accept the best hypothesis without any further investigation or dialogue, the judgment of the plausibility of the abductive reasoning needs to take this pragmatic factor into account. The strength of the abductive reasoning from the given premises to the conclusion should be judged in light of the progress of the dialogue on a burden-of-proof basis. Such an inference needs to be seen as based on both what is known and what is not known in the given case, as far as the collection of data and the process of questioning has proceeded.

THE DEFEASIBILITY ASPECT

The conclusion is drawn to accept tentatively the best hypothesis on the balance of considerations to that point, but acceptance should be based on commitment that is subject to retraction in the future unless the database and the dialogue are complete. In the most typical cases of abduction, the investigation should be seen as potentially subject to further dialogue as the data set is expanded or as more plausible hypotheses may be found. In other words, the argument should be seen as defeasible.

7

Unsolved Problems of Abduction

The aim of chapter 7 is to provide a platform for further research on abductive reasoning by indicating some key areas where problems need to be solved but where the dialectical theory of abduction as inference to the best explanation makes gains. It is easy to see that the theory put forward in chapter 6 cannot solve all the problems that have been raised. This is especially so with respect to problems in the philosophy of science that can only be solved by extensive case studies showing how abductive reasoning is used in classic cases of scientific discovery and problem solving. By concentrating on cases from legal and everyday argumentation and by using tools from argumentation theory, the new theory has put a framework in place that prompts precise questions that formulate a number of clearly definable problems. These problems have to do with abductive reasoning as a query-driven and dynamic form of argumentation that moves forward and evolves over the course of an investigation. In particular, a number of problems are posed about scientific discovery and its role in scientific inquiry as a framework of rational argumentation. One problem addressed is how an explanation can grow and evolve during a process in which it is examined and critically probed for gaps and weaknesses. These problems are shown to be amenable to solutions.

ABDUCTION AND ARGUMENTATION SCHEMES

One problem has surfaced time and time again. It is the connection between abduction and argumentation schemes. Obviously, abductive argumentation is itself an argumentation scheme, according to the theory presented in chapter 6. But several other argumentation schemes have appeared to be abductive in nature or to be closely connected to abduction. One case in point is the argumentation scheme recognized by Pollock (1995) and Prakken (2003) that, as noted in chapter 1, has the following form.

ARGUMENTATION SCHEME FOR ARGUMENT FROM APPEARANCE
If something looks like an x then it is an x.
This object looks like an x.
Therefore this object is an x.

Peirce noted that abduction is often based on visual observations, and his example of the fish skeleton from paleontology cited in chapter 1 tied in with the cases of visual abductive reasoning in archeology cited by Shelley (1996). What is indicated is that abductive reasoning, in science as well as in law, is often based on argument from appearance. Of course, argument from appearance is defeasible. Close inspection of data at an archeological site, at a crime scene, or in a medical examination of a patient often leads to a hypothesis. As more data come in, the hypothesis can be tested and then supported or defeated. Either way, the investigation can move along.

Three critical questions matching the argument from appearance are the following.

CQ1: Is there some reason why this object might look like an x but not really be one?
CQ2: Can the hypothesis that the object is an x be tested by collecting more data?
CQ3: Are there counterbalancing reasons for accepting the hypothesis that the object is something else, as opposed to being an x?

The first critical question can be illustrated by Pollock's example of the red object. I might find out that the object is illuminated by a red light, making it appear red. But a red light will make any object look red to a normal human observer. This is a reason why the object might look red but not really be red. The other two questions can be illustrated by the ancient example of the rope from Sextus Empiricus (*Against the Logicians*, 188). A man sees what looks to him like a coil of rope in a dark part of a dimly lit room. Thinking that it could be a snake, he jumps over it. At that point he turns back and sees that the object has not moved. He then draws the plausible inference that it is not a snake. To test this hypothesis he prods the object with a stick. It still does not move. He concludes it is a rope and not a snake. In this case, the second critical question is answered by testing the hypothesis, by prodding the snake, and by collecting more data. The third critical question is relevant because snakes are often dangerous in a way that ropes are not. If some doubt remains, it is better to assume that the object is a snake, as opposed to being a rope, until more evidence is in. This could be a reason for warning a child not to touch it.

Another argumentation scheme often based on visual evidence of one kind or another is argument from sign. This form of argument is so closely related to abduction that it might be tempting to hypothesize that the two forms are even equivalent. In the bear example, the best explanation of the observed tracks (or imprints that appear to be tracks) is that a bear passed this way. It is this abductive inference that seems to be at the basis of the argument from sign. But this apparent equivalence between abductive inference and the argumentation scheme does not work in all cases. In some cases, the inference is predictive rather than abductive. For example, if I say that dark clouds are a sign of rain, that inference is an instance of argument from sign. But it is not an inference to a best explanation from observation of the dark clouds to the hypothesis of rain as explaining the dark clouds. Josephson and Josephson (1994, pp. 22–28) cited other examples in support of this distinction between abduction and prediction.

Peirce's writings on semiotics, or the study of signs, were extensive (Hoopes, 1991). Important examples of argument from sign can be found in fields as diverse as forensic investigation, diagnosis in medicine, linguistics, and communication. Peirce defined a sign as something that stands for something else, called its "object," in such a way as to generate another sign, called its "interpretant" (Hoopes, 1991, p. 88). So defined, the notion of sign is very broad and can be stretched to include any kind of inference from some kind of data or given message taken to stand for something. The most resonant kind of example might be that of a detective finding something, such as a footprint or a fingerprint at a crime scene, and then taking this as evidence that some person had been at that location. Obviously, such examples are also typical cases of abductive reasoning. Thus there are important connections between the field of semiotics and the study of argumentation schemes. Certainly, argument from sign responds very well to an abductive analysis that views it as being based on an inference to the best explanation.

Generally speaking, the role of argumentation schemes in explanations is a source of much controversy, and it is so for various reasons. One is that although reasoning, in the form of sequences of inferences, undeniably plays a large role in explanations, especially scientific explanations, we must be very careful, as shown in chapter 2, to draw and maintain a distinction between explanation and argument. Another reason is that there is a tendency in the current philosophy of science to see all forms of rational argument in science as either deductive or inductive and hence a reluctance to admit plausibilistic argumentation schemes such as DMP as appropriate to model the kind of reasoning used in scientific explanations. This tension is apparent in recent unificationist theories of scientific explanation. According to the unificationist theory, scientific explanation provides a unified account of a range of different phenomena by exhibiting connections between phenomena previously thought to be unrelated (Woodward, 2003, p. 36). The chief advocate of the unificationist theory has been Philip Kitcher (1988; 1989). As mentioned in chapter 2, the notion of an argument pattern is fundamental in Kitcher's theory of explanation. Is an argument pattern comparable to an argumentation scheme? In some ways, it seems that it is, because it represents the schematic structure of a type of argument that can be applied over and over again to arguments (Woodward, 2003, pp. 36–37). But Kitcher seems to admit nondeductive argument patterns in scientific explanations with some reservations. He (1989, p. 448) wrote that there is "no bar in principle to the use of non-deductive arguments in the systematization of our beliefs" but added that "in a certain sense, all explanation is deductive." Perhaps Kitcher, like many philosophers of science, tends to concentrate on fairly well-established, advanced explanations in the natural sciences that have been worked out in a mathematical formulation that can be expressed using deductive logic. On the other hand, scientific explanations and abductive inferences based on them at the discovery stage are much better modeled using plausibilistic argumentation schemes such as those for DMP, argument from appearance, and argument from sign.

We should also remember that explanations are context sensitive and that an explanation used in a police investigation or in a trial may be based on argumentation quite different from argumentation that would be appropriate for a scientific explanation advanced within the scientific community and based on scientific research. Police investigators or lawyers presenting evidence in court often base their explanations on expert witnesses. Here the argumentation scheme for argument from expert opinion often plays an important role in the kind of abductive reasoning that is used. In a scientific explanation of the kind Kitcher seems to have in mind as his model, however, appeal to expert opinion would have no place at all.

There is also controversy about which argumentation schemes are associated with abductive reasoning. Some examples of argumentation schemes appear to not perform very well when one attempts to view them in an abductive model as inference to the best explanation. For example, consider argument from expert opinion (see chapter 1). You could try to view this scheme abductively as follows.

Expert E said proposition A is true.
Why would E say that A is true?
The best explanation of E's saying A is true is that A is really true.

Some would undoubtedly view this abductive reconstruction of argument from expert opinion as explaining how this argumentation scheme works and as revealing its warrant as an inference. But I would disagree. I would concede that one explanation of why E said A is true could be that E accepts that A is true or thinks that A is true. But there could be other explanations. For example, E could make a profit from saying that A is true. In effect, then, the other competing explanations play a role similar to that of the critical questions matching the scheme for argument from expert opinion. Thus I do not see any advantage in trying to structure the scheme for argument from expert opinion as an abductive inference. It could be harmless, but it is not all that useful or helpful in giving insight into how to use the scheme. I am sure that many commentators will disagree here, however.[1] Those attracted to the best explanation model tend to try to impose it on any kind of argumentation they may otherwise find hard to understand.

On the other hand, the best explanation model fits some argumentation schemes extremely well. For example, as noted in chapter 5, the argument from effect to cause can typically be viewed as an argument from observed data to a causal explanation of the data. Or consider the argumentation scheme from correlation to cause. Suppose, for example, a strong correlation has been observed between pattern baldness (moving outward from the crown of the head) and heart attacks. With the observation of such an interesting correlation, the question arises whether some causal explanation of it could be given. The mere correlation, even though it may be statistically significant, does not by itself warrant leaping to the conclusion that there is a causal link of some sort. But it is interesting enough to prompt a search for explanations. If an explanation is attempted, it might warrant a hypothesis stating a causal connection. In such a case, the argument from correlation to cause can nicely be viewed as an inference to the best explanation. At any rate, this model fits better here than it does in the case of argument from expert opinion.

There remains much controversy about the connection between abduction and argumentation schemes of the presumptive and defeasible sort. These presumptive schemes do not fit deductive or inductive models of reasoning, as indicated in chapter 4. It is tempting, therefore, to put them all in the abductive category, agreeing with Peirce's classification of all arguments as deductive, inductive, or presumptive. However, chapter 4 has already discussed the many difficulties with this approach, supporting the Josephsons' view that an adequate analysis of abductive reasoning resists the simple three-way classification. It would be nice if things were so simple. Instead, it appears that some of the presumptive schemes fit the abductive model very well, and others do not. As noted in chapter 6, in some cases and under certain conditions a presumptive argumentation scheme can take a form that is deductively valid. For example, argument from ignorance can sometimes be deductively valid if a condition of epistemic closure is imposed on the investigation.

ENTHYMEMES, ARGUMENTATION SCHEMES, AND THE DEFEASIBLE *MODUS PONENS* FORM OF REASONING

The problem of enthymemes was posed in chapter 3 and was shown there to be related to solving the problem of abduction.[2] As indicated, there are two different (but connected) problems. There is the problem of arguments with missing premises or conclusions. Second, there is the problem of the whole class of plausible (or abductive or presumptive) arguments that represent a third type of argument that is neither deductive nor inductive. This book is directed to solving the second problem, using a dialogue-based approach. But I would also argue that the other problem can also best be solved using the dialogue-based approach. To make clear how, we might find it useful to revert to the corporate income tax example from chapter 3.

The missing premise is said to be the statement, "Whatever encourages waste and high prices should be abolished" (Hurley, 2000, p. 289).

To make the argument into a categorical syllogism, this statement has to be taken to express a universal generalization, such as "All things (or perhaps practices) that encourage waste and high prices are things (practices) that should be abolished." One might wonder in this case whether the missing statement should be taken to express a strictly universal generalization. More plausibly it means something such as "In general, if a practice encourages waste and high prices, then that is a reason to abolish it." This version of the statement is defeasible, because it is compatible with there being reasons for not abolishing the practice. Thus it is properly classified as a defeasible or nonstrict generalization.[3] And this, of course, is the type of generalization that is the major premise of so many of the defeasible argumentation schemes.

Another observation about this case is that the argument depends on two additional missing premises. One is a statement that could be expressed as follows: a practice that encourages waste and high prices is, all other things being equal, a bad practice. The other is the statement, "If something is a bad practice, it ought to be abolished." A structure that is helpful in guiding an argument analyst on how to fill in these missing premises is the argumentation scheme for the argument from negative consequences (Walton, 1996a, p. 76).

Premise: if action A is brought about, bad consequences will occur.
Conclusion: therefore A should not be brought about.

This argumentation scheme can be used to give a reason to support the claim that an action should not be carried out, the reason being that bad consequences will occur. Below it will be shown that there is another argumentation scheme for what is called argument from classification. Using argument from classification, you could classify "waste" and "high prices" as being, generally speaking, bad things. Then, using argument from classification and argument from negative consequences, you could identify two generalizations that could function as unstated premises in the argument in the corporate income tax example.

Argument from Negative Consequences Premise: Any practice that has bad consequences should (other things being equal) be discontinued.
Argument from Classification Premise: Waste and high prices are (generally) bad things.

This way of reconstructing the argument is quite attractive, because the argumentation schemes can be used to identify the generalizations that naturally fit as missing premises. Although we can disagree about what the missing premises really are and exactly what form they should take, the analysis using argumentation schemes is a good fit.

One thing revealed by this discussion of the problem of enthymemes is that abduction, taken to represent reasoning backward (or literally "leading from"), is an ambiguous notion. In one sense, it means inference to the best explanation, as captured by the backward argumentation scheme for abductive inference. In another sense, it means reasoning backward from a given conclusion to see what premises in a given database that conclusion was supposedly derived from. As indicated by the corporate income tax example above, an enthymeme of the kind so often cited in the textbooks throws in an additional twist. The search for premises only produces a complete argument, one having all the premises needed to support the conclusion properly, if a missing or implicit premise is added to the explicit ones. This kind of backward or abductive reasoning could be called inference to the best reason to contrast it with the other kind of abductive reasoning called inference to the best explanation.

In the oatmeal example of an enthymeme studied in chapter 3, the original argument was: "Eating oatmeal lowers cholesterol, because Smith said so, and he is a physician." The nonexplicit premises were that Smith is an expert in a domain of knowledge (medicine) and that if an expert says something is so, then it is so. It was argued in chapter 3 that the best way to interpret this latter premise is as a defeasible conditional that is subject to exceptions. Judging from the corporate income tax example as analyzed above, one might think that the argumentation scheme for the argument from expert opinion (reprinted below from chapter 1) might be helpful.

ARGUMENT FROM EXPERT OPINION
Major Premise: Source E is an expert in subject domain S containing proposition A.
Minor Premise: E asserts that proposition A (in domain S) is true (false).
Conclusion: A may plausibly be taken to be true (false).

The argumentation scheme appears to help at first, because the first non-explicit premise, "Smith is an expert in a domain of knowledge (medicine)," matches the major premise of the scheme. But where does the other premise, the conditional premise, come from? This question can be answered by introducing a more explicit version of the scheme for argument from expert opinion from Reed and Walton (2003), where the scheme above is called "Appeal to Expert Opinion (Version I)." Version II would be as follows.

APPEAL TO EXPERT OPINION (VERSION II)
Major Premise: Source E is an expert in subject domain S containing proposition A.
Minor Premise: E asserts that proposition A (in domain S) is true (false).
Conditional Premise: If source E is an expert in a subject domain S containing proposition A, and E asserts that proposition A is true (false), then A may plausibly be taken to be true (false).
Conclusion: A may plausibly be taken to be true (false).

Version II of the scheme elicits the conditional premise of the oatmeal argument perfectly by matching it to the conditional premise in the scheme. Note that Version II reveals the *DMP* form of the argumentation scheme for appeal to expert opinion.

These cases show how many strands are now brought together. The argumentation schemes that have the *DMP* form can be applied to many common cases of enthymematic arguments in natural language discourse. When so applied, they can be used to make missing premises or conclusions explicit. A system such as *Araucaria* is a powerful device to exploit such connections, because it has the capability to represent argumentation schemes as well as chains of inferences in argument diagrams. Thus forward and backward chaining of the kind so characteristic of abductive reasoning can now be reconstructed using argumentation schemes to help fill in missing premises or conclusions that are links in the chain. The case study of causal abductive reasoning in legal argumentation presented in chapter 5 shows how all these strands are connected. The argumentation in this case was based on empirical causal generalizations of a kind that are defeasible. In computing, they are commonly called domain-dependent "rules." They are expressed by the plausibilistic generalizations or conditionals analyzed in chapter 4. In many instances of abductive reasoning, such as the case studied in chapter 5, these rules are the basis of defeasible *modus ponens* arguments. They are the missing premises that, once made explicit, enable the chain of reasoning to be completed. The job of filling them in is greatly assisted by the use of defeasible argumentation schemes. Thus the theory of abductive argumentation presented in chapter 6 reveals how argumentation schemes of the *DMP* form are useful for dealing with enthymemes.

THE ROLE OF EXAMINATION IN SCIENCE

The role of examination in scientific discovery and argumentation has not been appreciated or even recognized. Peirce's frequent association of abduction with the making of observations and the collecting of data does suggest, however, that there could be a role for examination in science.[4] Scientific discourse often takes the form of citing evidence to prove or disprove a hypothesis or theory. As such, it is a form of argument. But it also frequently takes the form of an attempt to explain some data. The functions of argument and explanation are of course intertwined in abductive reasoning. But there is another aspect of scientific discourse that is easily overlooked. This is the process of examination. Examination can take place in many instances even prior to the stage where an explanation of the data is proposed. The scientist is examining data not merely by collecting information but also by testing its sturdiness by asking questions about it. If data seem to be inconsistent, the scientist may try probing with a view to getting a consistent account. It is important to realize that the process of examination is not entirely passive. It is not a mere collecting of information. Examination involves a testing function to discard what may only look like genuine data. Examination is always based on asking questions, and such questions are organized and selective.

The role of examination has been evident in some of the examples of argumentation schemes cited. Prakken cited the example of the following conditional (rule) often relied on in legal reasoning: if it looks like an affidavit, it is an affidavit.[5] Pollock cited the example of the following defeasible rule: if it looks red, it is red.[6] The prominent example of argument from sign was the inference from the observation of what look like bear tracks to the conclusion that a bear passed this way. Peirce, as noted in chapter 1, also emphasized the importance of observation of data in his account of abduction. All such examples appear to indicate that abductive reasoning typically occurs in a context of examination of some given set of data or observations. The process of examination itself is not only one of carefully looking at the data but also one of asking questions about it and trying to explain it. The process of explanation in an examination is typically a preliminary one, however, prior to the formulation of any carefully worked out theory. You could even say that what characterizes examination as a type of dialogue is the dual process of carefully looking at the data and asking questions that attempt to make sense of them as a body of statements. The questions are typically requests for explanations. In the theory proposed in chapter 2, they are thus attempts to understand the data or to make sense of it. Of course, at the examination stage, however, explanations may be of a fairly superficial sort. Only at a later stage will sophisticated theories emerge.

This account of scientific argumentation suggests that there are three distinct levels in an examination. The first is the mere collection of data. Examination consists, first of all, in observing something and collecting information that reports or describes what was seen heard or recorded. The second consists of the testing of the data collected at the first level. The third consists in the processing of the findings of the first two levels by asking probing questions. The process of discovery in a scientific investigation begins with a set of data that has been collected or is in the process of being collected. But discovery is more than just the collection of data. It is based on an examination of the data and on asking questions about the data. Some of these questions ask for more details, but some ask for explanations of parts or all of the data. Thus the role of questioning is very important and shows that discovery can be viewed as a kind of dialogue process of questioning and answering. As Schum (1994, p. 458) emphasized in his account of discovery, "If we do not ask appropriate or important questions enroute during the discovery process, we may never even have at hand combinations of information from which we may, retroductively, generate possibilities or hypotheses that have some chance of being true." At the third level, the questioner tries to get a coherent account by drawing inferences from the set of statements collected at the first two levels using argumentation schemes. The argumentation at this third level has a critical edge. It is a testing of factual data, using different forms of argumentation that are not conclusive but that can raise doubts about the worth or accuracy of a finding. One important test is consistency. If the data appear to exhibit a contradiction, then looking for reasons that might help to explain the apparent contradiction can be useful.

Examination is distinct as a form of the diagnostic process in clinical medicine. It is also recognized as vitally important in the collection and processing of legal evidence in a trial. But it seems not yet to have been recognized as an important part of the process of scientific discovery. Future studies in the philosophy of science could benefit a lot from recognizing it. It would also seem to be vitally important for abduction. Abductive reasoning begins with data or observations and then proceeds to a best explanation of them. The dialectical framework, at this stage of a scientific investigation, can be seen as one not just of collecting "bare facts" but of examining the facts or data. Such an examination process has a cognitive structure. In some cases, it may be a simple attempt to explain the data. But because critiquing is involved, the explanation process may also contain argumentation. Thus abductive reasoning, as inference to the best explanation, needs to be seen as a process of argumentation using argumentation schemes and critical questions, just as proposed in chapter 6.

The analysis of the four phases of abductive argumentation in chapter 6 is based on a set of data D that represents the common starting points in the dialogue. In a forensic investigation, this set of data could be all the evidence collected at the crime scene. It could consist of measurements made by the police, videotapes of actions, or statements of witnesses. The data are not necessarily statements that are known or believed to be true. Rather, they are just taken as data. What they imply, and whether they are true representations of whatever they seem to be or are now taken to be, may be subject to later disputation. To take another example, consider the kind of data found at an archeological site excavated by a research team. Artifacts may be found, their locations may be recorded on a map of the site, and records may be taken of what artifacts were found, where they were found, and how they were found. All these records and artifacts are data. Or consider again the classic example of finding what look like bear tracks on a hiking trail. The tracks may be photographed. They may plausibly look like bear tracks. The investigators may make records of where they found them and so forth. These items are the data. Collecting them may take the form of an information-seeking type of dialogue. In the four-phase structure of abductive argumentation, data collection takes place at the dialogue setting stage.

The next phase is that of attempts at explanation. There may be more than one plausible explanation. In a case of scientific discovery, each theory will be shown to have deductive or inductive implications, and these implications can be tested empirically. At this phase, the dialectical tension between two sides may become more apparent. As new data come in from the test, one explanation may be shown to be better than its competitor. But the way the dialogue proceeds from this point may be quite different in a legal context than in a scientific context. Let us go back to the bear tracks example. A proponent may offer a causal explanation of the tracks. They were caused by a grizzly bear who passed that way on the trail. But a respondent may bring forward arguments that suggest a different explanation. The respondent may introduce an expert tracker, for example, who says that the prints do not look quite genuine. The respondent may also have some eyewitnesses testify that they saw two persons making artificial bear prints on the trail with a device made for this purpose from a bear's foot. The proponent may critically question these arguments. The proponent may argue that the witness is biased or not properly qualified as an expert, for example. There are photographs of the supposed bear tracks there as data, or common starting points. But each side may draw different inferences about what these show, and each side may critique the explanation of the other side, as well as the arguments used to support that explanation. This is the critiquing part of the dialogue.

What examination is and how it works varies with the type of dialogue the examination is supposed to be part of. It works in scientific argumentation in one way and in legal argumentation, for example in a trial, in a different way. In a trial, witnesses are examined by being subjected to questioning by advocates for the prosecution and the defense. In scientific argumentation, evidence is examined at the discovery stage by asking questions about it, particularly questions calling for an explanation of part or all of the evidence collected so far. But examination always has the three levels noted in chapter 6. First there is a collection of data. Then there is an attempt, or series of attempts, to explain the data. Then there is a critiquing or argumentation phase, where one explanation is pitted against another.

ACCOUNTS AND EXPLANATIONS

At the discovery stage of an investigation, abductive reasoning often looks like just a simple inference from premises representing some observations by drawing a single conclusion from them. But as the investigation continues, more and more evidence is typically collected. In a scientific inquiry, the single statement drawn by abduction becomes a hypothesis. As the inquiry proceeds, that hypothesis may become more and complex. The conclusion initially drawn may become carefully qualified, and the terms in it may be carefully defined. In a word, the hypothesis will be refined. The initial hypothesis may even grow into a scientific theory. Or it may be embedded in some existing scientific theory so that it comes to be expressed in a very precise way and connected to all kinds of additional assumptions and postulates. Along the way, the hypothesis may be criticized, and weak points found in it may be examined critically. If the holes in it appear to be impossible to repair, the hypothesis may be refuted and cast aside in favor of another more promising one. On the other hand, if it survives this process of testing and critical examination, a hypothesis may become quite complex. Although it may still be possible to sum it up by a single statement, a set of connected statements may have to be given in order to state the hypothesis fully and accurately. This set of connected statements is presumed to hang together so that the single statements or sets of statements in it are connected by logical reasoning with other single statements or sets of statements. We do not really have a good general word for a set of statements of this sort. Let us call it an account. The hypothesis drawn by abductive reasoning is an account that offers an explanation of some data. As the data multiply during the inquiry, the account inevitably becomes more lengthy and complex. This process of colligation makes the account a deeper and better explanation.

The role of the account as an anchored narrative given in the theory of witness testimony of Wagenaar, van Koppen, and Crombag (1993) was described in chapter 2. The testimony of a witness is seen in legal argumentation as a "story" or anchored narrative. A good or acceptable anchored narrative is one that hangs together internally, is consistent with other known facts or evidence in the case, and is plausible. For example, if the story offered by a witness appears to contain an inconsistency, that could count heavily against it. The lawyer who examines such testimony in court asks questions that probe into the weak parts of the story and may criticize it so effectively that it ceases to be plausible as an account of what supposedly happened (Pennington and Hastie, 1993). Witness examination in a trial is a more complex process than it might appear to be, however. Generally, the examiner already knows the answer to a question asked of the witness.

Using the case of Margie and the balloon as shown in chapter 2, we can make an account of an ordered set of statements that make sense not only independently but also as a whole set. As a set, the statements are tied together. Not only can inferences be drawn from subsets of this given set of statements, often by Gricean implicatures, but also the conclusions of such inferences can then be added to the original set, filling out the account even further or more explicitly. Schum (2001) showed how this process, which he called marshaling and Peirce called colligation, drives abductive reasoning. The role of implicit premises and conclusions in arguments traditionally called enthymemes (see chapter 3) is very important in this process. In legal cases and in examples of abductive reasoning in everyday argumentation, an account is colligated by adding unstated assumptions deriving from a body of commonsense knowledge (called a script in AI) (Schank and Abelson, 1977). But what about abductive reasoning of the kind found in the discovery stage of a scientific inquiry? Although it may be based on commonsense knowledge at a very early stage of the emergence of a hypothesis, once the inquiry proceeds and the hypothesis becomes more scientifically refined, commonsense scripts tend to play less and less of a role. The hypothesis will survive only if it can be situated within an exact scientific theory or if it is the basis of a new theory that can be expressed in some formal structure that fits in with the basic scientific concepts already known and accepted, and taken to be understood, in such fields as physics, mathematics, chemistry, and biology. The explanatory power of an account, according to the theory of explanation presented in chapter 2, derives from this existing understanding and acceptance.

In the EDGE user modeling system for explanations in Cawsey (1992, p. 134), two components of an explanation have to be matched. One is an account of some domain, in the form of a knowledge base made up of a set of rules and facts. For example, such an account might be about how a light detector works or about how to chop chocolate in a food processor (p. 135). The other is an account representing the user's knowledge of the topic. For example, the user may know only very little about the technology of light-detection devices. Or the user may know quite a lot about how a food processor works. To offer a successful explanation, the system has to know both what the user knows and what the user does not know about the domain. The system has to relate the one account to the other and to fill the gaps in the user's knowledge. The gaps are items of knowledge that are in the account of the appropriate domain as known to the system but are missing or incompletely represented in the user's account. The system, in other words, has to match the two accounts or compare them and fill gaps in the user's account.

In the dialectical theory of rationality presented in chapter 3, what counts as a successful explanation or argument depends on the context of dialogue or investigation to which that argument or explanation is supposed to contribute. In this theory, what is a successful explanation in law might not be a successful explanation in science and vice versa. Success in an explanation and the kind of explanation that is appropriate depend on the question that was originally asked in the context of some search, investigation, or inquiry. Thus it is not surprising, according to this dialogue-based theory, that abductive reasoning needs to be evaluated differently in different contexts of dialogue. Nor is it surprising that scientific explanation will, in general, be different from legal explanation of the kind that might be given by the prosecution or the defense in a trial. In a trial, as the evidence builds up and the argumentation reaches the closing stage, a rather large and more or less plausible story or account is built up on each side (Wigmore, 1913). The story put forward by the argumentation of the prosecution is opposed to the one put forward by the defense. Each side offers an account that purports to explain the facts. Abductive reasoning works differently in a scientific inquiry. The purpose of the dialogue is not, as in a court, to resolve a conflict of opinions on a basis of burden of proof but, using scientific knowledge, to answer a question or solve a problem by carefully collecting all the data relevant to proving or disproving a hypothesis. Thus abductive reasoning needs to be evaluated differently in science than in law. This context sensitivity of such reasoning raises some provocative questions about the meaning of the term "account" in contexts of scientific discovery and hypothesis formation. The theory that an account can be understood as an anchored narrative in legal argumentation has been very well articulated and supported by Wagenaar, van Koppen, and Crombag (1993). But an account in scientific argumentation is surely not a narrative or story. What is it, then, in that context? This question poses a fundamental problem for the philosophy of science that has not yet been solved. There is not enough space to try to solve that problem here. The best we can do is to work with relatively simple examples of explanation, such as the radiators case analyzed in chapter 5, to show how an account is built up through a process of query-driven colligation. But by drawing a comparison between legal and scientific abduction, some light can be shed on this process.

One of the biggest problems of abduction in scientific discovery concerns what role inconsistency plays as a hypothesis moves forward. If a hypothesis is found to be internally inconsistent or found to fail testing by being inconsistent with known data, then we have reasons for dropping it and moving to an alternative hypothesis. But why is this so? If abduction is inference to a best explanation, as outlined in chapter 2, then why should inconsistency play such a large role in abductive reasoning at the discovery stage of a scientific inquiry? The reason is to be found in the notion of a colligated account. A successful explanation yields understanding not just because it answers the question posed by the questioner but also because it yields a coherent account that the questioner can understand, or make sense of. If the hypothesis appears to be internally inconsistent or if it can be shown to not be consistent with other statements accepted as representing scientific knowledge, then it can rightly be subjected to critical scrutiny. If the apparent inconsistency cannot be removed, say by making changes in the formulation of the hypothesis, then the hypothesis will fail. The reason is that scientific knowledge is taken to be an account of reality, not a "web of belief," to use a common phrase, but a web of acceptance. Like any account, it is assumed to be consistent. Thus an apparent inconsistency found in a scientific explanation is a colligation failure. The apparent inconsistency must be examined and somehow dealt with. The reason is that a scientific explanation yields the sort of understanding appropriate for a scientific inquiry only if it makes sense, that is, if it is free of what appear to be inconsistencies.

Schum, even in an earlier work (1994, p. 488), recognized this process of binding together of a hypothesis with other statements during an inquiry, calling it the "marshaling" of evidence. Using Wigmore's theory of evidence, Schum (1994, p. 493) showed how discovery proceeds in legal and forensic investigations of the kind that provide evidence in a trial: "A refined hypothesis becomes more specific or detailed and therefore more extensive." A hypothesis may be very sketchy at first and will outrun the evidence that has been collected at that stage. This process of colligation proceeds as an account becomes more detailed and substantial as an explanation of the facts known at a given point in an investigation. As the investigation proceeds, new facts may have to be accounted for. Thus abductive reasoning is ampliative in the sense that it arrives at a tentative conclusion that is defeasible as an account expands in an open-ended process of discovery. As the dialogue shifts from a discovery stage through a testing stage to a proving or disproving stage, more evidence is marshaled, and the hypothesis is more and more refined as it survives each stage. The account may have started as a sketchy explanation that was little more than a clever guess. But at a later stage, many gaps in that initial account are filled in by colligating it with a mass of other statements marshaled as additional evidence.

THE PROBLEM OF INCONSISTENCY

Within recent studies of scientific discovery, there has been quite a marked concern with inconsistency. Case studies of scientific discovery have shown that inconsistency is a fairly common phenomenon in scientific discovery and theory formation. But, of course, classical deductive logic is limited in its ability to deal with inconsistency (Woods, 2003), for it is a well-known theorem of classic deductive logic that an inconsistency logically implies any statement you care to choose. Thus classical logic does not seem to provide any way of moving forward from the finding of an inconsistency in a set of statements to some statement that would be the conclusion to draw in order to move an investigation in a right direction. And yet a finding of inconsistency can, in some cases of scientific reasoning, help point the way to move ahead by resolving the problem.

Da Costa and French (2002, p. 114) argued that inconsistency plays a heuristic role in the discovery process in a scientific inquiry. They described the process as one in which an inconsistency found in a hypothesis enables the inquiry to move forward by replacing the inconsistent hypothesis with one that is consistent. This proposal is a dialectical one because the inquiry is seen as moving forward through several stages. At one stage the inconsistency is discovered, and at a next stage it is removed. But how exactly is such an adjustment made? Certainly it involves retraction. Removal of one or more of the statements that collectively produce the inconsistency is a first step. But how should such a retraction proceed? In a set of statements that hang together by logical inferences that join some statements to others, you cannot just retract one statement as if it were isolated from the others. Thus we are led to the problem of retraction.

The problem of inconsistency in scientific discovery is closely related to a more general problem in argumentation theory. There is also a tool from argumentation that is helpful. The argumentation scheme for argument from inconsistent commitment was introduced in chapter 6. This scheme helps to solve the problem because it presents the form of argument used to criticize an inconsistent set of commitments. This argumentation scheme, by itself, does not tell us how to solve the problem of inconsistency in scientific discovery. Other questions remain. But it offers a starting point. Clearly, one response to such a criticism by a respondent is for the proponent to give up one of the statements making up the inconsistency. But which one? And what if the one given up is closely connected by inference to another of the commitments? Should the proponent have to give up that one, too? This general type of difficulty in formal dialogue systems is called the problem of retraction, as noted in chapter 6.

The theory of accounts is very helpful in aiding with the perplexity often caused by inconsistency in logic and the philosophy of science. In a positivistic approach, scientific discovery aims at truth, and scientific knowledge is seen as a set of true propositions. Yet as all would seem to agree, if a set of propositions contains an inconsistency, it is not logically possible for all the propositions in it to be true. Thus it would seem to follow that an inconsistency in scientific knowledge can never arise. An account, on the other hand, is a set of propositions accepted by one party in a dialogue, representing commitment put forward in answer to a question. It is very clear that in dealing with an account, a finding of inconsistency can be quite a normal stage and one that needs to be overcome by confronting and dealing with it. In an account, various kinds of inconsistencies can turn up. But once a questioner probes into the account, the inconsistency can often be removed by asking further questions and specifically by confronting the author of the account with the inconsistency.

The dialectical solution to the problem of inconsistency in scientific discovery runs as follows. Suppose a researcher arrives at a conclusion by abductive reasoning. In the dialectical theory of abduction, this means that the researcher has offered a best explanation for a set of data. In scientific argumentation, such an explanation is said to take the form of a hypothesis. The hypothesis is normally not just a simple single statement, although it may sometimes be summed up that way. A hypothesis is more often a large set of related statements. Even though in its summary form it may be expressed as a single statement, it is normally a network containing many statements connected to each other by logical inferences. In the dialectical approach, the hypothesis can be viewed as an account. Accounts being what they are, it is evident that an account, although it may have initially appeared to be consistent, may, upon examination, reveal that it contains an inconsistency. When a respondent discovers the inconsistency, that individual should criticize the hypothesis, arguing that it cannot be an acceptable explanation as it stands because of its internal incoherence. The underlying logical form of reasoning in this kind of criticism is represented by the argumentation scheme for argument from inconsistent commitment. So far, then, the theory of accounts presents a model that enables one to understand what takes place when inconsistency is found in a case of scientific discovery and shows why the argumentation is, or at least could be, a rational sequence of moves in an inquiry. Accounts need to be consistent in order to maintain plausibility, and the reasons for this need are perfectly understandable in the dialectical theory of abductive reasoning.

But now we come back to the problem of retraction. How should the proponent of an abductive argument respond when challenged by a respondent who cites an inconsistency in the proponent's hypothesis? The best answer is that there is no one predetermined type of response. The proponent should be seen as having several options. One is that the individual can retract the old hypothesis and move to a different explanation, now held to be better because of the removal of the inconsistency in the old one. An alternative move that should be allowed is to attempt to repair the inconsistency. This move can be carried out in a number of ways. The simplest one is for the proponent to retract one or the other of the statements that make up the inconsistent pair. But if this kind of move is made, it may weaken the account so much that further modifications are needed to save it. The individual might have to retract other statements in the account that are related by inference to the rejected proposition. Or the retracted statement might have to be reformulated, for example by adding certain qualifications to it. Adding the qualifications may remove the inconsistency. In addition, changing the original statement to its modified form may require deleting some other statements in the account that had the unqualified version in it.

Once the notion of an account is added to the theory of abductive argumentation proposed in chapter 6, it becomes clear that formal dialogue theory can offer a useful way of dealing with the problem of inconsistency in scientific discovery. The discovery stage of a scientific investigation can be seen as having the dialectical structure of a critical discussion type of dialogue in which competing alternative hypotheses are elicited as explanations of the data found so far. But the problem is one of choosing which of a pair of opposed plausible hypotheses to commit to, at least tentatively, to move the investigation forward by collecting new data and testing the chosen hypothesis using the data found. The problem is to find a path to move forward, and hence it is one of choosing a heuristic that aims toward an ultimate goal of creating a carefully formulated and precise hypothesis that is proved, or at least confirmed, by empirical data that have been systematically collected. As soon as any hypothesis is found to be inconsistent with the data, it must be rejected. At least retraction is required if the data are accepted as accurate observations. As indicated above, such a hypothesis must be modified or a different one chosen instead. In the dialectical model of abductive reasoning proposed in chapter 6, the procedure works in three stages as follows.

1. The proponent puts an abductive argument forward.
2. The respondent asks a critical question based on what the individual alleges is an inconsistency found in the account presupposed by the explanation.
3. A burden of proof is placed on the proponent to argue that there is no real inconsistency in the account, to modify the account, or to move to a different explanation altogether.

The proponent is obliged to make this third kind of response because of the defeasibility of abductive argumentation generally. Otherwise the old argument defaults. In short, the problem of dealing with inconsistency in a hypothesis, and the general problem of evaluating abductive reasoning of any kind, is to be found in the dialogue structure of the argumentation. It is a matter of what argumentation scheme has been put forward, what the appropriate responses to it are, and on which side the burden of proof lies at any given point in the dialogue. What one especially needs to recognize is that at the discovery stage, scientific argumentation is based on decisions between competing hypotheses that are not yet proved or disproved. They are merely assumptions at this stage. Even so, a decision needs to be made on which one looks more plausible as a candidate for further exploration and testing. Testing can be costly, so a fortunate choice of a hypothesis that later turns out to be confirmable can save time and money in a research project. Thus although support for any hypothesis might be weak at this discovery stage, and the argument for it may be defeasible, there is a pragmatic justification for picking a hypothesis now.

HOW ABDUCTIVE REASONING MOVES FORWARD BY EXAMINING COMPETING ACCOUNTS

An account is a set of statements, $A_1, A_2, \ldots, A_n$, offered by one party in answer to a question put by another party in a dialogue. One important kind of question is the kind requesting understanding of something. An account may be a narrative, but it does not have to be. It could even be a single statement. At the other extreme, it could be an entire scientific theory. In a typical instance, it could be a set of statements at varying levels of generality, linking some events to others by causal relations or linking some actions to goals. In any case, some thread of reasoning, often practical reasoning, connects the account together into a coherent whole. It is characteristic of accounts of the kind found in everyday speech that the account, as presented, is incomplete. It has many gaps that can be filled through colligation by drawing inferences from the statements explicitly given in the account. Some of these inferences are based on linking together generalizations and specific statements, so-called facts, by means of argumentation schemes. Others are based on Gricean conversational implicatures. As the questioner asks more questions, the respondent fills in more gaps in the account. Through such a dialogue, the account grows and becomes more elaborate as more and more interconnections within its statements are filled in. This process could be called account expansion, and it works by colligation.

For example, suppose you want to explain to someone how a photocopy machine works. The account given should depend on who asked the question. Suppose a colleague who needs to photocopy an assignment for a class asked the question. What the person wants is practical advice on how to make copies with the machine. You might tell the colleague this is how it works. Insert your user number by pushing these buttons, push this button to indicate the number of copies, and then push the red button to make the copies. Indicating this sequence of actions tells the questioner how to do what needs to be done with the machine. Suppose a technician asks you how it works. You might have to give this person a more general account that emphasizes how repairs to the machine are made. Suppose a science student, writing an essay on photocopying technology, asks you how the machine works. To answer this question, you might have to offer an abstract account of the process whereby the toner powder is sprayed onto the paper from a drum using electrostatic charges. This account might be more general than the previous two. But in any of the three kinds of cases, you will begin with a set of statements in which groups of them are related to each other by logical inferences. The account might be sketchy at first, with many gaps in it. The respondent will tend to ask questions that indicate a need for more details to be filled in. A good account is one that answers these questions at the right level of detail. An account that leaves gaps open, so that the respondent still fails to understand what you are trying to explain, is one that is (at least so far) unsuccessful. An account that gives too many details, especially obscure or irrelevant statements that do not help the respondent to understand how the machine works in relation to the question asked, is one that can be criticized. Neither of these kinds of account is the basis of a successful explanation, or at least the explanation is one that could be improved by giving the kind of account the respondent needs.

An account does not have to be internally consistent. It can be an inconsistent set. But normally the inconsistency is not obvious. In other words, when you look at the explicit set of statements making up the account, you will not generally tend to find one statement A and another statement not-A. When inconsistency arises in an account, it does so more obliquely. For example, you might find one statement A in an account and then find two other statements B and "If B then not-A." When the questioner finds such a pair of statements, that individual can put them together and draw the conclusion not-A from them. In such a case what the questioner should do is to challenge the account by saying to the other party, "Your account is not consistent; therefore I do not understand it." In short, an account does not need to be internally consistent. But if a questioner finds an inconsistency in it, that person can demand that the one who offered the account either repair the inconsistency or cease offering the account as an explanation of something. In this respect, an account is much like a commitment set in a dialogue. It need not be consistent, at least to begin with. But if an inconsistency is found in it, that finding is a basis for a critical questioning of it by a questioner. Thus a second criterion of adequacy of an account is that if an inconsistency is found in it and challenged, the account needs to be modified to remove the inconsistency. The process of removal is normally carried out by retracting (deleting) one or more of the statements in the account. In some cases, however, it may also involve expansion of the account to fill gaps created by the deletion or otherwise to help solve a problem found by the questioner.

Another characteristic of accounts is that there is normally more than one account that can be given to answer a question. Normally there will be one account that has been offered to help a questioner understand a set of presumed facts that have been asked about, for example, but there may also be other accounts. In some cases, one account may be inconsistent with another. It could be that both accounts are useful to help the questioner understand the fact that was questioned, but if one is accepted, then the other is not needed. In such a case, we say that the one account is better than the other. Thus in a case of scientific inquiry, for example, there may be two hypotheses competing to explain the data. Both could be potentially useful for this purpose, but one, for some reason, may be more plausible than the other. In general, where there is a set of accounts to be compared, one is chosen as the best, based on criteria that vary with the context. Figure 7.1 outlines the process of how abductive reasoning moves toward a conclusion by judging accounts comparatively by questioning and critically examining each one. As shown in figure 7.1, the dialogue starts with a database representing what have been accepted as the facts, observations, or findings collected so far. A questioner then asks a question seeking a better understanding of some or all of these facts. A respondent answers the question by putting forward an account meant to explain the facts queried. But that respondent, or another, may present an alternative account that also explains the same facts. Indeed, many other accounts may be given, as indicated in the central line of argumentation in figure 7.1. As indicated above, however, in a case of a kind common in scientific inquiry, there may be two hypotheses competing with each other to explain the data. In figure 7.1, these are called account 1 and account 2. Let us say then, as indicated in figure 7.1, once each account has been examined individually, only accounts 1 and 2 survive as plausible hypotheses. Each of the others fails to stand up to examination and is rejected. Thus a choice has to be made between account 1 and account 2. Which is the so-called best explanation? The one that is most plausible is chosen, and it becomes the ultimate conclusion that the whole sequence of abductive reasoning has led to. The comparative plausibility of the accounts is judged by how well each stands up to the critical examination of the respondent.

The purposes of offering an account can vary, and the kind of account that is successful can vary, depending on the goal of a dialogue. The purpose of an account is not always to offer an explanation of something. In some cases, a witness might offer an account to tell what happened or to describe something that happened. For example, a participant in a famous battle may write a description of the battle as witnessed. The participant may not try to explain how the battle started or why one side won or lost. The person may just write the account representing what that individual witnessed from the viewpoint as a soldier who played a small part in one sector of the engagement. The small details described could be very useful to historians, assuming they are accurate representations of what the soldier saw and heard. Another case

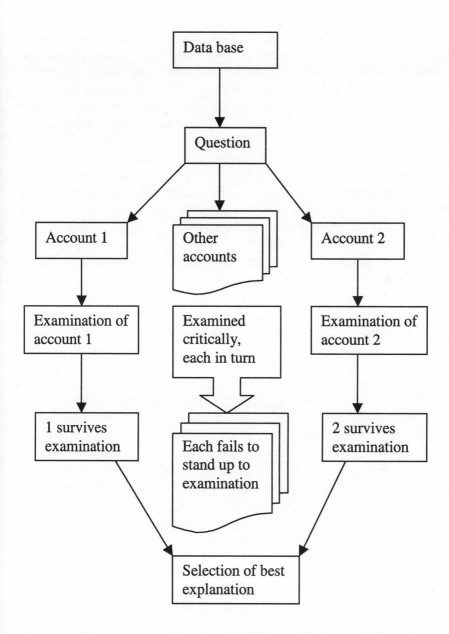

Figure 7.1 How abductive reasoning concludes to a best explanation.

in point would be that of an eyewitness in a trial asked to describe what was seen at a crime scene during a bank robbery. Although explanation may be involved in such a case, the main thing the witness may be attempting is to describe what was personally seen. Indeed, the lawyer questioning the eyewitness may object if that witness starts to draw inferences or make explanations rather than reporting the facts as seen by the person.

In cases of explanations, the purpose of offering an account is to help a questioner come to understand something that the individual claims is not now understood or only partially understood. The account is a set of statements offered by one party in a dialogue to another party who claims not to understand something. The purpose of offering the account is to remedy this party's lack of understanding. Thus an account should be defined in relation to how the party who offered it understands the lack of understanding of the other party. The purpose of an account is always to help the person who does not understand to make sense of something that, as the question indicates, is currently found to be problematic or puzzling. One important criterion of the usefulness of an account as a successful explanation that has stood up to examination is how well it fulfills this function.

When an account is examined, the examiner can ask many kinds of questions. The examiner can ask for clarifications, probe for weak points by asking critical questions, or cite separate parts of the account that do not seem to fit in with the account as a whole. The examiner can question specific statements in the account that do not seem plausible and can question a statement in the account that seems to be logically contrary to another statement previously accepted as factual in the case. Each type of question critically probes into aspects of the account that seem weak, are problematic, or are otherwise questionable. Thus to evaluate the success or failure of an account, one needs to judge how well it stands up to questioning. As the dialogue proceeds, the one who has offered the account will, as noted above, add some statements to it and delete others. But three factors can be cited as fundamental to judging the success or failure of an account. The first is how well the account performs its function of helping the questioner to make sense of something. The second is whether the account is internally consistent and how an alleged inconsistency is dealt with. The third is how plausible the account is generally and, in particular, how consistent it is with respect to other commitments that are not in question.

QUESTION-ANSWERING AND CRITIQUING
SYSTEMS IN ARTIFICIAL INTELLIGENCE

The new query-driven theory of abduction based on the dialogue theory of explanation seems like a novelty, but how could one go about applying it to computer dialogue systems that are currently in use? A new technology is moving in a direction that shows some potential for the development of the dialogue theory of explanation. In a question-answering system, a user asks a natural language question to a database of texts, and the system presents an answer. In the usual sort of search engine, such as *Google,* the user inserts key words. The system then cites a number of documents in which the user can find information elicited by these key words. Question-answering systems improve on this way of doing a search by allowing the user to express interest in the structure of a well-formed question so the system can focus more explicitly on what is wanted and can move to select some smaller part of a document that expresses the information requested. Question-answering systems now available on the Web include *AnswerBus, Ask Jeeves, Start,* and LAMP. The value of such a system is that it can answer questions that require specific factual information such as "What is the smallest bird in Britain?" "Who invented the first toilet?" or "How do worms multiply?"[7] Thus the user is saved the effort of scrolling through multiple Web pages that potentially contain an answer and can get the correct answer right away. One thing a question-answering system needs is an information retrieval system that can locate small segments of documents that provide an answer to a question. Another thing such a system needs is a question parser that recognizes different kinds of questions so the system can respond accordingly. And of course, one such question type is the why question of a kind calling for an explanation.

How the technology of question-answering systems relates to the dialogue theory of explanation that underlies query-driven abduction is still far from clear. But there does seem to be at least one interesting connection. When an answering system replies to a question, it must know what information is required and in what order the information should be presented. What is called an answer schema (Clark and Porter, 1999) specifies which components of information are required in an answer and how they should be presented. The answer schema tells which components are needed to answer a question and how to assemble the components into a specific structure (second to last page of Clark and

Porter, 1999). The answer schema for a question requesting an explanation performs a role comparable to that of an account in the dialogue theory of explanation. The account not only gives the statements required to answer the question that requests an explanation but also furnishes information of the sort that enables gaps to be filled in by drawing inferences from what was explicitly given. The account also has an order and fits together as a structure.

The dialogue-based theory of abduction goes beyond a static approach in which only a single question is asked; it concerns an extended dialogue sequence of questions and answers in which an account is clarified, questioned for more detail, or even critiqued by a questioner who probes into details of it. How could a question-answering system utilize technology that would enable this sort of task to be carried out? To make it possible, De Boni and Manandhar (2003, p. 48) have developed an algorithm for what they call a clarification dialogue, in which a series of questions is asked that enables the answering system "to refine its understanding of the questioner's needs." The problem they address is how the system can recognize whether a question is part of a previous series of clarifying questions or is the start of a new series. Solving this problem would enable a user of a question-answering system to ask a series of questions to clarify an initial question by probing more deeply into the details needed to get the specifics the user wants or to help explain something. It would also enable the system to deal with complex questions, such as "Does Sean have a house anywhere apart from Scotland?" (De Boni and Manandhar, 2003, p. 52). This line of research is very significant, because it indicates the promise of utilizing the notion of the clarification dialogue for developing more sophisticated question-answering systems. It is especially promising as a way of developing the explanation capabilities of such systems and thereby opening the way to technology based on a dialogue theory of explanation. In turn, this research opens the way to abduction technologies built around the notion of a query-driven collaborative search for a best explanation in a dialogue in which information is being collected by one party and presented to the party who questions it.

One of the central contentions of chapter 2 is that, as a sequence of argumentation proceeds, there will often be a shift to an examination dialogue.[8] Another central contention of that chapter is that examination dialogue is the most common and important context of dialogue in which explanations are offered. Thus examination dialogue is extremely important for providing the dialectical structure of explanations. But in fact, we know very little about examination dialogue. Indeed, it has not been recognized at all as a distinctive type of dialogue in the modern literature on argumentation and AI. On the other hand, the necessity for recognizing such a type of dialogue has been made abundantly clear by recent developments in expert systems. As indicated in chapter 2, an expert system is much more useful if it has an explanation function, with the user asking the system to explain assertions it has made to the user.

Some attempts have been made in AI to analyze explanation in a context of dialogue. In the view of Baker (1992), an explanation is a set of mutually held beliefs arrived at by negotiation. In this view, explanations are negotiated when two participants have a common task to be carried out, and they negotiate on goals and on how to divide the task responsibilities. This theory is indeed a dialectical view of explanation, but there is a problem with it (Moulin et al., 2002, p. 181). It departs from the view of explanation as a form of communication from one who understands something to one who does not understand it. In a word, it departs from the dialogue view of explanation proposed in chapter 2. This is a problem, according to Moulin et al. (p. 181), because it is precisely this transfer of understanding that is the basis of help functions in expert systems. Such a function is meant to provide assistance to a user who has some understanding, but not enough to solve a current problem.

As noted in chapter 2, the explanation systems that have been developed in expert systems in AI show a dialectical complexity. To begin with, the user asks the system a question or a series of questions, and the system generates answers. This part of the exchange can be seen as an information-seeking or advice-giving dialogue. But, of course, the user will often have problems trying to make sense of what the expert has said. Thus an important part of the system is the shift from a basic transfer of information or advice to a transfer of understanding. When the user asks the system for an explanation of something that is not understood, there has been a dialectical shift from the original expert opinion dialogue to an explanation interval. Presumably, this shift is an embedding. That is, the explanation interval is helpful in contributing to the goal of the original advice-giving dialogue. But the complication arises when, as often happens, there is a shift within the explanation interval to a more argumentative type of dialogue. In expert systems, this type of dialogue is called critiquing. Software critiquing systems, called critics, are now widely used in expert systems. As noted in chapter 2, critiquing involves a two-way communication that is a search for truth (Silverman, 1992). Thus described, critiquing comes very close to what is called the critical discussion or persuasion type of dialogue in the argumentation literature. Thus critiquing is a curious blend. It involves explanation and understanding, but it also involves argumentation. As Moulin et al. (2002, p. 182) put the point, "Critiquing systems provide a fertile ground for argumentation given that critical discussion is a prototype of argumentative discourse."

As AI moves closer and closer to the dialogue model of explanation, the problem of examination dialogue becomes more and more vital. Examination dialogue is the most common and characteristic form of dialogue in which explanations are used. So to understand explanation in the dialogue model, it is vitally important to come to understand the structure of examination dialogue. On the other hand, what is most characteristic of examination dialogue is that it contains explanations. Indeed, the goal of examination as a type of dialogue is for the examiner to make sense of the view being questioned and to come to a clear and coherent understanding of it. Thus we seem caught up in a circle. But the circle need not be a vicious one. We can partially come to understand examination dialogue by using the dialogue model of the speech act of explanation presented in chapter 2 as a starting point. From there, we can investigate examination as a complex process that begins with the goal of providing an explanation but then often shifts to a critiquing phase.

SUMMARY OF ABDUCTION AS A HEURISTIC

In general, how the process of abduction works has to be seen in the context of a search or investigation or any sort of goal-directed dialogue of the six kinds cited in chapter 2. The aim could be to prove or disprove some statement that has been brought into question, to collect information, to solve a practical problem, or to resolve a conflict of opinions. Whatever the ultimate aim, evidence will be collected as the dialogue proceeds through its stages, and if both parties agree not to dispute certain statements both are committed to, these statements can be called facts or data. The dialogue can be seen as a heuristic search process of the kind familiar in AI that collects data and draws inferences from the data. There is a first point at the opening move of the dialogue. Then each move is a transformation from the previous move by virtue of the four types of dialogue rules that defined permissible moves, permissible responses to moves, commitments of each participant at each move, and what sequence of moves counts as successful completion of the dialogue by a participant. At some point in such a dialogue, a question may be put forward to a respondent by a proponent asking for an explanation of some fact. A successful explanation given by the respondent takes the form of an account that enables the respondent to understand the fact in the respect indicated by the question. For example, the question may be how the event represented by the fact came about, and the answer may cite a cause. As the dialogue proceeds, the proponent may build up an account, and the respondent may question certain parts of it. The chain of reasoning as such an account is given and built up moves backward from the given facts to an explanation or several competing explanations of these facts. Successive colligated accounts produce a dialogue that increases the questioner's understanding of the facts through increasingly complete explanations.

In the evaluation of any case of an abductive inference, the best explanation generally is the one that best enables the respondent to understand the data that the proponent is trying to explain in answering the respondent's question. Such an explanation does not necessarily have to explain all the data, however. An explanation can be helpful to a respondent, and thus successful in a dialogue, if it gives an account better understood to the questioner than what the respondent asked about and presumably did not understand very well. Choosing what is the best explanation, or an acceptable explanation, is a contextual matter. An explanation that is appropriate and acceptable in one type of dialogue may be inappropriate and unacceptable in another type of dialogue. An empathetic explanation that is acceptable as legal evidence in a trial, for example, may not be acceptable as an explanation in a scientific investigation.

Understanding can be defined most precisely in terms of an agent's making sense of a given account. An account is a set of statements that can be expanded by filling in the missing assumptions through reasoning and scripts known to the proponent of the account and to the respondent who is trying to make sense of it. In empathetic explanations the account is an anchored one based on the assumptions that both parties are agents who share a capability for practical reasoning and knowledge of how everyday routines normally work. Because they are based on scripts and knowledge of how everyday routines work, the kinds of explanations commonly used in everyday conversations employ, for the most part, plausible reasoning. Plausible reasoning is based on how things seem to be as data that are normally acceptable but can be mis-leading and wrong in some instances.

There are two argumentation schemes for abductive inference. One is the reverse of the other. Both are useful. Both need to be evaluated dialectically by asking appropriate critical questions corresponding to the scheme. The forward scheme is evaluated using an argument dia-gram that shows the argumentation in a case chaining forward. The backward scheme works by eliciting an explanation from a set of facts, or a series of explanations as a series of deeper accounts is worked up through a dialogue process. Abductive inferences of the most common sort are based on conditionals in the form of defeasible generalizations, called "rules" in AI. Such rules are applied to other statements supposed by both parties in a dialogue to represent data, commonly called "facts" in AI and also in law. Such statements may later be shown to be false, when new information comes into a dialogue. But they are tentatively assumed to be true by both participants at a given point in the dialogue. In other words, "facts" are not being questioned by either party at that point, and thus it may be appropriate for one party to offer an explana-tion of them. Later on, they may come to be questioned, and at that point offering an explanation of them would be inappropriate.

The form of an abductive inference is that of a *modus ponens* argu-ment combining a rule and a fact. But it is not generally a deduc-tively valid version of it. Typically such an inference has the form of a defeasible *modus ponens* argument of the kind introduced in chapter 4. The defeasible conditional is contextual and presumptive. It says that if the proponent is committed to the antecedent as a presumption that can move a dialogue forward, and the conditional is generally acceptable and there are no known exceptions in the given case, then the respon-dent should accept the consequent or ask an appropriate critical ques-tion. Thus the dialogue can move forward provisionally. The same re-marks apply to defeasible generalizations. Arguments based on them are chained forward in abductive reasoning, as represented by an argument diagram. An abductive inference often has small evidential worth by itself, because it is merely a conjecture that may be based on localized evidence. Its primary value is that it can enable an investigation or dis-cussion to move ahead, building up a mass of evidence for one account, as opposed to a contrasting account that is supposed to enable better understanding of what was queried. As an explanatory dialogue pro-gresses, it allows information about the respondent's commitments to be updated. The proponent of an explanation must base it on some estimate of what the respondent currently understands about the subject being explained. The function of the explanation is to fill in the gaps in the one account by matching the one against the other to see what is missing. As a dialogue proceeds, the proponent will get a better idea of precisely what gaps need to be filled in and how they need to be filled in.

Once the dialogue has reached a given point, the evidence for a claim at that point can be modeled using an argument diagram. This diagram displays the reasoning from premises to conclusion in an extended sequence of argumentation. For example, in the broken knife case, the argument diagram was produced in *Araucaria* by filling in several implicit premises that took the form of defeasible conditionals. The whole forward-moving chain of argumentation took the form of a connected series of defeasible *modus ponens* steps. If the conclusion is a causal claim, the argument diagram will look like those shown in the car accident case study in chapter 5. Viewing such a diagram abductively, we can see it as representing the outcome of a sequence of backward steps, each of which is an inference to the best explanation. The argument diagram will change as new evidence comes into the dialogue. At the end of a dialogue, such an argument diagram could be quite large, as in the examples of legal evidence in court cases diagrammed by Wigmore (1931). At an early stage, or if not much is known about a localized example, the diagram could be quite simple.

Notes

1. ABDUCTIVE, PRESUMPTIVE, AND PLAUSIBLE ARGUMENTS

1. As shown in the second section below, Peirce divided reasoning into three categories: deductive, inductive, and abductive.

2. I will not try to define conditional probability here, but some traditional and nontraditional Bayesian ways of defining it are explained by Pearl (2000, pp. 3–5) using clear illustrations from rolling dice.

3. Greek philosophers were very familiar with forms of inference closely related to abductive inference, and there is a long but not well-known history linking these ancient notions to modern notions of plausible inference. Much historical work on the development of informal logic remains to be done, and much is simply not yet known.

4. Wellman's category of conductive argument showed the importance of a third category in ethical argumentation (Wellman, 1971). It is beyond the scope of this chapter, however, to go into the question of whether conductive and abductive arguments are the same or different.

5. Skyrms (1966, p. 4) put forward the view that "deductive" and "inductive" are not the names of kinds of arguments but should be seen as success criteria for arguments.

6. To say a statement is improbable means that it is unlikely that it is true, where "unlikely" is a Bayesian notion. This notion is based, in the typical Bayesian account, on placing the statement as one in a set of statements that are independent of each other and that together exhaust a set of outcomes. For example, the probability of getting a three when rolling a die may be calculated as one out of six, assuming that the probability of each of the six sides coming up is equal. To say a statement is implausible means that it does not seem to be true, based on appearances (usually in the form of some set of data in a particu-

lar case), including generally accepted opinions held by the majority and the experts in the subject domain. For example, the statement that Napoleon Bonaparte never existed is implausible (see note 7 below), but whether such a statement is improbable, or could somehow be shown to be so, is dubious (although some Bayesian may well undertake the task). Ordinary language does not appear to make this distinction between implausibility and improbability in any very clear or consistent way.

7. This example was analyzed in depth in Richard Whately's once-famous little book, *Historic Doubts Relative to Napoleon Buonaparte,* first published in 1819.

8. The assumption seems to be that *C*'s being a "matter of course" implies that *C* is true.

9. The account of presumption given here is quite simplified, and there are opposed theories of how presumptions work in law (Park, Leonard, and Goldberg, 1998, pp. 107–17). The view of them expressed above has been called the "bursting bubble" theory because it suggests that a presumption can easily disappear with no effect once contradicted by facts that have come to be known in a case. Some presumptions in law, however, are called "irrebuttable" because they operate as rules of law that change the nature of the facts to be proved. Park, Leonard, and Goldberg (p. 105) cite the example of the rule that the child of a wife cohabiting with her husband who is not impotent or sterile is presumed to be his offspring. Unless an exception applies, no evidence to the contrary is admissible in a trial. Using examples such as this one, some legal scholars reject the bursting bubble theory, claiming that presumptions are not always so fragile that they disappear when evidence is offered to rebut them.

10. In a linked argument, as contrasted with a convergent one, both premises (in the simplest case of an argument with only two premises) are required to support the conclusion. For example, in a *modus ponens* type of argument, both premises are required. If one or the other is assumed not to hold, support for the conclusion drops considerably.

11. Kienpointner's book has not yet been translated from German to English, but an article (Kienpointner, 1987) provides a summary of some of the schemes.

12. A controversial case in point is whether argument from sign is abductive. Many instances of argument from sign are clearly abductive, and viewing them as abductive inferences seems revealing and useful. But some arguments from sign are not abductive. For example, we take the presence of certain kinds of dark clouds as a sign that it will rain. Yet, as the Josephsons (1994, p. 24) have convincingly argued, predictions are not abductions.

2. A DIALOGUE MODEL OF EXPLANATION

1. A fourth source is ancient Greek philosophy, especially in the writings of Aristotle where he made a classification of different types of arguments that foreshadows the modern classification of different types of dialogue in argumentation theory.

2. Wesley Salmon reported that he was astonished when Professor J. J. C. Smart, a distinguished Australian philosopher, mentioned the problem of scientific explanation (Salmon, 1989, p. 4). Salmon thought the problem had already been solved by the promulgation of the DN model.

3. This process is called unification (Weber and van Dyck, 2002).

4. These considerations are steps leading up to the theory of accounts presented in chapter 7.

5. This example can be compared with a similar one used by Michael Scriven to raise doubts about the DN model of explanation in relation to necessary and sufficient conditions of actions. See the first section of chapter 5.

3. A PROCEDURAL MODEL OF RATIONALITY

1. The universal quantifier in modern logic and the all-statement (A-proposition) in syllogistic logic are absolute generalizations, meaning that one counterexample defeats the generalization.

2. Examining the long history of the subject starting from the earliest commentators on Aristotle's writings, Burnyeat (1994) showed that it was probably Alexander of Aphrodisias who first held the traditional view that the Aristotelian enthymeme is a syllogism with an unstated premise.

3. Tindale (1999, p. 9) has argued, however, that an examination of Aristotle's writings raises many questions about whether the traditional interpretation is accurate. Many other scholars have joined Tindale in arguing that Aristotle used the term "enthymeme" to refer to forms of plausible argumentation and that the traditional meaning of "ethymeme" attributed to him is a misinterpretation.

4. If Aristotle was not referring to syllogisms with missing premises or conclusions, what did he mean by "enthymeme"? The Greek term *enthymema* means "in the mind." That meaning could seem to favor the incomplete-syllogism interpretation. But this fairly inclusive phrase could refer to other things as well. What Aristotle really meant by "enthymeme," according to the very careful examination of the relevant passages by Burnyeat (1994), are the *eikotic* or plausibilistic arguments nowadays associated with presumptive argu-

mentation schemes. If this contrarian view of the Aristotelian enthymeme is right, the implications for logic as a discipline, and for other subjects such as rhetoric, are highly significant. It means that Aristotle was fully aware of argumentation schemes and that his writings on topics and fallacies can be seen as an attempt to establish informal logic as a systematic field in addition to the field of formal logic he is so well known for founding.

4. DEFEASIBLE *MODUS PONENS* ARGUMENTS

1. Of course, like all such disputes, much depends on how you define a key term. In this instance it is a question of how to define *modus ponens* as a form of argument.

2. Some might object that practical reasoning of the kind analyzed in chapter 3 requires an extension of classic deductive logic and thus goes beyond the domain of deductive validity, at least of the kind modeled by classic logic. I welcome this admission and think it supports my argument.

3. Some would admit straightaway that the argumentation in this case cannot be handled by deductive logic. They would argue that deductive logic applies only to propositions that are true or false and not to actions and deliberations. They would argue that you must apply practical reasoning to the case and that practical reasoning requires an extension of deductive logic. The questions are then raised: what is practical reasoning, and what forms of argumentation is it based on?

4. On the back cover of Hurley (2000), the text says that this book "is used by more students and instructors than any other throughout North America." But, of course, citing Hurley is an appeal to authority that could be wrong. The fact that this claim appears on the back of the textbook could also be classified as an *ad populum* appeal directed to potential buyers or adopters of the book.

5. There are more than three types of conditionals, as counterfactual logics show. Nevertheless, from a practical point of view, classifying into a three-way system is useful, I would maintain.

6. See Walton (1996a, pp. 46–47) for the argumentation scheme for argument from sign.

7. This issue is taken up in Walton (2002).

5. ABDUCTIVE CAUSAL REASONING

1. There is a complication to be mentioned here. By "necessary connection" Hume generally meant sufficient condition in the sense explained above.

6. QUERY-DRIVEN ABDUCTIVE REASONING

1. Such a suggestion can be found in Fann's interpretation anyhow, as indicated in chapter 1.

2. As noted in chapter 1, Peirce even used "hypothesis" as a synonym for "abduction."

3. The canonical example was introduced in chapter 1.

4. A form of the no-commitment problem was recognized by DeMorgan (1926, pp. 296–97). He described it as a "common occurrence" that arises in cases of the fallacy of begging the question. As he observed, "It is the habit of many to treat an advanced proposition as a begging of the question the moment they see that, if established, it would establish the question." Thus once such a respondent sees that the doubted conclusion can be proved by some premises, the individual immediately expresses doubts about the premises, seeing them as unacceptable.

7. UNSOLVED PROBLEMS OF ABDUCTION

1. For example, Schum (1994, p. 476) wrote, "The words a person utters in testimony are signs of this person's thoughts." If testimony can be seen as based on an inference from sign, then presumably argument from expert opinion could also be seen as a species of inference to the best explanation.

2. In view of the historical matters cited in chapter 3, some terminological clarification may be needed. First, we have to decide whether we are going to use the term "enthymeme" to mean an incomplete argument or a plausible argumentation scheme. Choice of terminology is somewhat arbitrary and will be decided by majority or influential usage in the field anyhow. Even though I think that the Burnyeat's interpretation of Aristotle is plausibly the right one, or anyhow the best one, it probably does little harm to continue to use the term "enthymeme" to stand for an incomplete argument.

3. So analyzed, the argument in the corporate income tax example falls into the category of enthymeme in the original Aristotelian sense of the term cited by Burnyeat.

4. Peirce (1965V, p. 116) wrote that it is difficult to make a clear and precise distinction between perceptual judgment and abductive judgment. The account of the form of abductive inference given by Peirce (see chapter 1) is his basis for making this distinction.

5. See chapter 1.

6. *Ibid.*

7. These three questions are taken from the list of sample questions on *AnswerBus* (http://www.answerbus.com).

8. Because so little has been written about examination dialogue in either philosophy or AI, the best source is, curiously, ancient Greek philosophy. Examination or peirastic arguments (*perastikoi logoî*) were defined in *On Sophistical Refutations* (165b4–165b6) as those "based on opinions held by the answerer and necessarily known to one who claims knowledge of the subject involved." Such arguments are "fitted to test someone's alleged knowledge and are based on the views held by the respondent" (Nuchelmans, 1993, p. 37).

References

Achinstein, Peter. 1983. *The Nature of Explanation*. New York: Oxford University Press.

———. 1993. Can There be a Model of Explanation? In *Explanation,* ed. David-Hillel Ruben, 136–59. Oxford: Oxford University Press.

Alexy, Robert. 1989. *A Theory of Legal Argumentation: The Theory of Rational Discourse as Theory of Legal Justification*. Oxford: Clarendon Press.

Anderson, Terence J. 1999. On Generalizations I: A Preliminary Exploration. *South Texas Law Review* 40:455–81.

Anderson, Terence, and William Twining. 1991. *Analysis of Evidence: How to Do Things with Facts Based on Wigmore's Science of Judicial Proof*. Boston: Little, Brown.

Aristotle. 1928. *On Sophistical Refutations*. Loeb Classical Library. Cambridge, Mass.: Harvard University Press.

———. 1937. *Rhetoric*. Loeb Classical Library. Cambridge, Mass.: Harvard University Press.

———. 1939. *Topics*. Trans. E. S. Forster. Loeb Classical Library. Cambridge, Mass.: Harvard University Press.

Audi, Robert. 1989. *Practical Reasoning*. London: Routledge.

Austin, John L. 1962. *How to Do Things with Words*. Oxford: Clarendon Press.

Baker, Michael. 1992. The Collaborative Construction of Explanations. *Actes des Deuxiemes Journees du PRC-GDR-IA du CNRS* 1:25–40.

Barth, Else M., and Erik C. W. Krabbe. 1982. *From Axiom to Dialogue*. New York: de Gruyter.

Bartley, William Warren, III. 1962. *The Retreat to Commitment*. New York: Alfred A. Knopf.

Bench-Capon, Trevor. 1997. Argument in Artificial Intelligence and Law. *Artificial Intelligence and Law* 5:249–61.

Best, Joel. 2001. *Damned Lies and Statistics*. Berkeley and Los Angeles: University of California Press.

Blair, J. Anthony. 1999a. Walton's Argumentation Schemes for Presumptive Reasoning: A Critique and Development. In *Proceedings of the Fourth International Conference of the International Society for the Study of Argumentation,* ed. Frans H. van Eemeren, Rob Grootendorst, J. Anthony Blair, and Charles A. Willard, 56–61. Amsterdam: SicSat.

———. 1999b. Presumptive Reasoning/Argument: An Overlooked Class. *Protosociology* 13:46–60.

———. 1999c. Review of Walton, 1996. *Argumentation* 13:338–43.

Boman, Magnus, and Walter Van de Velde, eds. 1997. *Multi-Agent Rationality: Eighth European Workshop on Modeling Autonomous Agents in a Multi-Agent World.* Berlin: Springer-Verlag.

Bratman, Michael E. 1987. *Intentions, Plans, and Practical Reason.* Cambridge, Mass.: Harvard University Press.

Burke, Michael. 1985. Unstated Premises. *Informal Logic* 7:107–18.

Burnyeat, Myles F. 1994. Enthymeme: Aristotle on the Logic of Persuasion. In *Aristotle's Rhetoric: Philosophical Essays,* ed. David J. Furley and Alexander Nehemas, 3–55. Princeton, N.J.: Princeton University Press.

Carberry, Sandra. 1990. *Plan Recognition in Natural Language Dialogue.* Cambridge, Mass.: MIT Press.

Cawsey, Alison. 1992. *Explanation and Interaction: The Computer Generation of Explanatory Dialogues.* Cambridge, Mass.: MIT Press.

———. 1998. *The Essence of Artificial Intelligence.* London: Prentice Hall.

Chandrasekaran, B. 1986. Generic Tasks in Knowledge Based Reasoning. *IEEE Expert* 1:23–30.

Clark, Peter, and Bruce Porter. 1999. A Knowledge-Based Approach to Question Answering. *AAAI '99 Fall Symposium on Question Answering Systems.* Available on the Web at www.cs.utexas.edu/users/pclark/papers.

Clarke, David S., Jr. 1985. *Practical Inferences.* London: Routledge and Kegan Paul.

Collingwood, Robin G. 1939. *An Autobiography.* Oxford: Oxford University Press.

———. 1946. *The Idea of History.* Oxford: Clarendon Press.

Copi, Irving M., and Carl Cohen. 1998. *Introduction to Logic.* 10th ed. Englewood Cliffs, N.J.: Prentice-Hall.

Curd, Martin V. 1980. The Logic of Discovery: An Analysis of Three Approaches. In *Scientific Discovery, Logic and Rationality,* ed. Thomas Nickles, 201–19. Dordrecht, Netherlands: Reidel.

Da Costa, Newton C. A., and Steven French. 1993. Towards an Acceptable Theory of Acceptance: Partial Structures, Inconsistency and Correspondence. In *Correspondence, Invariance and Heuristics,* ed. Steven French and Harmke Kamminga, 137–58. Dordrecht, Netherlands: Kluwer.

――――. 2002. Inconsistency in Science: A Partial Perspective. In *Inconsistency in Science,* ed. Joke Meheus. Dordrecht, Netherlands: Kluwer.

De Boni, Marco, and Suresh Manandhar. 2003. An Analysis of Clarification Dialogue for Question Answering. In *Proceedings of HLT-NAACL 2003,* 48–55. Edmonton: Association for Computational Linguistics.

DeMorgan, Augustus. 1926. *Formal Logic.* London: Open Court Company. Reprint of the original Taylor and Walton edition of 1847.

Dieks, Dennis, and Henk W. de Regt. 1998. Reduction and Understanding. *Foundations of Science* 1:45–59.

Doty, Ralph. 1986. Carneades, a Forerunner of William James' Pragmatism. *Journal of the History of Ideas* 47:133–38.

Dray, William. 1964. *Philosophy of History.* Englewood Cliffs, N.J.: Prentice-Hall.

――――. 1995. *History as Re-enactment: R. G. Collingwood's Idea of History.* Oxford: Oxford University Press.

Fann, K. T. 1970. *Peirce's Theory of Abduction.* The Hague: Martinus Nijhoff.

Finocchiaro, Maurice. 1975. Cause, Explanation and Understanding in Science: Galileo's Case. *Review of Metaphysics* 29:117–28.

――――. 1980. Scientific Discoveries as Growth of Understanding: The Case of Newton's Gravitation. In *Scientific Discovery, Logic, and Rationality,* ed. Thomas Nickles, 235–55. Dordrecht, Netherlands: Reidel.

Fox, John, and Subrata Das. 2000. *Safe and Sound: Artificial Intelligence in Hazardous Applications.* Menlo Park, Calif.: MIT Press.

Franklin, Stan, and Art Graesser. 1996. Is It an Agent, or Just a Program? A Taxonomy for Autonomous Agents. In *Intelligent Agents III: Agent Theories, Architectures and Languages,* ed. Jorg P. Muller, Michael J. Wooldridge, and Nicholas R. Jennings, 21–35. Berlin: Springer.

Freeman, James B. 1991. *Dialectics and the Macrostructure of Arguments.* Berlin: Foris.

Friedman, Michael. 1974. Explanation and Scientific Understanding. *Journal of Philosophy* 71:5–19.

――――. 1988. Explanation and Scientific Understanding. In *Theories of Explanation,* ed. J. C. Pitt, 188–98. New York: Oxford University Press.

Gagarin, Michael. 1994. Probability and Persuasion: Plato and Early Greek Rhetoric. In *Persuasion: Greek Rhetoric in Action,* ed. Ian Worthington, 46–68. London: Routledge.

Galilei, Galileo. 1914. *Dialogues Concerning Two New Sciences* (1638). Trans. Henry Crew and Alfonzo de Salvio. New York: Dover.

Goldman, Alvin I. 1995. Empathy Mind and Morals. In *Mental Simulation: Evaluations and Applications,* ed. Martin Davies and Tony Stone, 185–208. Oxford: Blackwell.

Goodwin, Jean. 2000. Wigmore's Chart Method. *Informal Logic* 20:223–43.

Gordon, Thomas F. 1995. *The Pleadings Game: An Artificial Intelligence Model of Procedural Justice*. Dordrecht, Netherlands: Kluwer.

Gough, James, and Christopher Tindale. 1985. Hidden or Missing Premises. *Informal Logic* 7:99–106.

Grice, H. Paul. 1975. Logic and Conversation. In *The Logic of Grammar*, ed. Donald Davidson and Gilbert Harman, 64–75. Encino, Calif.: Dickenson.

Hage, Jaap. 2000. Dialectical Models in Artificial Intelligence and Law. *Artificial Intelligence and Law* 8:137–72.

Hamblin, Charles L. 1970. *Fallacies*. London: Methuen.

———. 1971. Mathematical Models of Dialogue. *Theoria* 37:130–55.

———. 1987. *Imperatives*. New York: Blackwell.

Hanson, Norwood Russell. 1958. *Patterns of Discovery*. Cambridge: Cambridge University Press.

Harman, Gilbert. 1965. The Inference to the Best Explanation. *Philosophical Review* 74:88–95.

Hart, H. L. A., and A. M. Honore. 1962. *Causation in the Law*. Oxford: Oxford University Press.

Hastie, Reid, Steven D. Penrod, and Nancy Pennington. 1983. *Inside the Jury*. Cambridge, Mass.: Harvard University Press.

Hastings, Arthur C. 1963. "A Reformulation of the Modes of Reasoning in Argumentation." PhD diss., Northwestern University.

Hempel, Carl G. 1965. *Aspects of Scientific Explanation*. New York: Free Press.

Hintikka, Jaakko. 1998. What is Abduction? *Transactions of the Charles S. Peirce Society* 34:503–33.

Hitchcock, David. 1985. Enthymematic Arguments. *Informal Logic* 7:83–97.

Hitchcock, David, Peter McBurney, and Simon Parsons. 2001. A Framework for Deliberation Dialogues, Argument and Its Applications. In *Proceedings of the Fourth Biennial Conference of the Ontario Society for the Study of Argumentation (OSSA)*, ed. H. V. Hansen, C. W. Tindale, J. A. Blair, and R. H. Johnson. Compact disk. Also available on Peter McBurney's Web page at the University of Liverpool, Department of Computer Science: http://www.csc.liv.ac.uk/~peter/.

Hoopes, James. 1991. *Peirce on Signs: Writings on Semiotic by Charles Sanders Peirce*. Chapel Hill: University of North Carolina Press.

Hurley, Patrick J. 2000. *A Concise Introduction to Logic*. 7th ed. Belmont, Calif.: Wadsworth.

Jamieson, Patrick W. 1990. A New Paradigm for Explaining and Linking Knowledge in Diagnostic Problem Solving. *Journal of Clinical Engineering* 15:371–80.

Johnson, Ralph H. 2000. *Manifest Rationality: A Pragmatic Theory of Argument.* Mahwah, N.J.: Erlbaum.

Josephson, John R. 2001. Abductive Inference: On the Proof Dynamics of Inference to the Best Explanation. *Cardozo Law Review* 22:1621–43.

Josephson, John R., and Susan G. Josephson. 1994. *Abductive Inference: Computation, Philosophy, Technology.* New York: Cambridge University Press.

Keppens, Jeroen, and John Zeleznikow. 2002. On the Role of Model-based Reasoning in Decision Support in Crime Investigation. *Report of the Centre for Forensic Statistics and Legal Reasoning.* University of Edinburgh. Available on the Web page of Jeroen Keppens.

Kienpointner, Manfred. 1987. Towards a Typology of Argumentative Schemes. In *Argumentation: Across the Lines of Discipline,* ed. Frans H. van Eemeren et al., 275–87. Dordrecht, Netherlands: Foris.

———. 1992. *Alltagslogik: Struktur und Funktion von Argumentationsmustern.* Stuttgart: Fromman-Holzboog.

———. 1997. On the Art of Finding Arguments: What Ancient and Modern Masters of Invention Have to Tell Us about the *Ars Inveniendi. Argumentation* 11:225–36.

———. 2003. Perelman on Causal Arguments: The Argument of Waste. In *Proceedings of the Fifth Conference of the International Society for the Study of Argumentation,* ed. Frans H. van Eemeren, J. Anthony Blair, Charles A. Willard, and A. Francisca Snoeck Henkemans, 611–16. Amsterdam: SicSat.

Kitcher, Philip. 1988. Explanatory Unification. In *Theories of Explanation,* ed. J. C. Pitt, 167–87. New York: Oxford University Press.

———. 1989. Explanatory Unification and the Causal Structure of the World. In *Scientific Explanation: Minnesota Studies in the Philosophy of Science,* ed. Philip Kitcher and Wesley Salmon, 13:410–505. Minneapolis: University of Minnesota Press.

Krabbe, Erik C. W. 1991. So What? Profiles for Relevance Criticism in Persuasion Dialogues. *Argumentation* 6:271–83.

———. 1999. Profiles of Dialogue. In *JFAK: Essays Dedicated to Johan van Benthem on the Occasion of his 50th Birthday,* ed. Jelle Gerbrandy, Maarten Marx, Maarten de Rijke, and Yde Venema, 25–36. Amsterdam: Amsterdam University Press.

———. 2001. The Problem of Retraction in Critical Discussion. *Synthese* 127: 141–59.

Kuhn, Thomas. 1970. *The Structure of Scientific Revolutions.* 2nd ed. Chicago: University of Chicago Press.

Leakey, R. E., and R. Lewin. 1992. *Origins Reconsidered: In Search of What Makes Us Human.* New York: Bantam Doubleday Dell.

Lipton, Peter. 1991. *Inference to the Best Explanation*. London: Routledge.

Lodder, Arno R. 1999. *DiaLaw: On Legal Justification and Dialogical Models of Argumentation*. Dordrecht, Netherlands: Kluwer.

———. 2000. Review of Thomas F. Gordon, The Pleadings Game: An Artificial Intelligence Model of Procedural Justice. *Artificial Intelligence and Law* 2:255–64.

Loui, Ronald P. 1998. Process and Policy: Resource-Bounded Nondemonstrative Reasoning. *Computational Intelligence* 14:1–38.

Mackenzie, Jim. 1981. The Dialectics of Logic. *Logique et Analyse* 94:159–77.

———. 1990. Four Dialogue Systems. *Studia Logica* 49:567–83.

Mackie, John L. 1965. Causes and Conditions. *American Philosophical Quarterly* 2:245–64.

Magnani, Lorenzo. 2001. *Abduction, Reason and Science: Processes of Discovery and Explanation*. New York: Kluwer Academic/Plenum Publishers.

McCarty, L. Thorne. 1995. An Implementation of Eisner v Macomber. In *Proceedings of the Fifth International Conference on AI and Law, 276–86*. New York: ACM Press.

McGuinness, Deborah L., and Paulo Pinheiro da Silva. 2003. Infrastructure for Web Explanations. In *Proceedings of the Second International Semantic Web Conference (ISWC)*. Sanibel, Fla.: Springer.

Moore, Johanna D. 1991. A Reacting Approach to Explanation: Taking the User's Feedback into Account. In *Natural Language Generation in Artificial Intelligence and Computational Linguistics*, ed. C. L. Paris, W. R. Swartout, and W. C. Mann, 3–48. Dordrecht, Netherlands: Kluwer.

———. 1995. *Participating in Explanatory Dialogues*. Cambridge, Mass.: MIT Press.

Moulin, B., H. Irandoust, M. Belanger, and G. Desbordes. 2002. Explanation and Argumentation Capabilities. *Artificial Intelligence Review* 17:169–222.

Nettler, Gwynn. 1970. *Explanations*. New York: McGraw-Hill.

Nickles, Thomas. 1980. Introductory Essay: Scientific Discovery and the Future of Philosophy of Science. In *Scientific Discovery, Logic, and Rationality*, ed. Thomas Nickles, 1–59. Dordrecht, Netherlands: Reidel.

Nuchelmans, Gabriel. 1993. On the Fourfold Root of the *Argumentum Ad Hominem*. In *Empirical Logic and Public Debate*, ed. Erik C. W. Krabbe, Renee Jose Dalitz, and Pier A. Smit, 37–47. Amsterdam: Rodopi.

Park, Roger C., David P. Leonard, and Steven H. Goldberg. 1998. *Evidence Law*. St. Paul, Minn.: West Group.

Patel, V. L., and G. J. Groen. 1991. The General and Specific Nature of Medical Expertise: A Critical Look. In *Towards a General Theory of Expertise: Prospects and Limits,* ed. A. Ericsson and J. Smith, 93–125. Cambridge: Cambridge University Press.

Pearl, Judea. 1984. *Heuristics: Intelligent Search Strategies for Computer Problem Solving.* Reading, Mass.: Addison-Wesley.

———. 2000. *Causality: Models, Reasoning and Inference.* Cambridge: Cambridge University Press.

———. 2001. Causal Inference in the Health Sciences: A Conceptual Introduction. In *Health Services and Outcomes Research Methodology.* Dordrecht, Netherlands: Kluwer. Available on the personal Web page of Judea Pearl as Technical Report R-282.

———. 2002. Bayesianism and Causality, or, Why I Am only a Half-Bayesian. Available on the personal Web page of Judea Pearl.

Peirce, Charles S. 1965II. *Collected Papers of Charles Sanders Peirce.* Vol. 2, *Elements of Logic,* ed. Charles Hartshorne and Paul Weiss. Cambridge, Mass.: Harvard University Press.

———. 1965V. *Collected Papers of Charles Sanders Peirce.* Vol. 5, *Pragmatism and Pragmaticism,* ed. Charles Hartshorne and Paul Weiss. Cambridge, Mass.: Harvard University Press.

Peng, Yun, and James A. Reggia. 1990. *Abductive Inference Models for Diagnostic Problem-Solving.* New York: Springer-Verlag.

Pennington, Nancy, and Reid Hastie. 1993. The Story Model for Juror Decision Making. In *Inside the Juror: The Psychology of Juror Decision Making,* ed. Reid Hastie, 192–221. Cambridge: Cambridge University Press.

Perelman, Chaim, and Lucie Olbrechts-Tyteca. 1969. *The New Rhetoric: A Treatise on Argumentation.* 2nd ed. Trans. J. Wilkinson and P. Weaver. Notre Dame, Ind.: University of Notre Dame Press. First published as *La Nouvelle Rhetorique* in 1958.

Pollock, John L. 1987. Defeasible Reasoning. *Cognitive Science* 11:481–518.

———. 1995. *Cognitive Carpentry.* Cambridge, Mass.: MIT Press.

Polya, George. 1954. *Patterns of Plausible Inference.* Vol. 2. Princeton, N.J.: Princeton University Press.

Popper, Karl R. 1959. *The Logic of Scientific Discovery.* New York: Basic Books.

Prakken, Henry. 1996. A Dialectical Model of Assessing Conflicting Arguments in Legal Reasoning. *Artificial Intelligence and Law* 4:331–68.

———. 2003. Logical Dialectics: The Missing Link between Deductivism and Pragma-dialectics. In *Proceedings of the Fifth Conference of the International Society for the Study of Argumentation,* ed. Frans H. van Eemeren, J. Anthony Blair, Charles A. Willard, and A. Francisca Snoeck Henkemans, 857–60. Amsterdam: SicSat.

Prakken, Henry, and Silja Renooij. 2001. Reconstructing Causal Reasoning about Evidence: A Case Study. In *Legal Knowledge and Information Systems,* ed. Bart Verheij, Arno R. Lodder, Ronald P. Loui, and A. Muntjewerjj, 131–42. Amsterdam: IOS Press.

Prakken, Henry, and Giovanni Sartor. 1996. A Dialectical Model of Assessing Conflicting Arguments in Legal Reasoning. *Artificial Intelligence and Law* 4:331–68.

———. 1997. Argument-based Extended Logic Programming with Defeasible Priorities. *Journal of Applied Non-classical Logics* 7:25–75.

———. 2003. The Three Faces of Defeasibility in the Law. *Ratio Juris* 16:495–516.

Premack, D., and G. Woodruff. 1978. Does the Chimpanzee Have a Theory of Mind? *Behavioral and Brain Sciences* 1:515–26.

Reed, Chris. 1998. Dialogue Frames in Agent Communication. In *Proceedings of the Third International Conference on Multi-Agent Systems,* ed. Y. Demazeau, 246–53. New York: IEEE Press.

Reed, Chris, and Glenn Rowe. 2002. *Araucaria v1.0* Software. Available from the Department of Applied Computing, University of Dundee, Scotland, at the Web site: http://www.computing.dundee.ac.uk/staff/creed/araucaria/.

Reed, Chris, and Douglas Walton. 2003. Argumentation Schemes in Argument-as-Process and Argument-as-Product. *Proceedings of IL@25.* Windsor, Canada.

Rein, Martin, and Christopher Winship. 1999. The Dangers of Strong Causal Reasoning in Social Policy. *Journal Infosociety* 36:38–46.

Reiter, Raymond. 1980. A Logic for Default Reasoning. *Artificial Intelligence* 13:81–132.

———. 1985. On Reasoning by Default. In *Readings in Knowledge Representation,* ed. Ronald J. Brachman and Hector J. Levesque, 402–10. Los Altos, Calif. Morgan Kaufman Publishers.

Rescher, Nicholas. 1964. *Introduction to Logic.* New York: St. Martin's Press.

———. 1976. *Plausible Reasoning.* Assen, Netherlands: Van Gorcum.

Rich, E. A. 1989. Stereotypes and User Modeling. In *User Models in Dialog Systems,* ed. A. Kobsa and W. Wahlster, 35–51. Berlin: Springer-Verlag.

Russell, Stuart J., and Peter Norvig. 1995. *Artificial Intelligence: A Modern Approach.* Englewood Cliffs, N.J.: Prentice-Hall.

Salmon, Wesley C. 1989. Four Decades of Scientific Explanation. Vol. 13 of *Scientific Explanation,* 3–219. Minnesota Studies in the Philosophy of Science. Minneapolis: University of Minnesota Press.

———. 1992. Scientific Explanation. In *Introduction to the Philosophy of Science,* ed. Merrilee H. Salmon et al., 7–41. Englewood Cliffs, N.J.: Prentice-Hall.

———. 1998. The Importance of Scientific Understanding. In *Causality and Explanation,* ed. Wesley Salmon, 79–91. New York: Oxford University Press.

Schaffner, Kenneth F. 1980. Discovery in the Biomedical Sciences. In *Scientific Discovery: Case Studies,* ed. Thomas Nickles, 171–205. Dordrecht, Netherlands: Reidel.

Schank, Roger C. 1986. *Explanation Patterns: Understanding Mechanically and Creatively.* Hillsdale, N.J.: Erlbaum.

Schank, Roger C., and Robert P. Abelson. 1977. *Scripts, Plans, Goals and Understanding.* Hillsdale: N.J.: Erlbaum.

Schauer, Frederick. 1988. Formalism. *Yale Law Journal* 97:509–48.

Schiller, F. C. S. 1917. Scientific Discovery and Logical Proof. Vol. 1 of *Studies in the History and the Methods of the Sciences,* 235–89. Oxford: Clarendon Press.

Schlegloff, Emanuel A. 1988. Presequences and Indirection. *Journal of Pragmatics* 12:55–62.

Schum, David A. 1994. *Evidential Foundations of Probabilistic Reasoning.* New York: John Wiley and Sons.

———. 2001. Evidence Marshaling for Imaginative Fact Investigation. *Artificial Intelligence and Law* 9:165–88.

———. 2001a. Species of Abductive Reasoning in Fact Investigation in Law. *Cardozo Law Review* 22:1645–81.

Scott, A. C., W. J. Clancey, R. Davis, and E. H. Shortliffe. 1977. Explanation Capabilities of Knowledge-Based Production Systems. In *Rule-Based Expert Systems,* ed. B. G. Buchanan and E. H. Shortliffe, 338–62. Reading, Mass.: Addison-Wesley.

Scriven, Michael. 1962. Explanations, Predictions and Laws. In *Scientific Explanation, Space and Time,* ed. H. Feigl and G. Maxwell, 170–230. Minneapolis: University of Minnesota Press.

———. 1964. Critical Study of *The Structure of Science. Review of Metaphysics* 17:403–24.

———. 1976. *Reasoning.* New York: McGraw-Hill.

———. 2002. The Limits of Explication. *Argumentation* 16:47–57.

Searle, John R. 1969. *Speech Acts.* Cambridge: Cambridge University Press.

Sextus Empiricus. 1933. *Against the Logicians.* Vol. 2 of the Loeb Classical Library Works. Cambridge, Mass.: Harvard University Press.

Shelley, Cameron. 1996. Visual Abductive Reasoning in Archeology. *Philosophy of Science* 63:278–301.

Sidgwick, Alfred. 1884. *Fallacies: A View of Logic from the Practical Side.* New York: D. Appleton Co.

———. 1893. *The Process of Argument.* London: Adam and Charles Black.

Silverman, Barry G. 1992. *Critiquing Human Error: A Knowledge-Based Human-Computer Collaboration Approach.* London: Academic Press.

Simmons, Reid G. 1992. The Roles of Associational and Causal Reasoning in Problem Solving. *Artificial Intelligence* 53:159–207.

Singh, Munindar P. 1993. A Semantics for Speech Acts. *Annals of Mathematics and Artificial Intelligence* 8:47–71.

———. 1998. Agent Communication Languages: Rethinking the Principles. *Computer* 31:425–45.

———. 1999. A Semantics for Speech Acts. *Annals of Mathematics and Artificial Intelligence* 8:47–71.

Skyrms, Brian. 1966. *Choice and Chance: An Introduction to Inductive Logic.* Belmont, Calif.: Dickenson.

Stevenson, Charles L. 1944. *Ethics and Language.* New Haven, Conn.: Yale University Press.

Thagard, Paul. 1999. *How Scientists Explain Disease.* Cambridge, Mass.: MIT Press.

Tindale, Christopher W. 1999. *Acts of Arguing: A Rhetorical Model of Argument.* Albany: State University of New York Press.

Toulmin, Stephen. 1958. *The Uses of Argument.* Cambridge: Cambridge University Press.

Trout, J. D. 2002. Scientific Explanation and the Sense of Understanding. *Philosophy of Science* 69:212–33.

Tursman, Richard. 1987. *Peirce's Logic of Scientific Discovery.* Bloomington: Indiana University Press.

Twining, William. 1985. *Theories of Evidence: Bentham and Wigmore.* London: Weidenfeld and Nicolson.

———. 1999. Narrative and Generalizations in Argumentation about Questions of Fact. *South Texas Law Review* 40:351–65.

van Eemeren, Frans H., and Rob Grootendorst. 1984. *Speech Acts in Communicative Discussions.* Dordrecht, Netherlands: Foris.

———. 1992. *Argumentation, Communication and Fallacies.* Hillsdale, N.J.: Lawrence Erlbaum Associates.

van Eemeren, Frans H., and Peter Houtlosser. 2002. Strategic Maneuvering: Maintaining a Delicate Balance. In *Dialectic and Rhetoric: The Warp and Woof of Argumentation Analysis,* ed. Frans H. van Eemeren and Peter Houtlosser, 131–59. Dordrecht, Netherlands: Kluwer.

van Fraassen, Bas C. 1980. *The Scientific Image.* Oxford: Clarendon Press.

———. 1993. The Pragmatics of Explanation. In *Explanation,* ed. David-Hillel Ruben, 275–309. Oxford: Oxford University Press.

Verheij, Bart. 1996. Rules, Reasons and Arguments: "Formal Studies of Argumentation and Defeat." Ph.D. diss., University of Maastricht.

———. 1999. Automated Argument Assistance for Lawyers. In *The Seventh*

International Conference on Artificial Intelligence and Law: Proceedings of the Conference, 43–52. New York: ACM. Available on *http://www.rechten.unimaas. nl/metajuridica/verheij/contact.htm.*

———. 2000. Logic, Context and Valid Inference Or: Can There be a Logic of Law? Available on *http://www.rechten.unimaas.nl/metajuridica/verheij/contact.htm.*

von Wright, Georg H. 1971. *Explanation and Understanding.* Ithaca, N.Y.: Cornell University Press.

———. 1997. Explanation and Understanding of Actions. In *Contemporary Action Theory,* ed. Ghita Holmstrom-Hintikka and Raimo Tuomela, 1–20. Dordrecht, Netherlands: Kluwer.

Wagenaar, Willem A., Peter J. van Koppen, and Hans F. M. Crombag. 1993. *Anchored Narratives: The Psychology of Criminal Evidence.* Hertfordshire, U.K.: Harvester Wheatsheaf.

Walton, Douglas N. 1984. *Logical Dialogue: Games and Fallacies.* Lanham, Md.: University Press of America.

———. 1989. *Question-Reply Argumentation.* New York: Greenwood Press.

———. 1990. What Is Reasoning? What Is an Argument? *Journal of Philosophy* 87:399–419.

———. 1992. Rules for Plausible Reasoning. *Informal Logic* 14:33–51.

———. 1995. *A Pragmatic Theory of Fallacy.* Tuscaloosa: University of Alabama Press.

———. 1996a. *Argumentation Schemes for Presumptive Reasoning.* Mahwah, N.J.: Erlbaum.

———. 1996b. *Arguments from Ignorance.* University Park: Penn State University Press.

———. 1997. *Appeal to Expert Opinion.* University Park: Penn State University Press.

———. 1998. *The New Dialectic: Conversational Contexts of Argument.* Toronto: University of Toronto Press.

———. 1998a. *Ad Hominem Arguments.* Tuscaloosa: University of Alabama Press.

———. 2002. *Legal Argumentation and Evidence.* University Park: Penn State University Press.

———. 2004. *Relevance in Argumentation.* Mahwah, N.J.: Erlbaum.

Walton, Douglas N., and Erik C. W. Krabbe. 1995. *Commitment in Dialogue: Basic Concepts of Interpersonal Reasoning.* Albany: State University of New York Press.

Warnick, Barbara. 2000. Two Systems of Invention: The Topics in the Rhetoric and the New Rhetoric. In *Rereading Aristotle's Rhetoric,* ed. Alan G. Gross and Arthur E. Walzer, 107–29. Carbondale: Southern Illinois University Press.

Weber, Erik, and Maarten van Dyck. 2002. Unification and Explanation. *Synthese* 131:145–54.

Wellman, Carl. 1971. *Challenge and Response: Justification in Ethics.* Carbondale: Southern Illinois University Press.

Whatley, Richard. 1853. *Historic Doubts Relative to Napoleon Buonaparte and Historic Certainties Respecting the Early History of America.* New York: Robert Carter and Brothers.

Wick, M. R., and W. B. Thompson. 1992. Reconstructive Expert System Explanation. *Artificial Intelligence* 54:33–70.

Wigmore, John H. 1913. *The Principles of Judicial Proof.* Boston: Little, Brown.

———. 1931. *The Principles of Judicial Proof.* 2nd ed. Boston: Little, Brown.

———. 1935. *A Student's Textbook of the Law of Evidence.* Chicago: Foundation Press.

———. 1940. *A Treatise on the Anglo-American System of Evidence.* Vol. 1, 3rd ed. Boston: Little, Brown.

Woods, John. 2003. *Paradox and Inconsistency: Conflict Resolution in the Abstract Sciences.* Cambridge: Cambridge University Press.

Woodward, James. 2003. Scientific Explanation. *Stanford Encyclopedia of Philosophy.* Available at http://plato.stanford.edu/entries/scientific-explanation/.

Wooldridge, Michael. 2000. *Reasoning about Rational Agents.* Cambridge, Mass.: MIT Press.

Wooldridge, Michael, and Nicholas R. Jennings. 1995. Intelligent Agents: Theory and Practice. *Knowledge Engineering Review* 10:115–52.

Wright, Richard W. 1985. Causation in Tort Law. *California Law Review* 73:1735–1828.

Index